Fourth Edition

a career
in your suitcase

Jo Parfitt
and
Colleen Reichrath Smith

First Published in Great Britain 1998 by Summertime Publishing
Second edition published 2002 by Summertime Publishing
Third edition published 2008 by *www.bookshaker.com*
This edition published 2013 by Summertime Publishing

We greatly appreciate the copyright permissions granted by:
The Conference Board of Canada, *Employability Skills 2000+*, May 2000
Career Resources Publications, Government of Alberta, Alberta Human Services
Richard Knowdell, *www.CareerTrainer.com*

Cover and page design by *www.lemonberry.com*

Praise for *A Career in Your Suitcase*

'Research has shown why it's so important to maintain a professional identity when moving around the world. Jo Parfitt has literally written *The Book* on how to maintain this identity… full of practical advice and sage guidance, written from the heart by someone who's been there.'

Anne P Copeland PhD, Executive Director, The Interchange Institute, ***www.interchangeinstitute.org***

'In today's global economy, an international career can be built anywhere where electricity and a telephone line are available. In A Career In Your Suitcase readers will find the practical advice and encouragement to help make it happen.'

Lya Sorano, CEO, The Oliver/Sorano Group, Inc. *www.lyasorano.com*

'An awesome networker and intrepid traveller, there is nothing that Jo doesn't know about creating, sustaining and growing a portable career whilst moving round the world. Yes, there really is a career in your suitcase and Jo ensures that you unpack it safely.'

Gill Cowell, Publisher, *The Weekly Telegraph*

'Having watched Jo in action during one of her Career In Your Suitcase workshops, I wistfully wondered why I couldn't have met her twenty years ago when I first went abroad. Developing my professional life would have gone a lot more smoothly.'

Robin Pascoe, Expatriate Press

'If anyone can write about a career in your suitcase, Jo Parfitt can. Her experience, knowledge and network of global contacts are clearly demonstrated in her A Career in Your Suitcase series… true enlightenment for any mobile individual who aims for eternal blue skies.'

Assunta Mondello, Expatriate Adviser, *The American Hour*

'Through her Career In Your Suitcase program, Jo Parfitt helps people everywhere think outside the traditional boxes. She not only teaches but models how each of us can make all the pieces of our lives work together to form something new and satisfying in the middle of a changing world. I recommend this book highly to all who want to learn how to begin seeing the possibilities of new beginnings they may not have recognised before.'

Ruth E Van Reken, Co-author: ***Third Culture Kids: The Experience of Growing Up Among Worlds,*** **Co-founder: Families in Global Transition**

'Jo's workshops and book provided me with the tools, realisation and independence to operate outside "the conventional box".'

Marian Weston, Swift Transitions, author of ***At Home Alone*** ***www.swiftransitions.co.uk***

Contents

Praise for A Career in Your Suitcase...3

Contents..6

Acknowledgements..8

Foreword...10

Who should read this book?..12

How to use this book...13

Part One: Find Your Direction

Chapter 1: Introduction — Setting The Scene....................18

Jo's Story...22

Colleen's Story..23

Chapter 2: Finding Your Passion...29

How I (Jo) Found My Passions...30

Find Your Passion...41

Chapter 3: What Can You Do..90

Time For Some New Skills?...100

What is a Perfect Portable Career?...103

Food for Thought..111

Putting It All Together...113

Part Two: Find Your Opportunity

Chapter 4: Creating Your Career...121

What Do You Believe?..122

A Changing World...124

Manage your Expectations..125

Cultural Considerations..127

Influencing Factors..129

Purposes..133
Your Career Evolution..136
Getting Ideas...138
Ways of Working...149
Researching Options...156
Evaluate Your Options..159
Living Your Mission..160

Chapter 5: Networking..175
The Importance of Relationships..176
Building Your Network...178
Networking Skills..193

Part Three: Putting it Together

Chapter 6: Marketing Your Skills......................................223
Finding Opportunities..224
Creating Your Own Opportunities.......................................239
Self Marketing Tools..247

Chapter 7: Working for Yourself.......................................267
Starting Your Own Thing..268
Forms of Entrepreneurship...273
Do You Have What It Takes?...274
Your To Do List..277
Working From Home...304

Chapter 8: For the Journey...313
Change...314
The Challenge of Change..320
Work-Life Balance...328
Need A Career Development Professional?............................339

Chapter 9: My Career Passport...351

Acknowledgements

Since I first conceived this book, back in 1996, in Stavanger, Norway, I have watched the idea of a career in your suitcase evolve, pick up speed and grow into what I consider to be the number one solution to finding meaningful work wherever you may live in the world. It has been well over 15 years now and many people, from all over the world, have inspired me and added to my vision. However, one person in particular has to be held responsible for this book. Back in 1996, Kit Prendergast asked me to tell the members of the professional women's group she chaired about the career I had sustained while I had lived abroad in three different countries. She then encouraged me to develop my knowledge into the first ever Career in Your Suitcase workshop. Kit made me believe I had something to say. She gave value to my experiences.

Thank you to the contributors to previous versions of *Career in Your Suitcase,* whose footprints are still to be found scattered throughout this fourth edition: Galen Tinder, Mary Farmer, Gail MacIndoe, and Huw Francis. The Expatriate Archive Centre, The Trailing Spouse, Careerinyoursuitcase.com and CareerByChoice.com provided many pertinent quotations but the majority came from the mentors and bloggers at ExpatWomen.com and our gratitude goes to Andrea Martins who sourced them for us.

Inevitably, I give huge thanks to my husband, Ian, for making my career in my suitcase possible in the first place. I have immense gratitude to my children, Sam and Josh, for respecting the fact that I often work from home and for always being supportive. But it is my parents, Peter and Jenny Gosling, who have believed in me and shown their pride in even my smallest achievement, since the day I was born. And that has made all the difference.

Jo Parfitt
March 2013

I am extremely grateful to have met Jo and been offered the gift to build on the success of *Career in Your Suitcase*. It has been more than a two year journey from our initial discussion to the realization of this fourth edition. I appreciate Jo's flexibility and collaborative approach which has allowed this edition to unfold in a natural way. In coming up with examples from my own life to share, I was reminded of many other gifts I have received along my career journey; gifts from colleagues and mentors and ultimately my parents who continue to be role models for me in life. Most of all, I thank my husband, Sven, for his belief in me and my abilities as well as the gift of time and space in which to follow through on this dream. And of course it is because of him that I have developed a portable career. This book truly is the realization of what, when I first moved to the Netherlands seven years ago, seemed like a wild and crazy idea.

Colleen Reichrath
March 2013

Foreword

The Hague, the Netherlands, is known as the International City of Peace and Justice. It is home to the International Criminal Court, the International Criminal Tribunal of the former Yugoslavia and Peace Palace as well as countless other UN organizations, Europol, the European Patent Office, European Space Agency and NATO – the list of International organisations goes on and on. With several multinationals based in the city, and the most prominent being the Shell Global Headquarters, The Hague is a hub for expatriates from all over the world.

This vast number of global migrants converging in one place to work means the ratio of partners to spouses is almost equal. These individuals are often highly educated with a tremendous amount of experience. However, they find themselves searching for new career opportunities and meaningful work in a very different context and circumstance from the one they left behind.

In 2005 I founded the Women's Business Initiative International, a business incubator and professional network, based in The Hague, to support women (and men too) as they explored new business opportunities, created new entrepreneurial ventures or started on the path of self-employment. It is through the Women's Business Initiative that I had the pleasure to meet both Jo and Colleen.

Making a global move can often be a unique opportunity to pursue a lifelong dream of starting your own business or being your own boss, but it is surely not for everyone nor is it the only option. A Career in Your Suitcase is the ultimate tool to help individuals consider and explore all the options available to them. Thanks to all the examples and success stories that illustrate the practical information in the book, it provides reassurance that you are not alone in the way you are feeling; the loss of identity, the frustration, the fear are common emotions. Others have come before you and have found success and you can too.

Thank you, Jo and Colleen, for transforming this edition into the stunning new workbook format. It inspires action from the outset, particularly when those first crucial steps seem so difficult. We need to get this empowering resource into more people's hands.

Suzy Ogé

Director – Women's Business Initiative International
www.womensbusinessinitiativeinternational.net

Who Should Read This Book?

'Work is love made visible.'

Khalil Gibran

This book is for anyone who lives or hopes to live in another place and has to start again. If you want to find fulfilling, enjoyable work that is a meaningful expression of who you are and what you want from your life, and can be taken to wherever you are living then this is for you.

You may be about to emigrate, to retire, to return to work, to move elsewhere temporarily or permanently. You may be what is termed an 'accompanying partner' of an expatriate employee and about to move once or many times. You may be someone with a thirst for change and adventure. You may be about to move alone, as part of a couple, or with a family and want to work in a new location. You may want to run a business from your kitchen table or home office, find part-time, full-time, freelance or contract work. You may want to develop a one-off successful company or you may want to find something to do that can be sustained and grown as you move from place to place.

This book has much to offer the global nomad who needs a career with global networks and about which they can stay motivated despite upheaval. Yet it also speaks directly to anyone, anywhere, who has ever wanted to discover, once and for all, what they really really want to do for a living and how to turn that dream into reality.

How to use this book

The content of this book is organised around the Career/Life Infinity Model of Pamela Lester (see page 341 for further explanation). The first section is Find Your Direction and focuses on the internal journey. The second section is Find Your Opportunity and takes you through the external journey of learning about opportunities. Section three is Putting it Together and provides information, exercises and support to take action and follow through on your dreams.

Each chapter contains a wealth of information and resources alongside the inspiring examples of Jo's and Colleen's stories. We have chosen to use the pronoun 'I' for all these stories while including our name in brackets to help you know which story the example stems from.

Within each chapter or section you will find our recommended exercises to help you create your own personally meaningful portable career. When you see this exercise symbol:

it means that it's over to you. We have also provided an estimate of the amount of time you will require to complete each exercise using this time symbol:

30
mins

You may require more or less time based on how you like to complete this type of workbook. Remember that there are no right or wrong answers so don't overthink responses. Your answer will serve you best for these exercises. Start writing and see what happens.

The last chapter of the book is a Career Passport in which you can summarise the results of the work you have done throughout the book. This summary of your work here will help open doors and give you insight and access to the portable career of your dreams. When you see this symbol go to Chapter 9 and record your results.

Use the glossary at the end of the book to understand the difference between words like career and work. This will increase the clarity of the book's message for you.

At the end of each chapter you will also find a list of the resources and websites related to these tasks. The forms used in the exercises can be downloaded from *www.careerinyoursuitcase.com.*

We hope that region specific versions of this book will be available in the near future. Check our website *www.careerinyoursuitcase.com* to find out how you can get involved.

The Career in Your Suitcase website has more resources and will inspire you with additional career stories. Comment on these and add your own story to help others like yourself. The more we share the more there is for everyone.

Part 1
Find your
direction

'Your reason and your passion are the rudder and the sails of your seafaring soul.'

Khalil Gibran

Chapter ONE

Introduction - Setting The Scene

Until 1987 I (Jo) had enjoyed a successful career as a partner in a computer training business. I made my living from teaching and writing and had already published more than ten computer handbooks. Then I got married and my husband was posted to Dubai. Telling me I would regret it for the rest of my life if I refused to join him, my new husband persuaded me to become what is sometimes rather unflatteringly called a 'trailing spouse'. In this politically correct world the term has become the more anodyne 'accompanying partner'. It is perhaps the men in our number who have created the most compelling term - that of STUDS which stands for Spouse Trailing Under Duress Successfully, while Apple Gidley, author of Expat Life – Slice by Slice, created the new acronym STARS at the 2011 Families in Global Transition Conference. This stands for Spouse Travelling and Relocating Successfully. I like that.

In the 25 years that have followed, I have come to agree with my husband. I am glad I made the journey and yes, I would have regretted it for the rest of my life had I stayed behind. During these intervening years, I have developed what I call a career in my suitcase, a portable career that moves when I do. A career that is mobile, sustainable and keeps growing despite moving country every few years.

The first ten years were a struggle, in which I did my fair share of door-slamming and sulking. But it was around 1997 that I read Robin Pascoe's *A Wife's Guide* and realised, at last, a) I was not alone and b) I was not mad. In fact I was part of something often called the Dual Career Issue. It was around this time I published the first edition of *A Career in Your Suitcase.*

Fifteen years ago I began to study the phenomenon. I attended conferences, interviewed countless experts and talked with many women, and men, who shared my interest in portable careers. As a journalist, I was able to learn about this at the source and then share what I knew in the best way I knew - by writing about it.

Today, few international corporations remain ignorant of the dual career issue. It is on the agenda of almost every multinational corporation. Sadly though, many organisations find it a bit of a hot potato and offer the same kind of support they always have - with work permits, language and training. But it is impossible to create a one size fits all solution to this dilemma. Few mobile spouses will be able to climb their chosen career ladder, stay in the same field, or even the same company. Few will find it easy to hop from permanent employment to permanent employment. For even if there were work available, other hurdles get in the way, such as a lack of work permits or fluency in a new language. Perhaps your qualifications will not be accepted in a new country? Or maybe your usual career just does not exist in your new location? And then, with the demands of conducting an international relocation and all the domestic duties that entails, not to mention the responsibility of looking after a mobile family, it can be hard to find suitable work which fits round everything else.

At the same time, globalisation, increased mobility and self-employment alongside the desire for adventure are encouraging more and more people to consider developing a portable career for themselves. If you plan to make just a single move or move within the same country, then thankfully issues such as language barriers, work permits and unrecognised qualifications are likely to be less of a problem. But you may still find it difficult to obtain work similar to before the move. A fisherman would have to find a creative solution if he moved to an inner city. Someone with a shop selling tartan in Scotland may find it hard to establish the same business in the south of England. While there are many barriers likely to hinder your progress, there are skills to be learned and techniques that will support you to develop your own personally meaningful portable career.

What is a portable career?

A portable career is work that you can take with you wherever you go. It is based on your own unique set of skills, values, passion and vision and is not based in a physical location. Lower costs of travel and technological advances have made the global labour market a more accessible option for more workers and businesses than in the past. Megan Fitzgerald, expat career and entrepreneur coach defines a portable career as location independent, using skills that are in high demand, providing virtual products and services. It is non-jurisdictional, not housed in brick and mortar, and is a good fit for subject matter experts. Examples include working in administrative support, accounting, IT services, coaching, writing, graphic design, teaching and consulting, or anything 'virtual'. Technology opens many doors for portable careers, but other careers can be portable without using technology. The only real limit is your ability to imagine and create it.

A note for accompanying spouses

If the need for a portable career is driven by the fact that your partner is pursuing a career track involving international assignments, then there are additional factors to consider. A dual career couple is one where both are similarly educated and equally wish to pursue a career.

DUAL CAREER STATISTICS

- The 2012 Brookfield Global Relocation Trends Survey, now in its 17th year, indicated the top reasons for refusal of an international work assignment as: 1. Family concerns, 2. Partner's career, 3. Quality of life at the location.
- This survey also shows that while 49% of spouses were employed before an international assignment, only 12% were employed before and during the assignment.

WHAT CAN STOP YOU FROM WORKING?

The key reasons that accompanying partners do not work include:

- No work permit.
- Lack of fluency in the host language.
- Incompatibility of certification.
- Lack of suitable opportunities.

THE IMPACT ON IDENTITY

> 'It is more stressful to not have work when you want it than to do something you dislike.'
>
> **Tom Jackson, Author, *Guerilla Tactics in the Job Market***

If an international work assignment imposes a career hiatus on one partner, that partner will experience an identity shift alongside the physical relocation. One of the main reasons for spousal unhappiness on international assignment is the difficulty he or she has in maintaining a professional identity or career. Without the security the job title, the colleagues, the income, the routine and satisfaction that can be derived from a career, you can start to lose sight of who you are. It is a major shift in life roles.

This can be very frightening.

With a loss of identity often comes a loss of self-confidence and self-esteem. Enforced idleness can be hard to deal with. Without something 'interesting' or purposeful to focus on, it is easy to become stressed or depressed. This is where learning the skills to develop a portable career can create much more life satisfaction for the accompanying partner.

'Due to my inability to be employed for the first time in my working life I am dependent on another person. I feel trapped and observed all the time. This raises the stress level enormously.'

'My loss of job, loss of self-esteem, and an imbalance in the relationship is very stressful. Prior to this last relocation we were at the same level job wise.'

'By not being able to continue with my career I am made to feel like a second-class citizen… It is a lonely life, and we, the trailing spouse, are left to re-invent ourselves after every relocation. It's exhausting and unrewarding. I regret my life.'

'My self-esteem has taken a beating because I don't feel that I am contributing to our household finances.'

'I had no idea how much my sense of self-worth was tied to my career.'

'I felt that I had given [up] my real "self", and had become less of a person.'

'Companies need to support the spouse in allowing them to further their career. I do not live for my husband, nor do I live for his work, and they just couldn't understand that my work/career was, and is, as important as his. He did not marry a housewife and I will never be one.'

'I was a barrister in Australia who thought it might be fun to take a year to live with my husband in far north Finland. It wasn't. I couldn't work. I was ignored and my whole identity disappeared. We now live apart for 5 days a week – he in far north Finland, me in Helsinki. I am working, but it is not the senior job I had in Australia and this has caused intense bitterness.'

Yvonne McNulty, Author, *Being Dumped In To Sink or Swim in Human Resource Development International Journal*, 2012

Jo's Story

Let's go back to my arrival in Dubai back in 1987. I was a new wife unaccustomed to idleness. We were living in a fully serviced apartment and it was not many weeks before I tired of sunbathing and small talk around the pool. I found it hard to do what I considered to be 'nothing' all day. My identity, until my marriage, had been tied up with my career. I liked to work, to feel I was achieving something and to be financially independent. I liked the camaraderie of colleagues and the opportunity to keep learning and developing. With no support or inspiration from my husband's employer, I decided to make my own luck and, over the next 20 years on the move, acquired a range of skills that would allow me to create, maintain, pick up and pack my portable career. Despite living in five different countries, in the end I learned how to look inside myself to discover what I most enjoyed doing and how I might adapt my interests and my skills to match them up with opportunities in each location.

During the first decade I made and sold chutney, and taught French, creative writing and computer skills. I became a journalist, wrote manuals and newsletters and self-published a cookery book. When I noticed how desperate the local expatriates were for books I turned to network marketing and sold Dorling Kindersley books and CD-ROMs. When I heard my dinner guests commending the delicious curry our Indian housekeeper had prepared, I ran a small take away service. I soon realised problems are opportunities in disguise.

When we returned to England for a few years in 1997 with our two children, I noticed things had changed. People no longer had careers for life back home either. Mothers wanted some work-life balance and their frequent domestic relocations meant they wanted portable careers too. By 1998 I had formed Summertime Publishing and published the first edition of *A Career in Your Suitcase*. Since then, not only has that book sold out and been well received all over the world, but its message has inspired thousands of men and women, mobile and non-mobile, and encouraged them to create a career based on their passions. Since the first edition was released I have travelled the world speaking about my own experience and sharing the knowledge I have acquired. Along the way I've also been inspired by other people who have also created careers for their suitcases, and have learned from them.

After seven years back 'home', and a second edition of this book, we moved abroad again, to the Netherlands this time and my career came too, continuing to grow and develop along the way.

Writing has always been my first love. At the time of this writing I've had 30 books published and countless articles. I also teach writing locally, online and via residential courses. However, a few years ago I realised I needed to grow my business in such a way as to develop some passive income. In 2008 I decided to take the publishing company I had formed in 1997 to publish my own books to another level and to offer this service to my mentoring clients. Today, Summertime Publishing has over 70 titles in print and Kindle format and sells its books via Amazon and *www.expatbookshop.com*. My niche and specialisation, is books by and for people who live overseas.

This fourth edition is a culmination of everything I have learned and all the people I've met — not only since the first book came out but from the very beginning, more than 20 years ago, when I inadvertently became involved in a dual career partnership.

I believe a successful portable career is possible for anyone. First we must look inside ourselves to find our passions, then we must look outside ourselves to find the opportunities in the locality, and finally we must find a way to blend this together so we can tailor-make a career that fits our values, aspirations and lifestyle.

A Career in Your Suitcase is here to inspire, inform and support anyone who wants to find work they love. It's for all those people who, like me, want to continue working despite relocation. It's for everyone who believes challenges are merely opportunities in disguise and our world is full of surprises. Enjoy working through this book, be inspired by it and its accompanying website *www.careerinyoursuitcase.com*, Tweet with us and share your own stories on the website and LinkedIn *Career in your Suitcase Group*.

Colleen's Story

My story involves ten relocations within my home country of Canada before making an international move to the Netherlands in 2005 when I married a Dutch man. While a number of these moves may have given me some of the characteristics that define a third culture kid (TCK — see glossary), and others involved career transitions — from Recreation Therapist to Career Consultant — with this last move I took my career on an international adventure.

As a self-employed career consultant I believed that a move to the Netherlands would allow me to put the career development principles that I teach my clients to the

ultimate test. I gave myself some time to make the transition and focused on learning the language first. Two years later I was again delivering career development training on a freelance basis. Only this time it was in Dutch! Though my language skills then were nowhere near the fluency I would have required of myself, I was offered a contract to provide training in my second language by an employer who saw that I could be a role model for some of the training recipients.

It was through networking and offering my skills freely that I was able to go almost seamlessly (in hindsight that is) from one opportunity to the next, ultmately landing a paid contract. As I look back over the course of this transition I see a number of key events as well as some important qualities that helped to create this result. The steps to my successful transition were:

1. I took the time to reflect and re-evaluate what my values, interests and passions are at this stage of my life.
2. I was open to new learning and updating skills. In this case it was my language skills and the dynamics of the Dutch labour market.
3. I networked and met people working in my field. My Canadian network provided some great connections for me here in the Netherlands. Through volunteering and joining networking groups I quickly broadened this network.
4. I maintained momentum and self-confidence, even though there were times when they wavered and I felt lost. In addition to my support network, my professional portfolio (see Chapter 6) was most helpful.
5. I allowed myself to create a mental image of the life I wanted. Here in the Netherlands it meant taking advantage of the uniquely Dutch biking culture and going to work on my bike instead of sitting in traffic jams in a car.
6. I said yes to opportunities that came along even though there was no sign at the time they would lead to the work opportunities I wanted. I let go and allowed the journey to unfold.

I remember clearly some advice my mother gave me when I was moving to a new city on my own for the first time. She called it the *Rule of Three* that she developed for herself as a stay at home mom during the many moves we made as a family. These three components allowed her to achieve a sense of balance in her life wherever it led her, also helping her to transition back into the workforce after raising kids. They have also served me well.

The *Rule of Three* is:

1. Do something that allows you to learn.
2. Do something that contributes to the community.
3. Do something for your own enjoyment.

For me a 'career' encompasses incorporating all three of these elements in your life and more; it includes your work, learning, leisure and life roles. Seeing career from this type of holistic perspective instead of focussing only on the part that gives you a pay check will open up many opportunities to create the career that will best suit wherever you happen to be.

You can see the connecting theme in the *Rule of Three* is *doing*. This book gives you many tools and ways to take action for yourself to create a career which will travel with you wherever you go. These tools are provided within the context of Jo's compelling experiences and stories of life abroad, expanded upon with my own examples. The combination is inspiring and practical. After reading this book and completing the exercises, you will believe it is also possible for you to create an ideal career from your own suitcase!

> The fine art of a successful career in your suitcase doesn't mean having a big bag, but having a big imagination and the enthusiasm to carry it out.
> **Huw Francis, *Author of Live and Work Abroad: A Guide for Modern Nomads***

TEN STEPS TO A CAREER IN YOUR SUITCASE

1. Find your passions, values, mission and meaning.
2. Assess your skills, talents, strengths and uniqueness.
3. Discover what you want and need from a career at this stage in your life.
4. Brainstorm the perfect portable career for you.
5. Adjust your career to fit your current location and the opportunities it holds.
6. Do the research and learning you need to prepare for transition and your chosen career.
7. Create the marketing materials you need (CV, website, cards, brochures).
8. Network to meet the people you will need as they become your clients, employers, role models and support team.
9. Consider hiring a Career Development Professional to join you on your journey at any or all stages of the process.
10. Make it happen by setting goals, staying motivated and developing the self-belief and confidence you need.

'What you love is what you are gifted at and there is no exception.'

Barbara Sher

Chapter TWO

Find Your
passion

Your Calling

Finding our passions, which we can also think of as our vocation or the work we were uniquely designed to do, can be a challenge. Converting these passions into a career requires ingenuity and persistence. To unearth our passions we need to look inside ourselves. When we seek to translate what we love into work, then we need to look outside ourselves, the topic of subsequent chapters.

How I (Jo) Found My Passions

We firmly believe you can do what you love and earn money from it. I (Jo) had always believed this — until the day at school when my careers adviser informed me, at age 14, that writing was not a career option, but just an indulgence! That was when I began my attempts at conforming. And though I had written my first poem at six, my first play at 13, kept a diary since age 11 and penned hundreds of letters, I shelved my dream.

I loved French though. And for me that included the literature, the language, the people and the country. I found my French teacher, Mr Feather, inspiring, and received my best marks in French. So I went to university to study French. I knew I didn't want to be a teacher, nor a translator. Somehow I realised I had to be creative, and so it was during the year I spent abroad in France, teaching English conversation to a group of despondent teenagers, that I found the perfect outlet. I would write a book called French Tarts. Not once did it strike me that I couldn't cook. I knew I had a great idea and a great title, and my pursuit of authentic recipes from real French people would get me a few dinner invitations.

My plan worked. Octopus, the first publisher whom I approached with my idea, snapped it up. I quickly taught myself to type and use a word processor so I could produce the manuscript. The book came out in English in 1985 and then in French, in France. I put this immense good fortune down to beginner's luck. I had become a writer after all. I was 24 years old. I was doing something I loved and earning money.

Yet, despite getting an agent and deluging her with many other ideas for cookery books, I guess I was let down by the fact I was neither a trained nor an experienced chef. With hindsight, I realise my enthusiasm didn't quite match my skill and some of my ideas left a lot to be desired. After spending a year churning out synopses while I worked as a temporary word processing secretary, I decided it was time to change direction.

Instead of finding more work as a cookery writer, I found myself teaching word processing — the skill I'd only learned in order to produce the manuscript for *French Tarts*. But I found I loved the work, particularly when I was required to create typing exercises for the students. I also liked producing the documentation and course handouts.

Surprisingly, the work energised me. I would never have dreamed my creative soul would enjoy something as technical as word processing — but it did. I found I enjoyed the lessons, meeting new people and watching the students learn and grow. In my own small way I was changing people's lives for the better. My enthusiasm must have shown because one of my clients asked me to go and work for him, developing new computer training materials. The idea excited me and so, aged 25, I went freelance and have never looked back.

A few lucky breaks later, I found I had written 13 computer handbooks in plain language for some of England's largest publishers. Two years later I was in partnership with two others, running a thriving computer training and writing company.

Then I fell in love with Ian and we decided to get married. The trouble was my new husband had been 'temporarily' posted to Dubai and refused to cut short his assignment and come home. So I moved abroad.

Life without work

When I (Jo) arrived in Dubai the day after my wedding, they put a stamp in my passport that read 'not permitted to take up employment'. I was devastated. I had a few writing contracts to complete that I'd brought with me, but would have to spend six weeks waiting for my computer to arrive so I could begin work. Until this moment my work had been my life and my passion. I'd developed few other interests and knew no one in Dubai. With no company support, I had no idea where to look for friends or things to do. Work was all I knew. By then, ironically, I had become quite a good cook, but knew no one to invite for dinner.

Six weeks later and two days before my computer arrived, Ian came home from the office to find me crouched on the floor of our beautiful apartment, ripping a newspaper to shreds and crying my eyes out from sheer frustration. Without work I was a fish out of water.

Of course I could have attended Arabic language classes, or learned to paint in watercolours. I could have joined the gym, or asked my husband to introduce me to the wives of his colleagues and friends. I could have taken advantage of the wonderful swimming pool and tennis courts that went with our apartment. I could have taken a taxi and explored the city. But all I wanted to do was work, and nothing else would do.

I had lost my professional identity. My personal identity too was so intertwined with work I had forgotten who I was without it. I had no idea that volunteer work or taking classes might have fulfilled me. Being beholden to my husband and his company made me feel impotent, invisible. We had maid service in the apartment, so I had little to do. Shorts and tee-shirts didn't need much ironing. Despite the fact I soon had a driving licence, I was nervous about taking to the roads alone. I felt like a 'hollow woman' as Valerie Scane, writer and speaker on expatriate issues, would say. I didn't feel whole without my computer and some work to do.

Women, returning to work after taking time off to have children often find their confidence at a new low. But this is not reserved for mothers. It happens to lots of people after a career gap or during a career transition. Add to this living in a strange place, maybe with a new language, unfamiliar customs and unfathomable laws and your confidence can sink lower still. After so many knocks it can be hard to get going again and start looking for work.

It had always pleased me to have a label. I was a 'writer' and a 'computer trainer'. I was not 'just a wife' and the very idea made me feel hugely uncomfortable. I realised I had a personal need, not only to have a professional identity, but also to earn my own money — however little. I didn't want to have to ask my husband for the money to buy him his own birthday present.

'You need guts. You need to have the courage to say "I am going to do this."'

Belinda, Dutch, The Expatriate Archive, OAC5/3/3

'It is like this everywhere, change. Everything is new, so your confidence needs to be very strong just to say "Okay, here I am, wait for me, I am coming." … I came over here at 24 with my first born son, three month old, and I didn't know where to go, what to do. My husband was flying round the world … [I thought] Okay, what do I do here? And you just feel you don't really know where to go, what to do, or if you are doing things right.'

Flavia, Italian, The Expatriate Archive, OAC5/3/3

'I have only been here for two or three months. My role has changed… because my wife is here [as the lead employee]. I am now house husband and father… fundamental change… so much that it creates a spiritual crisis… the whole identity has changed from the real one and the new one has not appeared yet… there is a shift in the whole of the little ground on which I stand. It is giving way and sinking, sinking. Then I ask myself why? Why is this so? Behind this is fear… Am I able to touch this fear? Am I able to embrace this fear? Or am I avoiding it? Sometimes I find I do avoid it because I don't want to [face] it. So I [focus on] TV, BBC news and so on so that all my projection is on something external and this is perhaps a way to cushion this crisis… .The mental crisis inside is so deep… then as I come to terms with the gap within, it starts to open up the whole empty space, that I haven't seen [before] and I don't want to look at it.'

Wong, Malaysian in Europe, The Expatriate Archive, OAC5/3/3

'The reality of experience was different from our expectations. Although I consider myself extremely lucky to have had that one-year time with our first daughter, studying from home the first year in a new country prevented me from developing my own network of friends and my own social circle. In addition, it was the first time for me to find myself without a job. I underestimated the impact it would have on myself not to have a status or a more social and structured occupation.'

Francois-Xavier Groleau, Global Outpost Services Advisor, Shell International, the Netherlands

How passions become portable

Well, my computer did arrive and I completed my book contracts. But once they were finished, I soon learned that editors found it difficult to liaise with overseas authors. This was before we had Skype, email and even fax machines and so, reluctantly, I realised I had to go back to the drawing board and create a new career for myself. Today, happily, things are very different for writers working around the world.

Ian had promised me we would only be abroad for six months or so — but the thought of even a few months' sabbatical filled me with horror. I simply had to look for alternative employment.

Despite the stamp in my passport that apparently didn't allow me to work, I discovered not all hope was lost. In fact, working in Dubai was remarkably easy. Provided you found a local company to sponsor you and supply a labour card, you could do almost anything at all.

Over the next six years in Dubai, and three in Oman, I developed a range of complementary and changing careers I dipped into when the opportunity arose. Fortunately, I was also happy to discard some career streams when the opportunity disappeared. This ability to reinvent myself and be flexible has been key to my success. Each reinvention has taken place because I first looked inside myself to see which skills, interests and passions most excited me at that time. Next I looked carefully at the local market, to see where the gaps lay, or where I might find the most luck.

If I (Jo) look inside myself, I see the following key skills and values, all of which have grown out of my passions:

- Creativity
- Writing
- Teaching
- Helping people to grow
- Flexibility
- Willingness to learn
- Desire for variety
- Being with people
- Communication
- Computer skills

- French
- A love of food and cooking
- Connecting people through informal networking
- Helping people to get published

These core skills and values have led me to become a journalist, author, a teacher of creative writing, a teacher of French conversation, a copy writer, a publisher and co-author of a cookery book called *Dates*, a copy typist, a curriculum vitae producer, a computer teacher, a trainer of trainers, a computer training centre course developer, a manufacturer of Christmas decorations, a Dorling Kindersley book distributor, a manufacturer and marketer of date chutney, a founder of writers' circles, a keynote speaker, teacher, trainer and a newsletter editor. I have edited two international expat magazines, started helping others to write their books in 2002 and been a serious publisher since 2008.

When I look inside myself, I can also see the values that motivate me and make my professional life work for me. Some people value money, others value fame, free time, flexible hours or variety. Values change over time and it's worth taking a look at yours regularly. If you want to be true to yourself, you need to consider your values as well as your passions. My values, right now, are:

- Sharing
- Supporting
- Making a difference
- Using my passions
- Interacting with people
- A balance of introversion and extroversion
- Being accessible and affordable
- Developing a specialism within a variety of projects

When living abroad, we were lucky enough not to need me to produce a solid second income. This has been a terrific opportunity and has given me permission to do only what I most enjoy. But when your family needs a second income, as ours did on repatriation to the UK for seven years after a decade overseas, your dreams may take a little honing.

'Going abroad and moving from one part of the country to another forces you to take a look at why you do things and how you think. You have to look inside yourself and find an inner strength. The people you usually turn to for that strength are not around. No one ever comes to you. You have to go out there and do it yourself. You have to be self-reliant. I feel that all these problems have, in time, turned into my personal strengths. It has been a totally positive experience.'

Cheryl, American, *www.careerinyoursuitcase.com*

How Jo's career in her suitcase came home

When we repatriated I (Jo) had to earn some money. Overnight I became responsible for paying two sets of school fees and for family holidays. The first project I worked on when we came home was the publication of the first edition of *A Career in Your Suitcase.* I formed Summertime Publishing and, during 1998, launched this title and one called *Forced To Fly.* This took a lot of work and investment, and the returns were relatively small at first - so I decided to develop a range of seminars and workshops on the theme of portable careers. I soon discovered that, on average, about a quarter of delegates would buy a book too. And while these seminars were successful and well received, the marketing response was slow to start with. Along the way, I discovered those who most wanted me to speak, and whom I most loved addressing, tended to be non-profit associations and international conferences — who had little, if any, budget. If I was to meet my financial target I had to think again.

Once more I looked inside myself, and decided I had to calculate which among my many careers had the most earning potential. I had to think hard about which of my skills would earn me the most money per hour and for which there was also a market. During my soul searching I realised it was time to take my journalism to UK based magazines and newspapers. I love writing and in order to give me the most satisfaction, I needed to write about subjects that interested me. It became clear I had picked up a few more skills and passions to add to my list. I could now call myself an expert on expatriate living and portable careers. I began in earnest to look for opportunities. Within a few months I was writing for *Resident Abroad* (later called *FT Expat*), *The Weekly Telegraph, Women's Business Magazine* and the *Smart Moves* section of *The Independent on Sunday.*

Journalism was the work that paid the bills. Portable career presentations and publishing were *the expression of my passion*. At first my work funded my passion but over time the two merged until I was able to pick and choose my writing projects and my presenting started to earn me money.

When, in 2000, three years after we came home, I was offered the chance to edit a new magazine called *Woman Abroad*, I jumped at the chance. Without a doubt, this position was the culmination of my career experiences to date and it allowed me to exercise all my skills and values at once. I was flying. Sadly, after the tragedy of 9/11, the magazine was forced to fold as living abroad lost its allure for a while. In 2002 I had to go back to the drawing board and this time I emerged as what I first called a Book Cook, specialising in editing books for clients and helping them to go from pipedream to publication. You can find out more at *www.summertimepublishing.com*.

But it was not enough for me to just help others to produce their books. I had to write my own too and in 2002, *Grow Your Own Networks* was published as well as a second edition of *Career in Your Suitcase*, followed in 2004 by *Find Your Passion*. Yet I need a balance of introvert and extrovert activities in order to be happy and so this was when I developed a range of writing workshops to add to the career workshops that first began in 1997. My love of travel meant I took every opportunity to run these courses overseas.

In 2005, we moved abroad again, this time to The Hague, Netherlands, and having been careful to make my business global, many of my clients came too. I continued to help people write their books, marketed my workshops locally and, of course, kept on writing my books. In 2006, *Expat Entrepreneur* was published. In 2007 a second edition of *Find Your Passion*, a third edition of *Career in Your Suitcase* and a new one, *Release the Book Within* joined the list as well as a second edition of *Dates*.

More recently I've published two writing courses, an anthology of poetry and a novel, and created the online Expat Bookshop. Summertime Publishing now publishes about 12 books a year for expat authors.

We believe it's a *right* to be able to do what we love for a living. If we want to be energised by work, to look forward to each morning, to be authentic and enthusiastic, then it is vital we're passionate about our work. If we do what we love then our enthusiasm and energy will do our marketing for us. If you take a look back over my

(Jo's) long list of specialisations you may be able to spot the themes or patterns that have run through everything I do. I first wrote the list of values that appeared a few pages back 13 years ago. When I revisit them, it is clear little has changed. The 'red threads', the common denominators, that have sustained me despite those ups and downs and five moves, remain:

- Sharing
- Supporting
- Making a difference
- Using my passions
- Interacting with people
- A balance of introversion and extroversion
- Being accessible and affordable
- Developing a specialism within a variety of projects

Like many, my values are my passions. I need to incorporate them into my daily life in order to be happy. They are, to me, as vital as fresh air, food and water. It is easy for me now to seem complacent, and to point out exactly where my passions lie. But it was not always like that. It is only now, with the luxury of hindsight I can look back and see the patterns and the 'red threads' emerge. I believe very strongly that finding your passion is the fundamental first step to creating a portable career which will sustain you from move to move and will keep you motivated. A career based on your passion is more likely to earn you money, because if you truly believe in what you do, people will notice and they will believe in you too. And then, of course, they will buy!

Why our passions can be hard to find

Back when I (Jo) was 14 and my school careers adviser told me I couldn't make it as a writer, as I mentioned earlier, I picked another path. You may have noticed that my passion for French doesn't feature much in my most recent portfolio of careers. As a result, it would be easy to assume this was never a true passion yet, even as my second choice, its value is now apparent. I love to travel, to meet people of other nationalities, to mix with other cultures and to communicate with them and learn about their food. Not content to be ever the tourist, for me, studying French meant I also lived in France and had French friends. As a teenager I had many pen pal friends, and visited them on my own, in Germany and France, each summer. My potential love for expatriate life was written in my stars long before I chose to study French at university.

Sometimes we need to look more closely at the choices we make in order to spot the elements that excite us. Sometimes we are persuaded away from our passions for a variety of reasons.

Between the ages of 11 and 15 I loved drama and took classes in speaking and acting. I was nervous about improvisation and preferred to have a script. Yet, at 15, at a local drama festival, I walked away with five first prizes. I was featured in the local paper and some of my friends made sarcastic comments about my showing off. I quit, never to act again. While there was no doubt I loved acting and was good at it, I didn't want to lose friends over it. Rather than ostracise myself from my peers, I chose to give up something I enjoyed. Do you recognise this pattern in yourself? Often we suppress our passions because we want to conform. I decided not to flaunt my success and was never picked for the major parts in the school plays when I did audition. Deeply disappointed, I became convinced I must have lacked talent.

When I was 18, I was picked for an interschool debating competition. I had such a crisis of confidence that I learned a script, when I was supposed to speak from cue cards. We lost. For the next 20 years I was quite sure I did not belong on a stage at all.

In 1997 we were living in Norway. I'd started to compile notes for the first edition of *A Career in Your Suitcase*. One of the mothers from my son's preschool, Kit Prendergast, commented that my story was inspirational and I should do a short presentation to the business women's network there. Not one to pass up an opportunity or a challenge, I agreed. Then I worried myself silly! I was desperately nervous and, typically, wrote a complete script, word for word. On the night, however, I found people were genuinely interested and I dared to ad lib a little. The evening was a success and the catalyst for a three-hour workshop I designed and ran with an American named Elizabeth Douet.

Nine months later we presented our workshop at the *Women on the Move* (later called *Global Living*) conference in Paris. We were to speak in the auditorium to between 100 and 300 people. On a stage, with radio mikes, overhead projectors and sound engineers — I was terrified and suffered with nerves for three months beforehand. Huw Francis, who was at that seminar, says my voice trembled the entire time. Nevertheless the adrenalin rush I experienced afterwards was fantastic - and I was hooked.

Today, I have run this seminar and its many permutations all over the world, to thousands of different people. I know I belong on a stage. I prepare cue cards or PowerPoint presentations, but rarely look at them. In 2007 I was even invited to be the closing keynote speaker at the Families in Global Transition conference to talk about my portable career. My passion for being on stage was suppressed for so many years for reasons common to many of us.

Look to your past for clues as to where your passions may once have lain.

Another reason why we lose sight of what we love to do, is we become rather good at other things. We may not be particularly talented at music, but practise hard because we want to be in the school orchestra with our friends. We develop a competence in an area so we can fit in.

With practice we can be good at almost anything — whether it be music, sport, mathematics or driving — but this does not mean the subject fills us with energy. Sometimes it can be hard to separate the things we love to do and do well, from the things we like to do less, but still do well.

Remember back to when you were at school and had to make choices about the subjects in which you wanted to specialise. If you performed well in many subjects then it may have been difficult to decide where to focus. However, the chances are you elected to focus on the subjects that gave you the highest grades. Sadly, the subjects we do best in are not always the ones we love most.

You could be really good at maths, for example, and become a successful accounting firm partner only to realise one day that you are neither happy nor energised. As John Clark says in his book *The Money or Your Life,* you can get to the top of your chosen career ladder and suddenly realise 'you have the ladder against the wrong wall'. This is why it's so important, when you are trying to assess your interests, values and skills, you take account of the things you do at work *and* in your leisure time. Think about the activities that fill you with energy, even if they are not earning you money right now.

Don't expect it to be easy to find your passions. They may have been locked away for many years. You may have to dig deep to revive them. It may take a long time and you may be in for some surprises. But stick with it. The reward is well worth the effort.

Find Your Passion

When Richard Bolles published the first edition of *What Color is your Parachute* in 1972, he helped to popularize the idea that work is more than just a salary. Bolles writes both for people who are out of work and for those weary of work lacking in fulfilment and meaning. His annually revised and updated book, now in its 41st edition, provides readers with the blueprint for a journey of personal and vocational self-discovery.

Bolles recommends that we think of our work as the expression of our mission in life and he supplies us with many inventive exercises to help us identify the nature of this mission. Passion ignites the fuel of your skills and can keep you going when the going gets rough. It is an internal drive that finds expression through your values and skills. Poet David Whyte speaks of it as being 'wholehearted' about something (*http:// www.oprah.com/spirit/Poet-David-Whytes-Questions-That-Have-No-Right-to-Go-Away_1/2*).

> 'I've turned my passion into work by capitalising on France's interesting food and culture backgrounds. Last year, with the help of a colleague, I organised wine tasting weekends in the well-known Bordeaux and Burgundy wine regions in France. I am planning another weekend trip to the Champagne region. France's gourmet offerings — wine, cheeses, local delicacies — allow me to help my students discover the answers to the secrets of French gastronomy.
>
> Whether it is a pre-class trip to the local outdoor market to select fresh ingredients for the menu we will prepare, or a more involved weekend trip to a specific region, I enjoy teaching others to experience, understand and appreciate France's culinary offerings.'
>
> **Sue Y, British, *www.careerinyoursuitcase.com***

In the following exercises and suggestions you'll find a mixture of activities and inspiration we have picked up over the last 25 years or so. Each has merit. Some ideas are of our own invention, others were inspired by other people. If you decide you want to explore this topic in more depth then we suggest you refer to Jo's book, entitled *Find Your Passion,* available from Amazon.

Ways to get started

It is not surprising many people neglect the difficult task of self-scrutiny. After all, where do you begin? How do you get started? How do you know you're on the right track? And how do you keep yourself accountable for the results?

In order to create career ideas and assess our options we need a framework of self-knowledge. This framework will contain the skills and competencies most associate with finding work, but it is important to go deeper and assess your values, interests and drivers in order to find a truly satisfying career for you.

Here are several suggestions to prepare yourself for your own voyage of self-discovery.

BUY A NOTEBOOK

Prepare to do a lot of soul searching, thinking and writing. Buy yourself a large, lined notebook, preferably spiral bound, in which to write your thoughts and exercises. Choose a large one, about A4 or foolscap in size. Try not to succumb to doing this on a computer. If you want to be creative, it's more productive to have a pen in your hand than a keyboard beneath your fingers. Computers use the left, logical, side of your brain. A notebook and pen will use the creative, right side. Use your notebook to record all the 'aha' moments that stand out for you along the way as well as random thoughts and ideas. Later when you reread them with new perspectives, you may find gold you missed the first time round.

MAKE A SPACE

Give yourself permission to make a space in which to explore. This may mean you will have to give up something else in your life to provide time for your voyage of discovery. Ideas will only come to you if you have the space in your head in which to think and the space in your life in which to take action.

Practitioners of *feng shui* recognise the value of clearing clutter from their lives. *Feng shui* uses space clearing, clutter clearing and life laundry to help you to make the mental space in which to explore your dreams.

Your physical space is important too. Try to tidy your workspace at the end of each day, so each morning you're faced with a clear desk. Put your files and papers behind closed doors and remove mirrors from areas where they reflect clutter.

Create yourself a mental and physical space to provide a solid foundation for your portable career journey.

MAKE A COMMITMENT

Promise yourself you'll follow through on this. Picture yourself enjoying the fruits of all the efforts you will put in. But also tell someone else what you're doing. Make a commitment to someone else — a friend, counsellor or coach — whom you can trust to check up on your progress regularly and with love. Also, make a commitment to yourself that you'll be honest and listen to your inner voice. Trust your instincts. We don't mean to lie to ourselves deliberately, but through our efforts to capture what is true we can be influenced by what we would *like* things to be — as well as by what we *think* we should be, instead of what really is. Try hard to be honest about what you are and how you feel. Accept yourself as you are and believe this is all that is needed for your authentic, passionate portable career start.

MAKE A TEAM

Learning about yourself is very effective when you're able to talk with others who can provide perspective, balance and insight. Solitary self-assessment may invite self-delusion and frustration and the 'finding out what you want to find out' syndrome. We all need help in order to see ourselves accurately. Self-assessment is an interactive process. When someone else is there to probe and challenge it stokes our imaginations and sparks self-reflection. On the website of Barbara Sher, author of *Wishcraft*, is a link to her online *Idea Party* under the heading, "What's your dream? Isolation is a dream killer".

Barbara also has certified leadership materials to start your own success team available here: *http://shersuccessteams.com*. Who knows, maybe this is the portable career opportunity you've been looking for? Her bulletin board here is also a place where people can list unique ways to support yourself. Perhaps your ideas will be sparked by reading what has been posted?

To make an informal success team for your portable career, recruit supporters who will support you in finding out who you really are, and who believe in you. We all need to be encouraged and praised, and especially so in times of transition. If your closest family members are not with you in this, then prepare for a rough, but I hope not unbearable, ride. Find people you know well enough to feel that they can join you on the journey, and meet, Skype, text, Tweet or send emails each to other regularly to keep each other motivated and on track. You could form a Facebook page, Yahoo group or your own closed group on LinkedIn for this purpose.

You could kick off your team with a Blue Sky Party. We use 'blue sky' to refer to those magical times when we discuss dreams and make plans with someone else. It's a time for brainstorming — or 'random-entry listings' as it is now politically correct to call these sessions. It is a time for ideas. But we also take 'blue sky' to refer to the blue sky that can emerge from the clouds, and the hope it brings. A summer's day, with a blue sky above, is something many of us, particularly those further away from the equator, long for. Divide the time you have available by the number of guests you invite and take turns to 'blue sky' with each other. Read more on Blue Sky in *Chapter 4 — Create Your Career.*

If you can't build your own team of supporters, you should seriously consider hiring a Career Development Professional. I (Jo) know from painful experience that I won't go to the gym if I'm alone. On my own it's too easy to let myself down. Involving someone else makes it much easier to make a commitment. *Chapter 8 — For the Journey* provides suggestions on how to choose a Career Development Professional.

MONITOR YOUR PROGRESS

Start that notebook now. Write down your thoughts and your achievements each day under the appropriate date. This will help you keep track of your progress and make this process more concrete. Include all you achieve and the thoughts that come to you each day. Date each entry. When you write things down it will make your progress more real and encouraging. Read through it when you need some encouragement and confirmation that you are on your way.

MAKE A START

Take that first step. Start doing something right now, even if it is only for half an hour. Don't set yourself up for failure. The longer you put it off, the bigger it will become on a psychological level. Be realistic and do what will work for you. But start now and believe that in some way it will work for you. Once you begin, and you see patterns and insights emerging, you'll find it hard to stop.

CHECKLIST FOR GETTING STARTED

- ☐ Get a notebook
- ☐ Prepare my workspace
- ☐ Clarify my commitment in writing

  For example: I commit to the process of increasing my self-awareness and learning the skills to build a portable career for myself. I will keep track of and recognise my progress and reward myself for my efforts. I will share what I learn with others.

  Signed: _____

- ☐ Build my team
  Team members to invite:

  _____

  _____

  _____

  _____

- ☐ Keep track of progress:
  I will use _____to monitor my progress.

- ☐ Start date: _____

Put your passions on paper

The following range of exercises can help you discover and find words for your passions. Take time to allow your passions to emerge and clarify and keep going until you have got them written down and are able to express them simply and elegantly. Resist the temptation to jump to decision making before you are ready. The tendency for many people is to want to have it all resolved easily and quickly. Remember this is a process and something you will continue to do throughout your career. You will be learning these skills and often learning means buckling down and practising the skill until you have become comfortable with it.

The self-discovery tools that follow use both your rational and your intuitive capacities to help you explore. Brain research shows both are necessary to create the mental state needed for optimal decision making: that is, decision making based on experience and information rather than a knee-jerk reaction to a situation.

Choose one of the following exercises to get started. Skim through until you find one that clicks with where you're at and start there. Continue working through a variety of the exercises until you have generated enough insights to communicate who you are, and what your passion is, in a succinct way. At that point you are ready to go further and explore ways to turn your passion into action.

After completing the exercise, summarise the results in *Chapter 9 — Your Career Passport.* When you see this symbol at the end of the exercise:

go to *Your Career Passport* and summarise your results there. You will find leafing through this summary, once completed, will give you much support as you find your way towards your portable career.

VALUES

Your passion often stems from your values, interests and what is important to you. Knowing what's important to you can help you apply your skills in the work world in a personally meaningful way. You can be an accountant in a company that does work which is of no interest to you, or you can manage the books in a company that does something you find incredibly important. The latter means your work makes more sense to you from a values perspective while using your accounting skills.

The following exercise is adapted from Richard Knowdell's values card sort that I (Colleen) have used with many groups and individual clients. Write the following 64 values on Post-It® notes or little pieces of paper. On three other Post-It® notes write the headings: *always matter, sometimes matter, don't matter.* Sort through and organise the values into three columns under those headings. After making an initial sort, go through again until you only have eight in your column that always matter to you. If you feel like a value of yours is missing from this list, write it down and add it into your sorting process.

Values List

Accuracy	Fun & humor	Precision / detail work
Advancement	Group & team	Problem solving
Adventure	Help others	Profit / gain
Aesthetics / beauty	Help society / the world	Public contact
Affiliation / belonging	High earnings	Recognition
Artistic creativity	Honesty & integrity	Respect
Challenge	Independence	Responsibility
Change / variety	Influence people	Security
Community	Innovative ideas	Simplicity
Competence	Intellectual status	Spirituality
Competition	Job tranquillity	Stability
Contribute own ideas	Knowledge	Status
Diversity	Learning	Steep learning curve
Environment	Location	Structure & predictability
Excitement	Meaningful contribution	Supervision / be in charge
Expertise	Perceive intuitively	Tangible result / product
Fairness	Personal growth	Time freedom
Family	Personal safety	Tradition
Fast pace	Physical challenge	Work alone
Freedom	Power and authority	Work with others
Friendships at work	Practicality	Worklife balance
		Work under pressure

Adapted from the Knowdell Career Values Card Sort *www.CareerTrainer.com*

360° OF INSIGHT

Canadian Donna Messer started her career as a banker, which led to a variety of work roles until she went in search of a new career that embodied her skills and her passions. When she looked in the mirror she saw only education and experience. She had no idea what she wanted to do, nor what she could do aside from what she'd already done. So she asked three of her friends what they saw when they looked at her.

'You make things look nice,' said the first friend, referring to the wonderful decorations

Donna would make out of next to nothing to dress up the village hall or her home. 'You make things taste good,' said the second, reminded of the great food Donna would concoct from a random selection of ingredients and spices, and serve to the entire football team when they arrived on an impromptu visit.

'You bring people together,' said the third friend, as she recalled the way Donna could organise disparate people into a team and marshal their combined resources to create a successful project.

Thus inspired, Donna went on to create a company called Orange Crate, which sold original combinations of herbs and spices, packed into neat wooden boxes. She also created her team of associates from among the farmers in her community, who felt they could not yet contribute to the business, but who offered invaluable help with tasks such as driving, deliveries and book keeping.

Orange Crate began with a small loan from a local bank and ten years later was sold to a group of three companies who joined forces to buy it.

'They were a food company, a media company and a financial institution, so we must have done something right!' recalls Donna.

Donna no longer runs Orange Crate. She now travels the world speaking to large groups, conferences and corporations, inspiring them in turn, with her stories of resourcefulness and networking. She shares her secrets at *www.connectuscanada.com.*

Now it's your turn to ask others for feedback. If you formed a team as suggested under 'getting started' then this is a great task for you to do as a group. Go beyond your friends and include family, colleagues, clients (if applicable) and someone you've just met in your survey. You can email people, give them a sheet of paper to write on and give back to you, or call them. Some people may need some preparation time, but it's usually best if they just give their first reactions. Here is a text you can use to explain to people what you are asking for, or to print and distribute manually:

I am inventorying my career assets and would like your input. Could you please respond to the following questions honestly and openly? What kind of person would you describe me as? What are my best qualities? In what areas could I improve my personal effectiveness? What would you describe as fitting career choices for me?

15 mins

48

Resist jumping to conclusions when you receive your first reply. Journal your initial reaction to the response and then wait until you've heard back from everyone. Then look for the themes and patterns in the responses. Summarise the feedback you have received here:

30
mins

YOU: What do you say about yourself? How do you see yourself? What are your best qualities?

_____

_____

_____

FRIENDS: What do friends say about you? What do they appreciate most about you? What is their career wish for you?

_____

_____

_____

FAMILY: What does your family say about you? What do they appreciate most about you? What is their career wish for you?

_____

_____

_____

_____

COLLEAGUES / CLIENTS: What do colleagues/clients say about you?

_____

_____

_____

NEW ACQUAINTANCES: What first impression do you make? (Ask someone you just met - you'll be surprised how many insights they got from their first impression.)

_____

_____

_____

If you would like to focus more on these types of insights, go to *Chapter 6 — Marketing Your Skills,* and complete the exercises on personal branding, specifically the Johari Window.

I DO NOT LIKE

Sometimes it can be easier to work out what we do not want than what we do want. So make this list and be honest.

Write down all the things you do not enjoy doing, or that you feel you're poor at doing. Include all the things you leave until last and that make you yawn when you think of them. For example, we hate doing year-end accounts and making sales calls.

I do not like:

_____
_____
_____
_____
_____
_____
_____
_____
_____
_____

Identify the three things you hate most and consider what their opposites might be — since they may well be the very things you love. For example, the opposite for me (Jo) of *I hate doing my year-end accounts* is *I love holding a newly finished book — mine or my client's — for the first time.*

My top three and their opposites:

_____
_____
_____
_____
_____
_____
_____
_____

10 mins

ENERGY VAMPIRES

Now work with the next list, 'energy vampires', to find your possible energy drainers. Here you write down the things you do that make you feel tired. What activities bore you, and rob you of motivation and momentum? Also list the types of people who seem to drain you of energy. Think of them as energy vampires, these tasks and these people that suck life out of you. If 'types' of people don't come to mind, list actual people. Consider whether they are demanding or impatient people, perfectionists or people who can barely get one foot in front of the other. If you can calculate when you feel drained it can help you to see when you're energised. If you feel drained by people who are bossy, then think about working in an environment that allows you to be the boss. If you find it hard to be among needy or weak people, then think about working in a high energy, successful environment. If you feel uncomfortable among charismatic, dynamic people, then perhaps you would feel happier in a nurturing, supportive field. Knowing what you don't want can help clarify the vision of what you do what.

These types of people, environments and activities drain my energy:

10
mins

_____

_____

_____

_____

_____

_____

_____

_____

_____

_____

_____

_____

_____

_____

_____

_____

_____

_____

TIME FLIES

Write down all the things you have ever done when you realised afterwards that time had flown by. Who were you with? What were you doing? What were you talking about? Does it happen while you are gardening or shopping perhaps? In conversation, cooking, typing or driving? Think about it. When time flies so fast that you lose track of it, that's an activity worthy of repeating and finding ways to bring more of it into your life. These are also known as flow experiences. You can read more about flow online at Wikipedia with the search term 'flow (psychology)'.

Time flies when:

_____

_____

_____

_____

_____

_____

_____

_____

_____

_____

_____

_____

_____

_____

_____

_____

_____

15 mins

ENERGY SOURCES

It is widely accepted we expend far less energy doing the things we love than the things we don't. Some people claim we use an astounding 100 percent less.

Write down the things you do that energise you. What makes you feel like you're flying? What makes you want to sing? What makes you happy and puts a spring in your step? What do you do that leaves you feeling great and full of energy afterwards? These can be hobbies, domestic tasks and leisure activities as well as work related tasks. Think about the last time you did these things and use your creativity to bring

10 mins

more of them into your life now. They can help provide the fuel you need to keep
going in this process as well as give you direction for your portable career.

_____

_____

_____

_____

_____

_____

_____

_____

_____

_____

_____

_____

_____

_____

_____

_____

_____

_____

_____

_____

_____

_____

_____

10 THINGS I LOVE TO DO

This exercise is inspired by the work of Norm Amundson, author of *Active
Engagement.* Sometimes we forget to ask ourselves this question as we go through
our daily activities.

Write down ten things you enjoy doing, including those things you do on vacations,
in your leisure time, with your family, on your own and at work. Sometimes we take
these for granted as they can be very simple. If nothing comes immediately to mind,
then give yourself the time to reflect and go about your daily activities and the list
will come to you, especially if while you do things you note when you are enjoying
yourself.

15
mins

☐ _____
☐ _____
☐ _____
☐ _____
☐ _____
☐ _____
☐ _____
☐ _____
☐ _____
☐ _____

Place the applicable symbol beside each activity:

€ - if it costs more than €10
A - if it is something you prefer to do alone
P - if it requires planning
2 - if you have done it in the last two weeks

What do you notice about the activities: Are they diverse or do they have a great deal in common? Are you still actively involved or have there been changes in your life? Do you see any patterns? What new insights has this list inspired?

As an optional exercise to expand on the exercise above, you can ask yourself the following questions:

• What would I move mountains to be able to do?
• What topics grab my interest in a way that I am willing to spend time and money on them? What makes me sit up and pay attention? For example, what have I bought books about, got a subscription for, tuned in to, found myself searching for and reading on the web. What are my boards on Pinterest and groups on LinkedIn? What does my Facebook and Twitter page tell me about myself and who I friend and follow?
• What would I do if money were completely no issue?

FOLLOW YOUR CURIOSITY

If you feel your 'passion' has dried up and abandoned you or you don't have a 'passion', try doing what Elizabeth Gilbert, author of the bestseller *Eat, Pray, Love*, did when her writing passion dried up during the writing of her sequel. She followed the sage advice of a good friend to follow her *curiosity* for a while. This worked brilliantly for her as she immersed herself in gardening and eventually came to the 'aha' she needed to get the sequel back on track.

Don't pressure yourself into a state of panic if you find your passion is missing in action. Give yourself the time and space to explore the world and follow your curiosity for a while. Be like a tiny child exploring the world for the first time, full of wonder at the smallest things. Pay attention when your mind wanders and let yourself meander through an hour or a day. If you are in a new environment, because you have relocated for example, you are perfectly set up for this exercise. If not, go somewhere you have never been before and open yourself up to really experiencing it. It could be as simple as taking a walk in the opposite direction than you normally do, or buying your food in a different location. Take your camera with you and photograph the things you notice. Later you can review the images to discover common threads and make a collage if you wish.

Take note of the things that stand out to you during these experiences and record them here:

What did you notice?

_____

_____

_____

20 mins

What are you curious about? What questions arise out of what you noticed?

_____

_____

_____

Repeat this exercise often to foster your ability to see new things, dream new dreams and re-awaken your passion. Look for connections and patterns in what you are noticing and listen to what that says about you.

HOT TRACKS

Life Coach Martha Beck notes that following our 'hot tracks' can help us find our way in the ever-changing world around us. She explains research has shown the emotional side of our brain helps us to make choices and find our way and NOT the rational brain. She advises us to allow ourselves to go a little wild, to let our 'wild animal' help us find our way forward. Because as we all know, even animals are able to find their way to what they need in life — the right migration route, nesting ground, grazing area, water hole. We just need to allow this part of our brain to lead us forward.

It works like this: go to the place where you were last enthused and interested about something. This is your last 'hot track'. Now choose a direction, based on your knowledge of the animal (that's you!) and its behaviour as to where it would go next and follow that. If the trail turns cold return again to the place of your last hot track and make another educated guess.

When I (Colleen) moved to the Netherlands I felt I needed to reconsider my career direction. I wasn't sure if I would be able to continue in the field of career development with limited skill in the Dutch language. I considered a few other options to help me work and learn the language like teaching fitness classes again or working in a store for the first time. When I went to adapt my CV for this purpose, however, I got stuck. It was at that point, with the help of my portfolio, I found my hot tracks and again found a way to follow my passion.

Look back at what you wrote down under the headings, 'I Love' and 'Time Flies When'. These are some of your hot tracks. Now think about related activities which may also foster that sense of flow and engagement and also give you a little bit of room to grow and stretch from where you are now. Test one of these ideas to see if it's a hot track for you as well. If so, you're onto something. If not, try again with another idea. Your emotions will let you know if you're onto something, so pay attention to what they are telling you.

Three potential hot tracks for me to explore are:

_____
_____
_____

_____

Signs that tell me these are hot tracks:

_____
_____
_____
_____

Based on my current knowledge of 'the animal' the most likely direction this hot track could lead is:

_____

_____

_____

_____

_____

Allow your inner animal to take the lead and enjoy the adventure. Give yourself the time and space to find that path and follow one hot track to another. Eventually you will decipher your own individual route and journey. That's what having a portable career is all about anyway. Right?

Source: *http://www.oprah.com/money/Find-Your-Career-Path/1*

YOUR MENTAL PHOTOGRAPH ALBUM

This idea comes from Dr Phil McGraw, the psychologist doctor who came into the spotlight as a regular on the Oprah Winfrey show and now has his own show. He has written several useful books to help you understand yourself and your family better. His two books, *Life Strategies and Self Matters,* can be very helpful in a general way.

Dr Phil asks us to identify our Defining Moments, the moments in our lives that shaped us forever, the moments we can remember clearly with all of our senses. I (Jo) can remember distinctly how it felt that day the teacher told me I was too clever for her class. I can see the disdain on her face, feel the warm September day outside the classroom, remember how cold and saddened I suddenly became. This was a defining moment for me that shaped my life. Yet on a happier note, I recall the evening launch party for our date cookery book in Oman. The room smelled of incense and spice, the guests wore a mixture of eau de nil, traditional Omani dress and Western clothes. We ate miniature date and nut cutlets and dates stuffed with ricotta cheese and pine nuts and drank cardamom flavoured Arabic coffee. Outside the window of the Pearl restaurant at the Al Bustan Palace hotel, we could see the sea through the palm trees. This time I knew I loved the exoticism and opportunity of life abroad and I also knew I could succeed.

Similarly I (Colleen) remember a presentation I made during my Career Development studies when I suddenly noticed my fellow classmates taking notes on what I was saying. That was a feeling and moment which helped clarify my direction and develop my confidence.

Look out for your Defining Moments in your life and career. Sometimes they will be times that made you feel terrific, sometimes they made you sad and sometimes they will have filled you with so much energy you could almost feel your ego disappear. You were at one with the world.

Take a look at your mental photograph album now, seek out the snapshots that stay clear in your mind and work out what they tell you about yourself today. Add them into your professional portfolio as described in *Chapter 6 — Marketing Your Skills.*

25 mins

What are the snapshots that return to your mind's eye now as you look back over key moments in your life? Think about your childhood when you were around seven years old, your teen years when you were around 16 years old, your early adulthood around age 21 and so on. Record the following information for these snapshots:

Location/Situation/People involved:

_____

_____

_____

_____

_____

Age: _____

Key memory(s) associated with this:

_____

_____

_____

_____

_____

Feelings/Emotions:

_____

_____

_____

_____

WHEN I GROW UP

Think back to when you were a young child. What did you want to be when you grew up? We both wanted to be an actress or a singer! We can see now we wanted to be on a stage. And perhaps we both did realise that dream in its own way, since our work now puts us in front of people in various ways. Think about your own childhood aspirations. What did you want to do and be when you grew up? Have you fulfilled any of these hopes, even if only indirectly? Is there more you can do to work towards them now?

Write down what you wanted to do when you were young and how these aspirations may still be alive in you.

When I was 7, I wanted to be:

10
mins

_____

When I was 14, I wanted to be:

_____

When I was 17, I wanted to be:

_____

When I was 24, I wanted to be:

_____

Write down the themes you see connecting the different snapshots in your mental photo album and the different career ideas you have had over the course of your life. Look deeper than the job titles. **For example:** do they all include helping people?

_____

_____

_____

FAMILY INHERITANCE

Think about your parents and your grandparents. Taking each of them in turn, write down what you think their passions may have been. Now write down what you think their values may have been, and their strengths. Which of their passions, skills and characteristics do you think they passed on to you? I (Colleen) think of my grandma's values every time I roll out dough and try to use the minimum amount of flour necessary. Remember your own stories connected to these people in your life and use these stories to connect to the values that have been passed on.

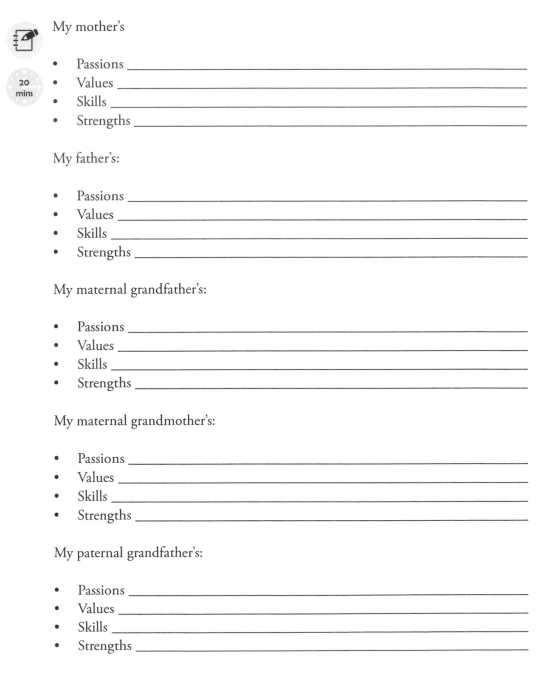

My mother's

- Passions _____
- Values _____
- Skills _____
- Strengths _____

My father's:

- Passions _____
- Values _____
- Skills _____
- Strengths _____

My maternal grandfather's:

- Passions _____
- Values _____
- Skills _____
- Strengths _____

My maternal grandmother's:

- Passions _____
- Values _____
- Skills _____
- Strengths _____

My paternal grandfather's:

- Passions _____
- Values _____
- Skills _____
- Strengths _____

My paternal grandmother's:

- Passions _____
- Values _____
- Skills _____
- Strengths _____

FEAR OF SUCCESS

Contrary to popular belief it is not always a fear of failure that stops us from doing something — it is just as likely to be a fear of success. When I (Jo) was a five-year-old, I had to change schools because my family moved house. I have a vivid memory of that first day at my new school when the teacher asked me to stand up and recite the alphabet. I did so, using the adult pronunciation of 'ay, bee, see'. The teacher told me I was wrong and it should be pronounced phonetically, 'ah, buh, kuh', which is the standard teaching method in England. I felt uncomfortable. Children stared at me. The teacher said I was 'too clever' so I was moved up a class, away from my peers. I saw this as a punishment. When I look closely at my life I can see many instances later on where I 'dumbed down' in order to fit in. My experience is corroborated by Dr David George, the eminent education expert, who notes that England is one of very few countries where it is not cool to be clever. For the remainder of my school life I forced myself to be average, and my grades reflected this. Only since my fortieth birthday have I realised that deep down I may actually be academic.

Recently I have braved talking about this to my English girlfriends, only to find that, so far, each one of them, like me, had feigned being average. I also remember a time when my then 11year-old son said he was pleased we had chosen for him a school that encourages academic competition, because he could not bear to be bullied and called a geek elsewhere.

Consider the times in your life when you may have sabotaged your success. I sabotaged mine by dumbing down. Think about your motives. Think about the passions you may have suppressed as a result. Add these to your list of passions.

Dr Susan Jeffers classic book, *Feel the Fear and Do It Anyway* has helped many to deal successfully with fear. I (Colleen) found it extremely helpful to gain an understanding of its psychological basis in our nature and discovering tools to work with these natural drives and ultimately go past the fear. If fear is holding you back in some way, get yourself a copy of this book.

Reflect on your own life experience to answer these next questions.
A time I sabotaged my own success was when:

20
mins

_____

_____

_____

My motives were:

_____

_____

_____

I can more effectively express these protective urges by:

_____

_____

_____

WHEN SUCCESS WAS EASILY WON

In *I Could Do Anything if I Only I Knew What it Was,* Barbara Sher provides many revealing exercises about success. She believes we are blocked more by our fear of success than by our fear of failure. Sadly, we receive more attention from others if we recount tales of failure instead of success. It is not as socially acceptable to be one who 'blows their own horn' and this is exactly why many have difficulty writing their CV or recounting their strengths effectively in a job interview.

In the process of self-discovery you are now on, you will need to take time to rediscover (if necessary), learn from and enjoy your successes. Think of the times in your past when you did allow yourself to succeed at something, times when you did not give in to peer pressure or fears. The following exercise allows you to record and reflect on some of your shining moments.

YOUR SHINING MOMENTS

Review the experiences that have brought you the most joy; that have allowed you to shine, be at your best and accomplish the most. By analyzing these moments in your life, you will be able to use the information to continue to put yourself into situations which will make use of the skills that support you to be joyful and shine. These moments don't have to be out of this world. They can be from different aspects of your life; from work achievements to things in the personal realm, like hosting a successful dinner party. They can be from different periods of your life or from different ages. The most important thing is that they brought you joy, a deep satisfaction, and a sense of pride.

Write down at least five of these stories. Perhaps one of the previous exercises has reminded you of a story or stories? After you have written your five stories, your task will be to look for similar patterns between stories. When you discover patterns you will be able to identify which elements are key to bringing you joy in your life. This is not only an important part of getting ready to choose your next move but also preparing to market yourself for your portable work.

Learning how to write these stories is a skill in itself. You may have more difficulty at the beginning, but once you get going and get a feel for it, you will be on your way to some great discoveries about the wonderful things that you have accomplished.

Here is an example to help you get an idea of how to go about this:

Situation:

Give a brief description of what was happening at the time.

Upon moving to the Netherlands I (Colleen) discovered I would need to pass a driver's theory exam and practical test in order to get a driver's license. After over 20 years driving experience I would have to be re-tested. It came as quite a shock.

Task(s):

What needed to happen or be done?

I needed to study for the theory test, arrange to take the test, get registered for driving lessons and get my license within six months as then I would no longer be able to use the driver's license from my home country. I also needed to build up my confidence and experience driving a manual transmission car.

Action:

What did you do? Get as specific as possible about what you actually did.

I researched driving schools and found one that met my criteria: it would give me lessons in English, was located in the town where I live and also had the best pass-rate for students. I arranged to take the driving theory exam in English. I studied and practised for the theory exam using an English translation of the driver's manual and a CD-ROM in the local language. I took as many driver's lessons as recommended by the instructor to ensure I was ready for the practical exam and to reinforce through practice the ways of traffic here while using a manual transmission car. I did a practice exam so I would know what would be expected in an exam here and to help deal with exam stress (which I had never experienced to this degree before).

Result:

What was the result that gave you satisfaction or made you proud? Why did you feel that you shone?

I passed both the theory and practical exam on the first try. I was proud I had re-established my level of independence in a new country, that I had proven my driving skills were safe and adequate in this country, that I had the self-discipline to study for something I thought I already knew; that I was open to learning things over again if needed; that I was able to succeed even under stress. While on one level this seems small, it felt like a huge accomplishment to have successfully gone through the process to obtain my driver's license for this country.

Okay. Now it's your turn!

Shining moment story 1

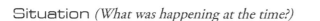

20
mins

Concisely describe below something you have accomplished which gave you a feeling of satisfaction and brought you joy. It can be something very simple and non-work-related, like cooking a nice dinner. The key is that you felt a sense of satisfaction or joy as a result.

Situation *(What was happening at the time?)*

_____

_____

_____

_____

Task(s) *(What needed to be done? What was the obstacle?)*

_____

_____

_____

_____

Action *(What did you do?)*

_____

_____

_____

_____

Results / satisfaction / benefit *(What was the result?)*

_____

_____

_____

_____

Reflection *(What did you learn? What would you do the same/differently next time?)*

_____

_____

_____

_____

_____

Shining moment story 2

20 mins

Concisely describe below something you have accomplished which gave you a feeling of satisfaction and brought you joy. It can be something very simple and non-work-related, like cooking a nice dinner. The key is that you felt a sense of satisfaction or joy as a result.

Situation *(What was happening at the time?)*

_____
_____
_____
_____

Task(s) *(What needed to be done? What was the obstacle?)*

_____
_____
_____
_____

Action *(What did you do?)*

_____
_____
_____
_____

Results / satisfaction / benefit *(What was the result?)*

_____
_____
_____
_____

Reflection *(What did you learn? What would you do the same/differently next time?)*

_____
_____
_____
_____
_____

Shining moment story 3

Concisely describe below something you have accomplished which gave you a feeling of satisfaction and brought you joy. It can be something very simple and non-work-related, like cooking a nice dinner. The key is that you felt a sense of satisfaction or joy as a result.

20 mins

Situation *(What was happening at the time?)*

_____

_____

_____

_____

Task(s) *(What needed to be done? What was the obstacle?)*

_____

_____

_____

_____

Action *(What did you do?)*

_____

_____

_____

Results / satisfaction / benefit *(What was the result?)*

_____

_____

_____

_____

Reflection *(What did you learn? What would you do the same/differently next time?)*

_____

_____

_____

_____

Shining moment story 4

20 mins

Concisely describe below something you have accomplished which gave you a feeling of satisfaction and brought you joy. It can be something very simple and non-work-related, like cooking a nice dinner. The key is that you felt a sense of satisfaction or joy as a result.

Situation *(What was happening at the time?)*

_____
_____
_____
_____

Task(s) *(What needed to be done? What was the obstacle?)*

_____
_____
_____
_____

Action *(What did you do?)*

_____
_____
_____
_____

Results / satisfaction / benefit *(What was the result?)*

_____
_____
_____
_____

Reflection *(What did you learn? What would you do the same/differently next time?)*

_____
_____
_____
_____
_____

Shining moment story 5

20
mins

Concisely describe below something you have accomplished which gave you a feeling of satisfaction and brought you joy. It can be something very simple and non-work-related, like cooking a nice dinner. The key is that you felt a sense of satisfaction or joy as a result.

Situation *(What was happening at the time?)*

_____
_____
_____
_____

Task(s) *(What needed to be done? What was the obstacle?)*

_____
_____
_____
_____

Action *(What did you do?)*

_____
_____
_____
_____

Results / satisfaction / benefit *(What was the result?)*

_____
_____
_____
_____

Reflection *(What did you learn? What would you do the same/differently next time?)*

_____
_____
_____
_____

Reflect on your *Shining Moments* and create a personal definition of success, noting when you have been successful and what your key ingredients needed for success are.

Adapted with permission from *Advanced Techniques for Work Search,* published by the Government of Alberta, Human Services, *www.alis.alberta.ca/publications.* For more career planning exercises, visit *www.alis.alberta.ca/careerinsite.*

ECLECTIC CAREERS

Some people have one full time work role and that is sufficient for them. Others take on a variety of roles in order to create their full time work scenario. We can work on lots of projects at once, each project drawing on different strengths. When I (Jo) was in Oman I made date chutney, taught creative writing and wrote as a journalist. Accept that you can do many seemingly disparate things.

10 mins

Write down as many things as you can think of that you'd like to do. Don't limit yourself by only writing down the things you know to be possible right now, or only those that might earn you money. This is a form of bucket list; a list of all the things you want to do in your life before you die. You may have seen the film of the same name starring Jack Nicholson and Morgan Freeman. What is on your bucket list? Do you want to: Cook with Jamie Oliver? Sing with a live orchestra? Volunteer to build a school? Write them all down. Don't stop until you have run out of dreams.

This is the unlimited list of all the things I want to do:

_____
_____
_____
_____
_____
_____
_____
_____
_____
_____
_____
_____
_____
_____
_____
_____

(Note: Don't let the end of these lines stop you from continuing!)

Now, from this list, put a box around the ideas which are impractical right now, and circle the ones that are more feasible. Look again at the ideas marked as impractical and ensure you have gathered all the needed information before you decide not to pursue them. Be aware you may be able to do some of these things consecutively, and others concurrently.

Choose four things you could do almost right away and keep your eyes open for ways to incorporate them into your current situation. Write them down here. Writing down your goals increases your chance of realizing them without limiting you, as you can always change and adapt them as you go along.

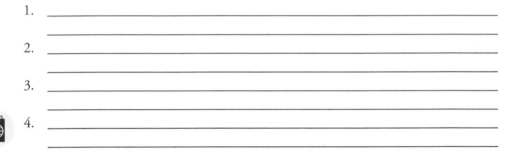

1. _____
   _____
2. _____
   _____
3. _____
   _____
4. _____
   _____

YOUR CAREER VISION

What does your dream for the future look like? What are some of the elements that make up your dream and help give it shape and form? Athletes have discovered that, after their natural talent, having a vision of their success is as important as their physical training regime. 1988 Winter Olympics downhill ski champion Alberto Tomba made headlines for his activities off the hill as well as on. Many questioned how someone as undisciplined as he appeared to be could win so many medals. The key difference was he had a clear and powerful *vision* of what winning would be like for him. It included not only seeing and hearing the crowds roaring at the bottom of the hill, but his family celebrating him and welcoming him home afterwards, and receiving a Ferrari and a car sponsorship deal. It was a vision he could not only see but also *taste, hear and feel.* It made a huge difference for his performance that year as he won two gold medals. This technique can also be used by people who have a different set of values, talents and vision from an Olympian. Use this process to maximize and focus your potential, to achieve what you most want to achieve in your life and to fuel your endeavours.

'Live out of your imagination, not your history.'
Stephen Covey

Create the time and space you need to do this exercise effectively. Make sure you have 30 minutes of uninterrupted time in a space that is just for you. You may want to pre-record the following text so your mind is free to take you where it chooses as you listen to it being replayed. Wherever you see three dots in the text, make sure you pause to allow your thoughts to form. This is also an excellent exercise to do with your support, success or blue-sky team. Make sure to read it slowly and pause between sentences so your mind can create a visual for the scene and fill in some details.

When you are ready to start, close your eyes and make yourself comfortable in a chair, feet firmly on the ground, breathing and body relaxed. Take the time to ensure you are relaxed, have let go of other thoughts and are ready to hear what is going to be said. When you are comfortable, relaxed and your mind is clear, start the text.

Visioning Text

You are waking up ten years in the future after a perfect night's rest. Your life has gone exactly as you hoped it would and you are completely satisfied with everything that has happened. As you wake up, you look around you. You see the room you are in…, how it is furnished…, and who is there with you. You look out the window, enjoying the view and the elements that make it up, be it nature, bustling city or somewhere in between… You recognise where you live… what type of dwelling…, what town, city or rural area…, province, state or region…, and what country. You get out of bed and walk to the closet to select your clothes appropriate for the day's activities. You see what is in your closet and how it reflects your life roles…, work… and leisure activities…. As you walk through your home you notice how you have arranged everything to perfectly suit your ideal life, including your hobby equipment. Enjoy how it looks…, sounds…, smells… and feels to be living your ideal life… Now you are ready to head out into the day. Outside, you run into an old friend you haven't seen for the past five years. You fill them in on what you have been doing since you last saw them… Once you have finished talking to your friend, you can come back to the present.

Adapted with permission from *Radical Change in the World of Work: The Workbook*, published by the Government of Alberta, Human Resources and Employment. For more career planning exercises, visit *www.alis.alberta.ca/careerinsite*.

Following this visualization it is important to take the time to record what you saw. Use the questions that follow to do this.

Take the time now to write down what you saw and experienced in this visioning process.

1. This is a description of my home:

_____

_____

_____

_____

_____

2. This is who I am living with:

_____

_____

_____

_____

_____

3. This is where I am living (location):

_____

_____

_____

_____

_____

4. This is what I will do today (activities):

_____

_____

_____

_____

5. This is what I have done over the last 10 years:

_____

_____

_____

_____

6. My hobbies are:

_____

_____

_____

_____

7. My work is:

_____

_____

_____

_____

8. My lifestyle is:

_____

_____

_____

_____

9. What is most important to me is:

_____

_____

_____

_____

10. I am most proud of accomplishing:

_____

_____

_____

_____

Did this process work for you? Was it difficult or easy? Were you able to open yourself up to this task, or do you find this type of activity too 'out there'? That's okay too as there are other ways to develop a vision or image of your desired future. If you had difficulty with this or didn't do the process, take note of the thoughts that kept you from engaging in this process.

Thoughts that interrupt dreaming for me:

_____
_____
_____
_____
_____
_____
_____
_____
_____
_____
_____
_____

My (Colleen's) own first experience of this process over 10 years ago informed me, among other things, of the importance of the role natural light plays in my life. It was present in all aspects of the visioning process and was something that stayed with me afterwards and which I began to notice more and more. Now living in the Netherlands, I appreciate on a whole different level that there is a law that states every work space (as appropriate to the work function) must have an adequate amount of natural light! And that Dutch architecture uses many large windows.

Come back to this visioning process from time to time as your vision will continue to evolve along with you.

Speedwriting

I (Jo) am a firm believer in speedwriting as a valuable way to get inside yourself and unlock your secrets. Speedwriting has nothing to do with shorthand. Instead it refers to the method by which you write really fast about whatever is on your mind. For this to work you must use a lined notebook with a spiral binding, so that it is easy for you to move from page to page. Some people call this kind of writing 'stream of consciousness'.

When you write fast like this, your thoughts may be random and that's fine. Put down each thought as it comes to you and keep on writing until you have no more to say. Let your mind wander. You must not stop writing to think or edit what you've written. If your ideas are slow in coming then write down words such as 'words words

words' or 'I must write I must write', but do not take your pen off the paper.

Speedwriting feels like magic. You can almost sense that the thoughts go straight from your soul to the page, bypassing your brain. Lose control; don't worry about spelling, grammar or punctuation. Just write.

In her book about speedwriting, called *Writing Down the Bones*, Natalie Goldberg talks about the process at length. She says speedwriting allows your subconscious to emerge and is a great way to find out what you really think and want and believe. As a fan of this method I (Jo) have to agree. Once I was unsure when to run my next series of creative writing classes. I agonised over the day of the week, the time of day and the pricing I would use in a new country. So I speedwrote around my thoughts for about 20 minutes, and miraculously the answer came to me. I would run them on a Thursday morning at 9am. Simple when you know how! You can speedwrite on any topic you like, of course, and the results can be therapeutic. I even know of several people who formed their own speedwriting group and met monthly to write together and share their experiences. Often it can be very painful to read out loud what you've written. So before you leap into starting a group be careful that you will be among firm friends.

Here are some ideas you could work with, to set you off with speedwriting:

- The job of my dreams
- When I was a child
- I wish
- I love
- I hate
- If only
- In a perfect world
- Next year
- In my teens
- Work

KEEP A JOURNAL

One of the biggest influences on my (Jo's) life has been a book called *The Artist's Way* by Julia Cameron. I completed this workbook as part of my personal journey of introspection back in 1994, when I was living in Muscat, and my friend Karen recommended it. So impressed was she with it, Karen would buy several copies every time she went home to England to give to her friends.

This book is particularly designed for people who want to unlock their inner creativity and to discover who they really are. Yet it is not reserved for artists — we all have creativity in our soul. Cameron asks readers to devote 12 weeks to her course, which includes speedwriting a journal for ten minutes every morning. In addition, Cameron provides a chapter on a different subject each week, asks questions and invites you to reflect on that topic for seven days.

Start writing your own dream journal every morning as close to waking up as you can. Through journaling you're likely to remember your dreams, which can be most revealing. It is interesting that once you start to anticipate writing down your dreams on waking, your dreams become more vivid and revealing than ever. I recall distinctly a dream I had about thirteen years ago while I was journaling daily. I saw that I was working in an attic surrounded by the colour turquoise, and people came to me and I gave them books. I now have an office upstairs in my house, and it is lined with books. Indeed people do come to me, usually through email, to buy these books. I have resisted painting the walls turquoise, but know this to be a colour that, for me, represents water, creativity, the sea and peace. Funnily enough, if I look at the pictures and cards I have pinned up around my desk, they all contain quite a splash of turquoise!

There are many ways to journal. Blogging, old-fashioned letter writing and even scrapbooking can be a form of journaling. If you are starting to journal for the first time and would like a journal with prompts in it, consider the 'Become' journal available at *www.gadanke.com* for your journey towards a portable career.

WRITE YOUR STORY

Most of us enjoy reading an autobiography. They can be insightful and revealing. Your own story can be equally insightful and compelling, so there is every reason for you to write it down in order to find out more about yourself and put your life into perspective. Often what appears mundane and ordinary to us is experienced as not so ordinary by another.

When we make an effort to see each of our career choices on paper we can begin to understand what motivated us to make each decision. It is important to remember the details of the actual context in which you made your decisions, as this will allow you to uncover what your real motivators are. For example, instead of assuming your choice to follow a particular course of study was solely motivated by you, consider the outside influences which played a role in your life at the time. They could be parents, friends, the economy, demographics and financial necessities. In school, I (Colleen) chose to specialise in working with seniors because the demographics showed this would be a growth sector in the future. After some experience I discovered I would rather work with other age groups and that making a decision based solely on demographics missed some important factors, like where my strengths would be most effectively applied in a personally satisfying way. Writing your own career story in this way puts you in a strong position to gain insights into your life as a story and continue the development of its main character and plot. You will have put yourself in the driver's seat of your portable career.

Writing your story can also help you to connect the past to your new reality, a reality that may seem so unlike anything you have experienced. This can open the door for increased receptivity to the opportunities that await you in your new location. In so doing you will move yourself in the direction of an 'examined life', becoming more conscious of how you have operated in the past and integrated these experiences into your understanding of yourself and the world. This level of conscious awareness can create the space needed for you to make new choices and take new directions.

I (Jo) would always suggest you write any of this soul-searching stuff longhand — but as memories are wont to return randomly, use whatever method allows you to record your story as it comes to you.

You may want to incorporate the tool of writing in the third person in order to create some distance and objectivity for your writing. For example. 'She went to language class expecting...'. Creating distance and objectivity from your own life will help you gain insights and perspective impossible to achieve without this psychological distance.

Write the different chapters of your life as distinguished by key transitions and crossroads. Include details of your situation at the time, recognizing what is now different for you. It is not uncommon for this process to take a significant investment of time and effort. This is required to allow your story to take shape as you see the connections, red threads and different interpretations that present themselves the more you work with it.

Start at the beginning and write about what you loved to do when you were a child, about your friends, your family, your achievements, who you admired, what frightened you and the things you did at play. Then proceed into your teenage years, your twenties and beyond, right up until the present day.

Write about your work, your education, your relationships and why they ended, or why they worked. What made you happy? Write about your successes, your failures, your passions, the things you spent most time with and the things you least liked to do. See if you can spot any of the catalysts that caused certain things to happen in your life, the reasons you had arguments with your friends, the reasons you did well in certain subjects and what made you choose them.

Write about what you do in your leisure time: What magazines do you read? What television program do you watch regularly? What is the storyline of your favourite book or movie and what does that tell you about what's important to you, your values and drivers?

When you've finished, look back and see if any patterns emerge or any links are made. See if this reflection holds some of the keys to what you love to do.

In her book *Work with Passion*, Nancy Anderson gives pages of instructions on how to write a highly detailed and insightful autobiography. Her version is likely to extend to 50 pages or more! If you feel you need help writing your story, few books are more thorough than hers. For example, Nancy asks you to begin your autobiography by writing about your grandparents.

My (Jo's) book *Release the Book Within* is another resource to consider.

If you want a Career Development Professional to work with you on this, find one who practices the career construction approach of Dr Mark Savickas or who has experience and training working with career narratives or biographies.

Self-Assessment Tools

There are a number of self-assessment tools available on the market and many can be completed online. Some are free of charge. The objective overview of your talents, gained through the use of these tools can be insightful, though you may find some seem complicated and others trite. You may find some discrepancies, but in general they have huge value and are great fun, particularly if you get a few friends together, do one each and then compare notes.

Gail MacIndoe (*www.gailmacindoe.com*) is a behavioural and values analyst and uses a number of time-tested and cross cultural validated assessment tools to help her clients gain an insight into their behaviour, attitudes and values. She believes such tools may provide:

- an increased understanding of self
- an increased understanding of others
- understanding of your motivations
- insight into how your behaviour affects and communicates with others
- awareness of your natural strengths and weaknesses
- understanding of what motivates your decisions
- insight into your causes of conflict

You may legitimately wonder whether you would be better off taking assessments under the guidance of a live Career Development Professional. Some people will certainly prefer this option, partly because you are not left to interpret the assessment results on your own and can pursue questions with a professional career guide.

Perhaps you completed an interest inventory in high school that came back with a suggested career you found initially unsuitable, like funeral director. A professional could have helped you analyse these results as well as your test approach (e.g. only filling in 'maybe' instead of a clear 'like' or 'dislike'). An analysis of the results could have helped you see you were looking for a work role that allowed you to sensitively support people during meaningful moments in life and use your organisational, event management, aesthetic and eye for detail skills. With this information you could have evaluated alternatives for a work role you found more fitting or it may have helped you get past the stereotype you have of this work role. A description of the different career development services available is provided in *Chapter 8 — For the Journey* to help you make an informed choice if you wish to retain the services of a Career Development Professional.

The following are some popular and effective assessments. It is important to use them as a tool for self-reflection and not take the results verbatim. If you decide to use an assessment or a few assessments, once you have the results, think of concrete examples from your own life that corroborate or contradict the results and hone those results into a summary of your own that accurately reflects what you know to be true for you and have demonstrated in the past.

MYERS-BRIGGS TYPE INDICATOR

There are many personality assessment tools available, and few are better known than the Myers-Briggs Type Indicator (MBTI). According to Jung's typology all people can understand themselves and others through three main functions:

Extroversion – Introversion

This first function defines a person's source and direction of energy. The extrovert's source and direction of energy is mainly expressed through the external world, while the introvert's source and direction of energy is mainly expressed through the internal world.

Sensing – Intuition

The second function defines how a person generally perceives the world. Sensing means that a person primarily trusts information he receives directly from the five senses. Intuition means that a person primarily trusts information he receives from a sixth sense.

Thinking – Feeling

The third function defines how a person makes decisions. Thinking means that a person prefers to make decisions based on logical analysis. Feeling means that, as a rule, he prefers to make decisions based on personal values.

Then Isobel Myers-Briggs added a fourth function:

Judging – Perceiving

The final function defines how a person implements the information he has processed. Judging means that a person is inclined to organise life events and acts according to his plans. Perceiving means that he is inclined to improvise and act spontaneously.

The different combinations of the functions determine a 'type', such as ISTJ *Introvert Sensing Thinking Judging* or ENFP *Extrovert iNtuitive Feeling Perceiving.*

There are 16 types, each one having a four-letter name (or formula such as ENTJ) according to the combination of criteria. No one type is better or preferable to any other type. Each type has its strengths and its weaknesses.

Using the Type inventory, a Type formula and quantitative measure of expression of each criterion (strength of the preference) can be determined. The corresponding type description provides you with insights into your personality type. One of the websites where you can access this self-assessment tool is *www.knowyourtype.com.* Many people have found this tool highly informative and insightful.

BEHAVIOURAL STYLE ANALYSIS ASSESSMENT

The Behavioural Style Analysis assessment (DISC) is based on the work of Dr William Moulton Marston. By means of personalised reports, respondents have the opportunity to increase their knowledge of themselves and how they interact with others, resulting in increased effectiveness and productivity. One free version of this assessment is available at *www.disc-personality-testing.com/test/index.html.*

PERSONAL INTEREST, ATTITUDES & VALUES ASSESSMENT (PIAV)

The Personal Interests, Attitudes and Values assessment (PIAV) is based on Eduard Spranger's book, *Types of Men,* and measures the relative prominence of six basic attitudes, interests or motives in personality. This assessment is widely used to provide insights into the *motivation* of a given individual. Attitudes and values help to initiate one's actions and are sometimes called the hidden motivators because they are not always readily observed. The PIAV report identifies these motivating factors and attitudes.

CAREER TACTICS ASSESSMENT

This questionnaire can be completed online in just a few minutes and is designed to help people think more systematically about the specific strategies they have used in their career.

Although management capabilities, professional and technical expertise are clearly major factors underpinning a person's effectiveness and future progress, in themselves they may not be sufficient. Career success and failure is not merely an outcome of talent. Critical to success and failure is the deployment of one's personal time and effort in responding to the realities of human nature and organisational life.

Career Tactics highlights this dimension: which *tactics* have you made most and least use of in the personal advancement of your career? What are the gains for deploying these tactics in the future; what are the potential risks?

FALSIFICATION OF TYPE

Dr Katherine Benziger, author of *Thriving in Mind*, whom we mentioned earlier in this chapter, has created a unique profiling tool, which focuses on natural competencies and Falsification of Type called the BTSA Assessment. Falsification of Type is when people rely on strengths of mind instead of their natural strengths and is strongly associated with burnout. This assessment can be accessed at *www.benziger.org*.

PSYCHOGEOMETRICS

In her book *Transform Yourself*, author and TV psychologist Ros Taylor describes a number of personality testing tools, including the Psycho-geometrics tool developed by Dr Sue Dellinger. This tool invites you to look at a number of shapes and decide which one best represents you. The results are most revealing.

For example, if you see yourself as a squiggle, you are likely to be creative, witty and messy. If you choose a triangle, you may be focused, decisive and athletic. See what your shape tells you about yourself for $10.95 USD at *www.psychogeometrics. com/onlinetest.php*.

KEIRSEY TEMPERAMENT SORTER

The book, *Please Understand Me* by David Keirsey, has provided many with key insights to help you understand yourself better, appreciate who you are and communicate more effectively with others. When I (Colleen) did it the first time, it provided insights into my own personality and how a personality clash with a former manager had developed. I had always thought I could get along with anyone but in this situation it seemed everything I tried only made things worse. By gaining insights into the manager's temperament as well as my own, I was able to put the whole experience into perspective and learn more effectively from it. There is a free online assessment at *www.keirsey.com* (click on KTSII in the upper right hand corner).

OTHER OPTIONS

If you want to explore additional assessment options, the Internet offers many career assessments of varying levels of validity and reliability, both for free and at cost. One way to narrow down the options is to visit *www.quintcareers.com* or another reputable and established career development website.

My assessments summary

Review your assessments and come up with as many concrete examples from your life experience to back them up. These examples will help you to apply the insights gained as well as prepare you to explain who you are when you are looking for opportunities. Now write in your own words a summary of your personality, temperament, competencies, career strategies, interests and attitudes:

_____

_____

_____

_____

_____

_____

_____

_____

_____

_____

_____

_____

_____

_____

_____

_____

_____

_____

_____

_____

_____

_____

_____

_____

CLARIFYING THE PICTURE

This has been a demanding chapter, involving lots of honest introspection from you. By no means does it contain all the exercises and lists you can work with. Give yourself some time now to let the dust settle and then return again in a week to what you have written in your notebook and on these pages. Make a date with yourself in your agenda to do this.

When you are ready, go to the next chapter to develop an inventory of your skills. Following that you will have the chance to integrate your passion with your skills and start looking at ways to apply them in the work world.

'Should one work to live or live to work? The majority do not want to simply get by because they have to work. Once passion is brought into the equation work does not feel like work at all. It becomes more enjoyable and one is usually more productive and stimulated resulting in greater achievements and performance.'

Carol, American, *http://delhi4cats.wordpress.com* and
www.expatwomen.com

'I think the key to success is to be working on something you ab-so-lute-ly love doing or feel very passionately about. It would be very difficult to stay focused and housebound doing something that you didn't believe in.'

Victoria, New Zealander in India, *www.expatwomen.com*

Chapter 2 – Resources for Finding Your Passion

B Sher, *I Could Do Anything if I Only Knew What it Was,* Dell Publishing
BR Anchor: Home Away From Home, Relocation 101, Let's Make a Move, and other books
D Dunning, *What's Your Type of Career,* Nicholas Brealey Publishing
D Keirsey, *Please Understand Me II,* Prometheus Nemesis Book Company
DR Bryson & CM Hoge, *Portable Identity,* Transition Press
E Kruempelmann, *The Global Citizen,* Ten Speed Press
F Trompenaars, *Riding the Waves of Culture,* Nicholas Brealey Publishing
Government of Alberta, Human Services, CAREERinsite,
www.alis.alberta.ca/careerinsite
J Cameron, *The Artist's Way,* Pan Macmillan
J Clark, *The Money or Your Life,* Random House
J Parfitt, *Expat Entrepreneur,* Summertime Publishing
J Parfitt, *Release the Book Within,* Summertime Publishing
J Parfitt, *Find Your Passion,* Summertime Publishing
J Parfitt, *Forced to Fly,* Summertime Publishing
JM Hachey, *The Canadian Guide to Working and Living Overseas 2003,* Intercultural Systems
K Benziger, *Thriving in Mind* KBA
M Landes, *The Back Door Guide to Short-Term Job Adventures,* Ten Speed Press
Norm Amundson, *Active Engagement,* Ergon Communications
N Anderson, *Work with Passion,* New World Library
N Goldberg, *Writing Down the Bones,* Shambhala Publications
N Snelling & G Hunt, *Laptop Entrepreneur,* Summertime Publishing
P McGraw, *Life Strategies,* Hyperion Books
P McGraw, *Self Matters,* Hyperion Books
R Bolles, *What Color is Your Parachute,* Ten Speed Press
R Pascoe, *A Broad Abroad,* Expatriate Press
R Taylor, *Transform Yourself,* Kogan Page Limited
S Jeffers, *Feel the Fear and Do it Anyway,* Random House

'Whatever you are, be a good one.'

Abraham Lincoln

Chapter THREE

What can you do?

What Can You Do?

So far in this book we have talked about finding your passion and working out what really matters to you. Along the way you may have come to realise not only your passions but also the things you can do. For some readers, you may have reached this stage clearer about what you love and how you like to feel, but less sure about what you can *actually* do.

In this chapter we look inside ourselves again to analyse our skills and find out what we are good at. In the chapters that follow we will think creatively about the best kind of portable career for us and finally we need to adapt that 'dream' to the market. We then look at our context, the location and environment where we're living, whether temporarily or permanently, and consider whether we want to work locally with the people and resources in our community, or beyond our community with the use of technology. We will also take into account all the factors important to our choice, including family responsibilities. We want to notice and investigate all the opportunities immediately around us, while also exploring the possibilities that lie beyond that. Let's begin by taking a look at what you can do.

Review your experience

Start with your own activities from previous jobs and experiences. You can also use significant school, community and volunteer experiences. Using the form below, extra copies of which can be downloaded from *www.careerinyoursuitcase.com,* answer the following:

Describe the responsibilities and tasks you performed

45
mins

- Which of these did you perform the best and enjoy the most? Which gave you energy?
- Which tasks and responsibilities did you like the least? Which were the most difficult to carry out? Which sapped your energy?
- What aspects of the work environment were conducive to doing your best work?
- What aspects of the work environment were unpleasant or de-motivating?

Position _____

Company _____

What aspects of the work environment were conducive to doing your best work?

_____

_____

What aspects of the environment were unpleasant or de-motivating?

_____

_____

What I found difficult									
What I disliked about this									
How well I performed this									
What I enjoyed about this									
Tasks / responsibilities									

What are your skills?

Now is the time to make an inventory of your skills. These are things you do that make up the tasks or responsibilities you have performed. They are practical things, like delegating, managing people; even woodwork or cooking are all skills. You have developed skills through work, learning, leisure and life experiences. Most of us take many of our skills for granted; we use them often and easily without thinking. If you look more closely at all the tasks and activities you do you will see just how many skills they contain. When considering your career options, it's important to take a closer look at all the activities you do, not only work-related ones, because they all hold a great deal of information about you and can help generate ideas for your portable career.

SKILLFULLY UNAWARE

Here is an example of a skill many people have, even took lessons in order to learn, but now take for granted because they can do this complicated task without thinking. It involves:

1. Getting the equipment ready for use.
2. Ensuring everyone is safe.
3. Checking the way is clear.
4. Shifting gears while at the same time: steering, accelerating or braking, looking in the mirrors, navigating a route and for many, conducting an engaging conversation with passengers or singing with the radio.
5. Arriving at your destination and locking the equipment.

Of course, this skill is driving. When you first learned how to drive, you had to concentrate on each step individually. Now you can do them all almost without thinking. For those of you who don't drive, take a look at someone behind the wheel taking driver's training and you will see for yourself by their facial expression just how hard they are working to be able to get the car to go safely where they want it to. For those of you who do drive and follow the same route regularly, have you arrived at your destination, stepped out of the car and suddenly realised you were there, that you had 'unconsciously' got yourself to your destination? This is an example illustrating when a certain skill level is achieved through repetition; you can do complicated and involved tasks without consciously being aware of them. Think how difficult it was to manage all the steps listed above when you first started driving. Now you can do it almost unconsciously!

COUNT YOUR SKILLS

Becoming consciously aware of all your skills again will help you explore different ways of combining them to discover work options. All the tasks and accomplishments of your experiences are made up of underlying sets of skills. For example, if you take the task of driving a car and break it into sets of skills, it could look like this:

1. Safe machine operation.
2. Machine maintenance.
3. Following rules.
4. Teamwork and consideration for others.
5. Physical coordination.
6. Clear communication through signals and behaviour.
7. Exercising self control.

This of course is something you never think of when doing the task itself, but these are just a sample of all the skills you use when you drive!

THE SKILLS CYCLE

Before making choices about your career, you need to think about how you want to and can apply your skills now. When I (Jo) was at school, we had a campaign to raise student and parental awareness of environmental issues. The slogan was 'recycle, return, re-use'. Be aware that in every location you may have to recycle, return or re-use some of your skills and interests. You may not always need to change careers completely, but you will probably be called upon to make creative adjustments. This is an area in which you will need to exercise resilience: be flexible and open to new ways of using what you already have.

'A career means there is a well-defined track, but when you leave the one you are on, you do not know what to do next. We have to rethink our identity, our role, everything. When you come off the track you can't just stand there. But there is nothing crafted out there ready, designed for us, to fit in ... The concept of work, of career, you have to redefine it all again.' (Paraphrased from original.)

Wong, Malaysian in Europe, The Expatriate Archive, OAC5/3/3

Recycle

In Dubai I (Jo) taught word-processing, but when I moved four hours down the road to Muscat I found there was little demand for this skill. So I recycled my talent and taught desktop publishing instead. To elaborate with a more fanciful example, had I sand-skied in the Middle East, I could have recycled this into snow skiing in Norway. The point is this: be prepared to adapt and modify some of your skills so they fit the needs and the market you find in each location. Realise in some countries you may need to secure local certifications for activities that are unregulated in the country from which you came. Flexibility and ingenuity are the keys to success.

'While I have had a prestigious career as an American diplomat as well as having held senior executive positions in corporate industry, these kinds of positions are not filled by foreign women in Saudi Arabia. As a result I have had to look for other challenges and opportunities where I can maximise the use of my skills and expertise, which ultimately resulted in the establishment of my own business, Global Watchers Arabia. However, even in spite of opening my own business, due to the culture and customs of the male-dominated Kingdom, many times I have had to take the back seat in discussions and negotiations rather than the forefront, which I had routinely done prior to locating to the Kingdom.'

**Carol, American, *http://delhi4cats.wordpress.com* and
*www.expatwomen.com***

Return

Some skills and passions are just not made for a given location. For example, dates were hard to come by in Norway in 1996, so there was naturally little demand for my (Jo's) date cookery books. In the Middle East I was able to find English language journalism work with local publications. But I was out of luck in Stavanger, where there was no commercial English language newspaper or magazine at the time. Sometimes you have to put skills in storage until you need them for a new time, a new place, or a new circumstance.

'... then you move on and you're back to square one and you're back to the struggle. I worked. I was senior manager in the health service ... and then moved out to Oman. I offered to write a ten-year health strategy for the government but they did not want me to. I was willing to do it for nothing. It was my area of expertise ... I retrained as teaching English as a foreign language ... I worked in the Shell school and the British Council and I got some interesting private clients and it was great fun. ... I had just got it all nicely set up and low and behold we're posted ... back to the UK and I thought right, what am I going to do now? So I decided to retrain as a therapist ... Did that. Did all my post-qualification client work, started doing some training, eventually got taken into a private group practice where we had a contract with the local hospital and police service so it just meant that I'd got myself beautifully set up. I was teaching three days a week, working in a GP practice one day a week and private practice one day a week and got moved here... same thing. The system's so different... none of the qualifications are registered.'

Julia, British in the Netherlands, The Expatriate Archive, OAC5/3/3

Re-use

Some skills transfer more easily than others from place to place. There are few dates in Norway and few snowy slopes in the Middle East. But people who want to learn the English language are nearly everywhere. So teachers of English as a foreign language can usually find work wherever they go, although they may have to adapt to a different group of learners. And while date cooking had limited portability, I was always able to teach creative writing. Take a hard look at your skills and evaluate their portability. If few of them are transferable, then think about what additional skills you may need to learn to make it workable in your current location. I (Colleen) considered teaching fitness lessons in the Netherlands, a job I had done during my university days, in order to practice my Dutch and make a start.

'Coming away forced me to think about diversifying. It made me push myself to the limit. You know, it is so easy for people in this situation to focus on the negatives and think about the qualifications or the language they do not have. Coming here made me see what I really was able to do.'

Kit, American in Norway, *www.careerinyoursuitcase.com*

Grow

I (Colleen) like to include a fourth element in the Skills Cycle which I call grow. Because of the recycling metaphor I'm tempted to think about composting and how interesting things often grow out of composting bins when they are left long enough. The idea is to identify which skills you wish to develop further. When I discovered my word processing skills needed some attention, I took a course. When my curiosity was raised by something like improvisational theatre, I took a series of workshops. Each of these has been useful in many more ways than I imagined when I first took the course.

Continue to develop your various skills based on your curiosity and your goals. Ask yourself how you can learn these skills. At an evening class? In a workshop? With a mentor, perhaps? By reading a book? Research online and in person what is being offered, where and in what format.

MAKE AN INVENTORY OF YOUR SKILLS

To become aware of all the skills you have, including those you are taking for granted, your task now is to make an *inventory of your skills*. To do this you will use the Skills Checklist that follows. Further review this checklist to gain more insights into what these skills mean for your future opportunities. First we'd like to provide you with a framework for deciding whether or not you can say you have a skill on the Skills Checklist.

How skilled am I?

You will likely be surprised when you do the inventory at how many skills you have. Before doing the inventory most people don't know all the 'skills' words to be able to list them so to help you we have added a list of possible skills in the Skills Checklist that follows. You will discover many skills you take for granted. Use the following as a guideline so you are confident you have honestly represented your skills on the checklist:

1. Have you taken a course or some training, read a book or manual, taught yourself or had someone show you in order to develop the skill?
2. Have you used the skill yourself a number of times after learning how to do it? Through practice you have become comfortable using the skills.

3. Have you developed your own way of doing it based on experience? For example, after trying a recipe a few times you have made some adjustments in order to better suit your tastes and style.

4. Have you been asked to show someone how you do that task? This is the highest level of skill acquisition when someone else recognises your ability and you are able to teach someone else to do the task. Teaching someone to do a task forces you to become consciously aware again of all the steps and skills needed in order to complete the task well.

If you can use a skill based on any of the criteria above, then you *have that skill* and you can place the corresponding number in the box on the Skills Checklist.

Transferability of skills

Some skills are task specific and some are transferable to different settings and situations. The Skills Checklist provided includes many *transferable skills* because these are most often the skills we overlook. Sometimes these are called *soft skills* as they are related to attitudes and behaviours. They are harder to teach someone and as a result a person will often be selected for work based on their soft skills. A person can usually be taught the *task specific* or *technical skills* if they already possess the soft skills. Alongside an awareness of your occupation-specific skills, knowing what your soft skills are, and being able to present them well, will give you a great advantage when you are looking for opportunities. These are some of the most important skills for your portable career!

Skills Checklist

Source: The Conference Board of Canada, *Employability Skills 2000+*, May 2000

This generic skill list was compiled after polling employers across all work sectors. As a result these skills are transferrable between industry sectors and are referred to as employability skills since they are a key element in your ability to access work opportunities almost anywhere. If you have other specific skills, add them to the list or elaborate on the skills listed here.

Go through the list and put a 1, 2, 3 or 4 from the list above in the box to indicate at what level you believe you have developed the skill. It's not about whether or not you are an expert at something, it's about whether or not you can do it and at what level.

15
mins

Personal Skills

- [ ] positive attitudes and behaviours
- [ ] responsible
- [ ] adaptable
- [ ] learn continuously
- [ ] work safely

Fundamental Skills

- [ ] communication skills
- [ ] information management skills
- [ ] numerical skills
- [ ] thinking and problem-solving

Leadership Skills

- [ ] administering
- [ ] delegating
- [ ] directing / supervising
- [ ] initiating
- [ ] making decisions
- [ ] managing

Technology Skills

- [ ] computer literacy
- [ ] keyboarding
- [ ] e-mail and social media
- [ ] Internet

Business Skills

- [ ] coordinating
- [ ] evaluating
- [ ] implementing
- [ ] negotiating
- [ ] organizing

- [ ] planning
- [ ] promoting
- [ ] revising
- [ ] understanding the mission / role / big picture
- [ ] contributing to organisational goals

Working with Information Skills

- [ ] attention to detail
- [ ] being precise
- [ ] following procedures
- [ ] information gathering / locating
- [ ] organizing data
- [ ] record keeping
- [ ] sorting
- [ ] verifying

Creative Skills

- [ ] adapting
- [ ] creating concepts / ideas / products
- [ ] designing
- [ ] improvising
- [ ] inventing
- [ ] perceiving intuitively
- [ ] performing
- [ ] visualizing / imagining

Communication Skills

- [ ] editing
- [ ] explaining
- [ ] interviewing
- [ ] listening
- [ ] mediating
- [ ] persuading
- [ ] public speaking

- [ ] questioning
- [ ] reading
- [ ] talking
- [ ] writing

Physical Skills

- [ ] manual dexterity
- [ ] motor coordination
- [ ] stamina
- [ ] physical fitness

Working with Others Skills

- [ ] advising / counselling
- [ ] assisting others physically or emotionally
- [ ] compromising
- [ ] cooperating
- [ ] protecting / guarding
- [ ] respecting the opinion of others
- [ ] serving
- [ ] sharing information
- [ ] teaching / training
- [ ] team playing
- [ ] artistic skills

Working with Difficult Situations Skills

- [ ] dealing with emergencies
- [ ] exercising self-control
- [ ] giving and receiving feedback
- [ ] managing change
- [ ] multi-tasking
- [ ] performing repetitive tasks
- [ ] resolving conflict
- [ ] taking risks
- [ ] tolerating discomfort

- [ ] willingness to learn
- [ ] working under pressure

Teamwork Skills

- [ ] work with others
- [ ] participate in projects and tasks

Reasoning Skills

- [ ] analyzing
- [ ] investigating
- [ ] researching
- [ ] remembering
- [ ] problem solving
- [ ] putting ideas together

Working with Numbers Skills

- [ ] budgeting
- [ ] calculating
- [ ] counting
- [ ] estimating
- [ ] measuring
- [ ] numerical reasoning

Other skills / Technical skills:

_____

_____

_____

_____

_____

_____

_____

_____

_____

Now read through the checklist again:

1. Place a second checkmark (^^) beside each skill you have that you would like to *reuse* in the future.
2. Which ones do you want to leave dormant for a while or *return*? We don't always enjoy using every skill we have. Put an X there.
3. What skills would you like to use again, or *recycle*, but in a different way? Draw a circle(*) here.
4. Draw an arrow (↑) beside each skill you would like to learn or *grow*.
5. Record all the items marked with one of the above symbols on the skills summary sheet in your Career Portfolio.

Time For Some New Skills?

Mobility skills

There are specific personality traits which are highly desirable in adapting to working and living overseas. Mary Farmer of Global TMC says they include:

- Empathy: also emotional intelligence
- Respect: able to value difference
- Interest in local culture
- Background: language skills, having lived abroad before
- Tolerance (or perhaps 'tolerance for ambiguity')
- Flexibility: do you see the big picture or live strictly by the rules?
- Initiative: achievement-oriented and independent
- Attitude: open mindedness to being exposed to another culture, race and religion
- Sociability: willingness to connect with others
- Positive self image: valuing your qualities and experience
- Team spirit: being able to work with and fit into the culture of the local team

Mary suggests you use this list as a guideline, where do your strengths lie? Which areas do you think you may need to work on? Language skills? How is your sense of self? How aware are you of your own culture and the influence it has on you? How good is your knowledge of the local culture, market, economy, political situation? If this matters to your work idea, then maybe you need to find out more.

Learn new skills

If your need and desire for a mobile career has arisen based on the progress of your partner's career, continues Mary, and you have a window of time in which to make this transition, then consider it a gift. This may be the time to learn new skills. What have you always wanted to learn but haven't yet made time for? Which skills did you put into the 'grow' category? What are you curious about in your new location and current stage of life?

Continuing to learn is key to finding and creating opportunities, for staying engaged with life and taking responsibility for your own growth and development. Look for work, leisure activities and volunteer opportunities which will allow you to grow in a direction you find desirable instead of trying to keep doing what you've already done.

Where can you go to learn? Check out local colleges and universities, community organisations or groups. Research distance learning opportunities as well, including webcasts and podcasts. Offer to trade skills with your contacts, acquaintances, friends and neighbours. Be open and ask questions and you will be able to learn anywhere at any time.

One time when I (Jo) was moving to a new country, I signed up for correspondence courses in short story writing and copy writing before leaving; that way I knew I would have something lined up to do when I arrived. Eventually that short story correspondence course led me to teach short story writing in Muscat, and the copy writing course led me to copy writing work in Stavanger; so both helped me with my career and kept me meaningfully occupied. Even while I was not actively working or looking for work, I felt I was moving forward.

Learning new skills is a great way to feel usefully occupied. Especially if you study a subject or skill that's in line with your career direction. You never know exactly where it will lead you. Take action and let your career adventure continue.

How do you learn?

Not everyone learns the same way, so perhaps the first step in learning is determining which type of learner you are. Harvard professor Dr Howard Gardner *(www.howardgardner.com)* has identified eight distinct learning styles (which he recommends should replace standard IQ testing, since they have such impact on how we gather and retain knowledge). Author and child development specialist Diane Schilling also matches your preferred style of learning with studying a foreign language.

An online test to find out what type of learner you are is available at *www.agelesslearner.com*. Learning expert Marcia L Conner's excellent website also offers free online assessments for motivation and engagement.

Learning styles suggested by Mary include:

- If you like words you may work best from books and audiotapes
- If you are logical and like numbers, you may enjoy learning rules, grammar and linguistics best
- If you are visual then you might be best learning from a course that is highly illustrated or from videos
- Intuitives, 'feeling' types, may work best from total immersion courses or from living in the home of a native speaker for a while
- Extroverts may like the interactive atmosphere of a classroom
- Introverts may prefer self-study

- Music lovers may like to learn through the music of a language, listening to songs, perhaps. If you are a parent you can learn along with your kids through children's songs in the local language
- And many may like to explore 'superlearning' techniques, sometimes called accelerated learning or effective learning, for which you listen to music of 60 beats per minute while absorbing the language aurally.

'My husband is a career diplomat and we have spent the last 27 years moving around the world. I have developed my own career as an educator and have had dream jobs that I've had to leave for the next international relocation. The last position I loved and had to leave was as the education and youth officer at the US Department of State. There I helped our American diplomatic families navigate all the issues they faced with international moves and the education and successful transitions of their children. I never would have wanted to leave that position, but when my husband received an ambassadorial appointment to Oman (our second tour here), I packed up once again and moved overseas.

'Only this time I did something different. I was tired of leaving behind work I

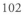

loved and did not want my Rolodex to grow cold. I wanted to build a business that I could do for the next 20 years. Therefore, I started laying the groundwork in advance, and launched my own international educational consulting business last year. Before leaving the States, I earned the right credentials to become a Certified Educational Planner, and used my State Department experience to become accepted as a full professional member of the best professional organisations in the US for my field, the Independent Educational Consultants Association and the National Association of College Admissions Counsellors. I am working from my home office here in Oman and have clients in various countries around the world. My portfolio includes choosing an international school, boarding schools, working with children with learning differences as well as those who are gifted and talented (and many times children are both), transition and TCK [third culture kids] issues, and lastly, one-on-one counselling for students who want help with the complex college admissions process for American universities. I have done site visits on almost 250 American boarding schools and universities in the States and Europe, so my advice carries the weight of experience. I also do public speaking on a wide variety of topics related to education and internationally mobile youth.

'I am pleased with the way many things have gone for me, but I still need inspiration and motivation for what often seems like an uphill climb. I'm taking additional advanced educational consulting classes online through UCLA that have been wonderful.'

Rebecca (Becky), American in Oman, *www.rebeccagrappo.com*

What is a Perfect Portable Career?

A career you can put in your suitcase and take with you anywhere in the world is a portable career. But we want you to find the perfect portable career for you, not just any career. If it does not allow you to express what is important to you, and make the difference you want to make in the world, then it will not be easy to sustain it through additional moves or a return home. The elements which qualify a career as *portable* are as follows:

- It is based on your passions, the things you love
- It expresses your values
- It uses your top favourite skills and talents
- It can operate in more than one location
- It is flexible enough to be adaptable to new opportunities and markets
- It allows you to build a global network that is not lost when you move
- It fulfills your needs
- It fits around your other commitments and life responsibilities
- It meets your objectives - financial, fame, making a difference, or whatever
- It motivates you so much that you can keep going regardless of new moves
- It is easy to transport, with no equipment to ship
- It can be set up quickly in a new location
- It is sustainable despite moves
- It continues to grow and evolve

Here are some examples of portable careers that may fulfil the above objectives.

Teaching

Teaching is a more transferable skill than most people realise. If you can teach one thing, the chances are you can teach another. I (Jo) taught computers in England, French conversation in Dubai, creative writing in Oman and how to create a portable career in Norway. Related to teaching are training and facilitating workshops. In a number of different work roles starting during university, I (Colleen) have facilitated fitness lessons, information sessions on healthy eating, events and activities, and finally career development workshops in the course of my career. Take a presentation, training or facilitation skills course and you will be able to deliver workshops for adults on subjects in which you specialise, in many cases without a teaching qualification. The role of personal trainer or fitness instructor also falls under this teaching category. You can teach and deliver training online too. Online tutors or e-tutors guide students through an Internet learning experience. If you have a teaching background, why not create courses that can be delivered electronically via email, online tutorials or webinars.

'In Japan I taught businessmen, school children and even a three year-old. The businessmen paid best but the children were better students. In Milan, Italy, I taught at a language school and in four companies. In Thailand I decided to teach on a voluntary basis to help deprived individuals to better themselves. Social interaction was as important as teaching. I could choose what I taught too. In Belgium I taught three retired ladies who had decided to expand their horizons despite being over 70.'

Fiona, British in many countries, *www.careerinyoursuitcase.com*

Virtual assistance

All businesses need some administrative support, yet we don't all have the time, skills or inclination to do it ourselves. Administrative duties include accounts, maintaining a database, upkeep of a website, sending newsletters, invoicing and copy typing. A virtual assistant (VA) offers a combination of services that can be done from anywhere in the world using a computer and the Internet. I (Jo) know several people who use a VA to answer their telephone and respond to email. I use one to work on my database, another to upload items to my websites and one to send out my press releases.

Coaching

Life coaching, business coaching and career coaching can be practiced from almost anywhere there are people looking to develop themselves. Many coaches operate face to face with clients; however, with Skype, email and web conferencing, in addition to the telephone, many coaches operate remotely. In addition to the natural qualities and skills, you need training and qualifications to be a good coach. You can study by distance learning to become a coach.

Network marketing

Companies like Tupperware, Avon, Forever Living and Usborne Books all operate in this way. You become a distributor, buy a start up pack at a favourable price, may receive some training and then you work at selling the product. Many network marketers sell directly to the public by hosting parties in people's homes. But you can also make money by recruiting others to work in your team. You are responsible for motivating your team and in return you get to earn a percentage of their income. This can be very rewarding, and, providing you choose a product about which you are passionate, and a company that allows you to operate in the appropriate countries, you stand to grow a very lucrative business.

Network marketing can be a perfect choice if you want to maintain flexible work patterns. Your success depends on the quality and reputation of the product (always check this out) plus your own natural people and organisational skills.

I (Jo) was a Dorling Kindersley Family Learning distributor in two different countries and found it to be hugely lucrative, as well as a good way to meet people and make friends. I picked the product because the countries I was living in had a shortage of good quality English books at the time and the market was ripe. Although I did my best to ensure my operations were legal, when in Oman, I discovered a local bookstore was not happy with what I was doing and put a stop to it. Not all network marketing companies have licences to trade in every country, so do make sure you check up before you barge on in, as I did.

'Many network marketing schemes such as this [Cabouchon] give their distributors no set monthly targets. You sell products at the usual retail price but you buy them from the manufacturer at discount. The discount increases as you sell more products. Cabouchon is a good choice of party plan product because jewellery is relatively easy to post. It is also quite affordable. By inviting people to host parties in their homes you help to add to the social scene. Generally expatriates have a bit of spare cash too.'

Pauline, British in Norway, *www.careerinyoursuitcase.com*

Online trading

If you enjoy investing in the money markets then you may enjoy trading both for yourself and even for clients. You could also organise investment clubs, teach others how to trade and offer an advice service, all while making money for yourself with your own investments.

Therapy, counselling, hairdressing or beauty

These options are grouped together here because they all involve building and maintaining a client base. Once you have trained in a skill such as reflexology, acupuncture, psychotherapy, beauty, hairdressing, colour and style analysis or similar areas there is a good chance this could become a portable career. While you cannot take clients with you when you move, you can take your skills and, with a good marketing strategy and networking skills, you can find new clients fast in a new location. You do need to check your qualifications are recognised in the new country though and that you will not be restricted by lack of language skills. Being a therapist can be a very portable career, but unless you can offer your services virtually it is dependent on you having a local client base. However, if you keep in touch with your clients and friends and have a global network, there is a good chance some clients and referrers will be around in a new location. The best way to keep this type of business alive, despite postings, is to add another string to your bow. Maybe you write a book on your specialism, which you can continue to sell online regardless of where you live? Or perhaps you could also become a network marketing distributor selling a product that complements your work? An aromatherapist could also sell essential oils. A beauty therapist could sell make-up. A massage therapist could sell aloe vera products and so on. You will find that there are a range of products suitable to complement most businesses.

'In Norway most of my clients came from my husband's company. Women hate having to change their hairdresser when they move. At least with me being English they knew I would understand what they wanted.'

Pauline, British in Norway, *www.careerinyoursuitcase.com*

Subject matter expert

A new and growing field of work is 'the subject matter expert'. Once you have written your book, blogged regularly on your area of expertise, contributed to other blogs and publications, presented at conferences, been interviewed for radio programs on and offline, been quoted in other media and reTweeted so you become a trending topic, you can call yourself a subject matter expert. Blogging on your topic and developing a large number followers means advertisers will pay to have their product on your blog page because of the niche group you give them access to. You can develop related products to broaden your income stream and thus create a portable career. Generally, you will need to work at this consistently over a number of years to get it going. An excellent resource for this area of work is Brendon Burchard who wrote *Millionaire Messenger*. His website is *www.expertsacademy.com* and he provides an abundance of sound advice in his free online videos.

Writing, editing, proofreading

Being a journalist can be a good source of income wherever you go. If there are no English language publications locally then now is the time to expand your horizons and write for international publications, airline magazines, papers in your home country and magazines and websites relating to your experience. Be an author and write books if that appeals to you. But if you prefer to write short, sharp pieces, consider writing public relations material, e-books or Kindle books, blogs, website content, brochure copy and so on. Jo's *Definite Articles* course can teach you how to write this way.

If you can write, then maybe you can edit and proofread too. Create information products such as eBooks, and you can sell those online and the customer can download them immediately, so there is no shipping involved. While you can make a career from writing non-fiction, creative writing, poetry and fiction also make great portable careers.

'Now that I have been successful with my portable career, I can happily call myself a househusband – though I still get strange looks from people who don't know what else I do. However when [my wife] adds, 'He's a writer and has a book published too,' you can see a lot of people visibly relax because they now have a pigeon hole they can more comfortably (for themselves) put me in.'

Huw Francis, Author of *Live and Work Abroad: A Guide for Modern Nomads*

Social media manager

Manage and monitor the online identity of a company and harness the power of social media for a company. All the information is online, so this is a new work role that is portable.

Graphic design

Learn to use the graphic design software used by printers and publishers of marketing and other material and you will never be short of work. Create business cards, company brands, layout books and articles, brochures and other things. Learn to use digital image software and not only can you work with photographs but you will find yourself in demand teaching others this skill too.

Website design and maintenance

Businesses need a web presence. Learn how to use the software, to upload material, and register with the search engines and you will be kept very busy. Many websites can be self-managed as the software has become very user-friendly and you don't need to know how to 'code' but many business people are too busy to take the time to learn how to do it themselves. If you have an eye for design, or can work with a designer, your websites will have the edge.

Anything online

You can sell goods online without ever having to hold the stock yourself. So, design a compelling website, take orders and collect the money, and then pass those orders onto suppliers who are responsible for the packing and shipping. Products sold on the Amazon Marketplace are sold by this same 'drop ship' method. Only those things you buy directly from Amazon are shipped by Amazon themselves. Selling any product online by this method creates a passive income stream for your business.

eBay is an example of an international online marketplace, making it a perfect business to operate from any country. eBay has sister sites in many countries. In fact, you can sell all manner of things through Amazon Marketplace too.

Gaming sites are also something that can be developed, designed and managed from anywhere with a good Internet connection. A friend of mine (Colleen) just relocated within North America from a big city to a small mountain ski village while working for a gaming company in London, England.

Art or photography

If you are already a professional artist or photographer you will have already thought of the portability of your skill. If you are an amateur in these areas, consider turning your hobby into a portable career for this chapter of your life. Perhaps your perspective is unique (and marketable) where you are currently located. Is there a market 'back home' for your greeting cards and other souvenir items? Create a website and sell to the rest of the world. You can teach your skill to others too, if that appeals. With a bit of research you may be able to take your art to a new level. Take a look at the business concept *www.artsumo.com* uses.

Entrepreneurship

In simple terms an entrepreneur is likely to be either selling a range of related products or services to one target market, or selling one main product or service to a range of markets. He may sell from business to business (B to B), from business to institution (B to I) or from business to consumer (B to C). Those who are living outside their passport country may like to consider a fourth option, that of expatriate to expatriate (E to E). My (Jo's) own workshops and books are a case in point. I specialise in teaching people to write about their overseas experiences so my market is expatriates. However, while marketing to the expatriate community may seem like the most sensible option, be aware that the market is not only a niche market, but also a moving target. You have to be very clear about your product and your marketing efforts. Additional typical entrepreneur choices include purchasing an existing franchise operation or signing up with a multilevel marketing company. These options are all discussed in more detail in *Chapter 4 — Creating Your Career.*

Want to know more?

A selection of in-depth reports on some of the careers mentioned above is available from *www.careerinyoursuitcase.com.* You are also invited to share your own career ideas, so please pay us a visit.

For more inspiration on which career to choose, please take a look at 'Sixty Brilliant Ideas' at *www.careerinyoursuitcase.com.*

Portable career areas I am considering
(at this point)

☐ Beauty Consultant	☐ Personal Trainer
☐ Coach	☐ Photographer
☐ Counsellor	☐ Proof-reader
☐ Editor	☐ Subject Matter Expert
☐ Entreprencur	☐ Social Media Manager
☐ Graphic Artist	☐ Teacher
☐ Hairstylist	☐ Therapist
☐ Network Marketer	☐ Virtual Assistant
☐ Online Sales person	☐ Website Designer
☐ Online Trader	☐ Writer

5 mins

Food for Thought

'Thus the task is not so much to see what no one yet has seen but to think what nobody yet has thought about that which everybody sees.'

Arthur Schopenhauer, 1788–1860

Schopenhauer wrote the original definition of 'build a better mousetrap' more than 150 years ago, and it remains one of the best ways to describe originality, innovation… and success.

Mary Farmer, management and organisation consultant, says a portable career requires constant introspection and reinvention - becoming too attached to what you've already been and already seen may be the biggest obstacle to your international career success. There are many inspiring stories in this book of non-traditional approaches to career management, of people who have demonstrated career resilience. Moving abroad is the perfect time to think outside the box. Prepare to see this box from a new perspective: imagine, just for a second, that perhaps you built the box yourself, climbed in, and nailed the lid down from the inside. With a little critical self-analysis, you'll be amazed to discover how many of the obstacles to your successful career development you are placing there yourself, perhaps through self-limiting beliefs about what constitutes a career, where to look for opportunities - and where your own talents lie.

Chaos theory

The principles of chaos theory have been applied to career development by Robert Pryor and Jim Bright. This theory calls for an *emergent approach* to careers and a move away from matching and linear-causal models. This theory suggests that taking a test and matching the results to an occupation is no longer effective in today's rapidly changing labour market. In a world of change and uncertainty, the chaos theory of career development provides a framework for understanding what approaches and skills will help you navigate your way. These approaches understand the importance of using creativity, intuition and openness, together with the more traditional career development techniques, to create possibilities which can be honed into workable career options. For the global nomad, these approaches will also be the most effective in developing a sustainable portable career.

Alternate paths

The Chinese believe while all the paths of your destiny are laid out at your birth, different ones are revealed to you at separate times in your life. Mary believes that the challenge for all of us is to recognise the opportunities being offered. Deepak Chopra calls this 'Synchrodestiny'.

'Very often we fall into ruts in our lives; we maintain the same routines and act in the same manner predictably day after day after day. We set our minds on a certain course of action, and simply proceed. How can miracles happen if we march mindlessly, unthinking and unaware, through our lives?'

Making a career and life change is a time of opportunity, to get out of ruts you may have been in, to change the way you approach your work, to set different goals and adjust your beliefs in how the world works based on the new experiences you will have. Some doors close, and others in turn open again, and that is how you can view your life, your career path and your skills set: as a journey, packed with jewels, treasures, opportunities and adventure around every corner.

'In Chinese, the characters for Challenge and Opportunity are the same. It really makes you think.'

Lisa, British in Italy, *http://burntbythetuscansun.blogspot.com* **and** *www.expatwomen.com*

Putting It All Together

All the exercises and activities you have completed to this point have generated a multitude of information for you. Now what do you do with it? As mentioned before, we are not looking for a knee jerk reaction, but a well thought out reflective conclusion. Review and refine your findings until you have a concise summary which captures who you are, your unique mix of passions, attitudes, motivators and drivers. Here are two ways to do this.

Write your mission statement

I (Jo) attended a workshop entitled 'Write Your Own Mission Statement', given by inspirational Danish holistic management expert Helen Eriksen. An actor at heart, Helen's workshop is a lesson in how to forget convention and follow our instincts to be different. She teaches how we can free our 'inner originals', claiming, as Jung did, that 'we are born original and die as copies'.

'When we know where we are going we approach everything differently,' explains Helen. 'When we don't know what we want we tend to act reactively and end up simply going wherever the wind blows. Often we find ourselves landed on a shore where we do not belong at all. Conversely, proactive people are conscious of where they want to go and why and then set their sails accordingly.'

The key here is to choose a direction and not necessarily a destination.

Helen shows us how to find out what our core values are by examining our achievements, both personal and professional, and working out which of our values motivated us to be successful at that time. Values such as 'transforming', 'sharing', 'learning', 'dreaming' or 'communicating' may come to mind.

When you have written down your successes and the values that inspired them, you might notice some values are not as important to you as they used to be - and you have acquired others which don't appear on your early lists. Double-check these with the values you selected earlier in Section Two.

I (Jo) last participated in Helen's workshop in January 2002, just before I embarked on the project of rewriting the second edition of this book. My core values that day were 'enthusiasm', 'creation' and 'sharing'. The mission statement I produced became 'to use my enthusiasm to create things that I may share with people who want to do what they love for a living'. Now it's your turn. Since then I have honed my mission to 'sharing what I know to help others to grow'. Ten years later it still holds true.

20 mins

Developing a mission statement can help you focus your passion in a desired direction. It will help you to communicate to yourself and others what it is you hope to achieve, who you want to serve and what you hope to contribute that's unique, by focusing your passion and values in a particular direction. It is something you can continue to tweak and refine as time passes; it is not meant to be written in stone. It is important to revise it until you are at a point where it satisfies you. However, if you keep changing it every week it will not be the North Star that helps you find your way when the road map changes to off-road travel. You will have the opportunity to further revise your mission statement again in *Chapter 4 — Create Your Career.*

Reread your Shining Moments Stories in *Chapter 2 — Find Your Passion.* What are the values you expressed during those key experiences?

_____
_____
_____
_____
_____

Reread your top eight values listed in *Chapter 3 — What Can You Do?* Compare them with the values in your Shining Moments Stories here:

_____
_____
_____
_____
_____
_____

Select three of these values, phrase them as verbs and put them into a sentence together. You will probably need to make a number of edits before you whittle it down to the nugget it is for you.

For example:
Values: authenticity, growth and meaningfulness.
Sentence: Meaningful careers support authentic self-growth.

_____
_____
_____
_____
_____
_____

Look at the purpose you identified in *Chapter 3 — What Can You Do?* and add that information in.

_____
_____
_____
_____
_____
_____

Now add *who* you want this to make a difference to. This will often be a group involved in some way with the problem in the world you most want to be part of the solution for.

_____
_____
_____
_____
_____
_____

Finally put in what makes you different from all the others. The key to this answer may be found by reading your Shining Moments Stories. Often it is something so fundamental to who you are, and what you are about, that you miss seeing it. Revisit the notes you made where others commented on your key qualities and characteristics, to see if it is already apparent to those around you. Work with this information until you find a satisfying way to phrase it and write it here:

_____

_____

_____

_____

_____

 Write this mission statement on a large piece of paper and post it near your computer, work area or where you will regularly see it.

Six word memoir

 If you are looking to use even fewer words, try summarizing your life in a six-word memoir. As described at www.oprah.com/omagazine: 'In November 2006, writer and editor Larry Smith issued a challenge to fans of his Web publication, SMITH Magazine. Inspired by Ernest Hemingway's poignant shortest of short stories ("For sale: Baby shoes, never worn"), Smith asked his readers to describe their lives in six words.' Oprah's example is 'seeking the fullest expression of self'. Jo's is 'sharing knowledge abroad, mostly with writers'. Colleen's is 'meaningful choices in life and career'. The process of reviewing your life's chapters and boiling down the essence for yourself can really help you clarify your focus on what is really important to you. Give it a try now. Choose the first six words that come to you having done the work of the previous chapters.

_____

_____

_____

Now organise them into an order that seems to make some sense.

_____

_____

_____

It is *your* mission statement and *your* memoir, so continue to revise and adjust it as you gain more insights or aha's in the coming months. If you want a workbook to help you with finding your passion, check into creative entrepreneur coach Michelle Ward's *www.thedeclarationofyou.com* or Jo Parfitt's *Find Your Passion. Chapter 5 — Marketing your Skills,* contains information on personal branding which can also be used here to summarise and capture who you are and what you have to offer. We have not yet touched on turning your passions and skills into a career. This chapter has focused on looking inside yourself. It is only once you have found where your passions lie, what you most enjoy doing and what your skills are that you can begin to create and navigate your way towards your own perfect portable career. In the following chapter you will group your skills and passions into potential expressions of your mission statement.

Chapter 3: Resources for Finding Out What You Can Do

B Burchard, *Millionaire Messenger,* Free Press

B Sher, *I Could Do Anything I Wanted if Only I Knew What it Was,* Hodder and Stoughton

C Eikleberry, *The Career Guide for Creative and Unconventional People,* Ten Speed Press

C Handy & E Handy, *The New Alchemists,* Hutchinson

C Longman, *Creating a Career,* The Times with Kogan-Page

C McConnell, *Soultrader,* Momentum

C Sangster, *Brilliant Future,* Momentum

D Freemantle, *How to Choose,* Momentum

G Pyke & S Neath, *Be Your Own Careers Consultant,* Momentum

Government of Alberta, Human Services, CAREERinsite, *www.alis.alberta.ca/careerinsite*

Government of Alberta, Human Services, My Choices, My Life, My Work, *www.alis.alberta.ca/publications*

H Gelatt & C Gelatt, *Creative Decision Making,* Crisp

H Ibarra, Working Identity: *Unconventional Strategies for Reinventing Your Career,* Harvard Business School Press

J Clark, *The Money or Your Life,* Century

J Krumboltz & A Levin, *Luck is No Accident,* Impact Publishers

J Parfitt, *Find Your Passion,* Summertime Publishing

L MacKinnon, *Cosmic Coaching,* Ryder

M Buckingham & D Clifton, *Now, Discover your Strengths,* Simon & Schuster

M Buckingham, *Go Put Your Strengths to Work,* Free Press

M Malewski, *Generation Xpat,* Nicholas Brealey

M Sinetar, *Do What You Love and The Money Follows,* Dell Trade Paperback

N Amundson, S Niles & R Neault, *Career Flow,* Pearson

N Williams, The Work We Were Born to Do, Element Books

R Nelson Bolles, *What Color is Your Parachute?,* Ten Speed Press

R Nelson Bolles, *How to Find Your Mission in Life,* gift edition, Ten Speed Press

R Nelson Bolles, *What Color Is Your Parachute Workbook: How to Create a Picture of your Ideal Job or Next Career,* Ten Speed Press

R Taylor, *Transform Yourself,* Kogan-Page

S Longman, *Choosing a Career,* The Times with Kogan-Page

Part 2
Find your
Opportunity

'Vocation is where our greatest joy meets the world's greatest need.'

Frederick Buechner

Chapter FOUR

Creating your
career

In *Chapter 2 — Find Your Passion* you obtained a clearer picture of what you love (passion) and in *Chapter 3 — What Can You Do?* you discovered all the things you can do (skills and talents) as well as ways of using those skills. In this chapter you will generate personally meaningful and creative ideas of how to apply your skills and talents and express your passion as well as explore the different ways of working.

What Do You Believe?

The beliefs you hold about the world and work, and the rules you think guide how they operate, are very important considerations. They are beliefs about what constitutes work and a career. They are beliefs about the world and how it works. For example, believing opportunities come to those who work hard will have an impact on the effort you are willing to put into achieving your goals. The beliefs you hold about yourself and your own abilities will also have an impact on what you see as an achievable and realistic goal for yourself. They can provide energy as well as drain energy. They can lead to opportunity or they can put up barriers to opportunity. You may have touched on some of these themes when completing the *Family Inheritance* exercise in *Chapter 2 — Find Your Passion*.

Take some time to journal some of the beliefs you hold that impact your career, and challenge the validity of these beliefs where you believe useful. Our tendency is, unfortunately, to generalise some (often negative) experiences and form a belief based on this generalisation. Challenge yourself to see where you are generalizing and look for stories (your own and other people's) that contradict this generalisation. Breaking through some of these beliefs can help you to recognise and respond to opportunities you may otherwise miss. If you discover a belief, and its resulting pattern in your life, that you wish to change and you are not successfully able to change it on your own, enlist the support of your Blue Sky Team or a professional.

Career resilience, an essential skill for expats and those creating a portable career, is defined by career coach Carole Pemberton as 'holding the beliefs that enable flexibility in thought, behaviours and actions when facing adversity'. Adversity can be seen as any situation which challenges your ability to come up with solutions and alternatives. According to Carole, career resilience is about holding onto the beliefs about yourself that allow you to maintain the flexibility needed for resilience.

Think about the life and work experiences you've had and the lessons you have taken from those experiences. They can be about how hard work will or will not be rewarded, working in teams and formal organisations, whether or not you will find support when you need it, and much more.

For example: In this economic climate no one is looking for new hires. I won't apply because who needs all that rejection? Or: My education and experience have prepared me for only one career path.

1. What are some beliefs you hold about the world and work?

_____

_____

_____   30 mins

_____

2. What are some of the rules you believe apply to finding work that's right for you?

_____

_____

_____

_____

Go back and underline any words in number one and two that locate the control outside yourself. Rephrase them in a way that gives you a choice as to how to respond and deal with them.

For example: With all the cutbacks, reorganisations and mergers...

> **First draft:** no one is looking for new hires. I won't apply because who needs all that rejection?
> **Rephrased:** there are new unplanned opportunities being created for someone just like me somewhere. I will keep looking to find those opportunities.

3. How can you rephrase any beliefs that do not serve you, so they produce a more constructive, helpful and resilient perspective? For example, self-reflection is essential for me to understand what I need to learn to make good choices in my work and life.

_____

_____

_____

_____

4. How will you use these rephrased beliefs and rules to better serve your portable career?

_____

_____

_____

_____

Changing how you think about the way the world and work operate will change the results you generate. Make sure your beliefs and understanding of what rules apply are well informed, positively formulated and give you the control of choosing a response that serves you. Gathering this information and challenging your beliefs as necessary can reduce the amount of frustration you may experience in your career travels. The Blue Sky Team you have created to work with in the last chapter may also help you find the beliefs you hold which need to be challenged, as they are usually easier to recognise in someone else. You will be able to do it much more easily for someone on your team than yourself. Having done this exercise and reflected on it, write down the beliefs you will use to guide you towards your portable career in *Your Career Passport*.

A Changing World

As the world continues its shift to a truly global economy, new kinds of leadership are required. According to some, this new leadership style will use many of the skills traditionally associated with women. Experts agree that women's focus on relationships, comfort with diversity, refusal to compartmentalise skills, talents and lives, innate scepticism of hierarchy and, most importantly, desire to lead from the middle (not from the top) are all key attributes required by tomorrow's leaders. These are leadership skills women have traditionally used to keep families together and to organise volunteers to come together to positively impact their communities, according to Dr Musimbi Kanyoro, the World YWCA Secretary General as quoted in New York Times' *About.com*.

Business and technology writer Daniel Pink in his book, *A Whole New Mind* says we are entering the 'conceptual age', a time when right-brain skills such as design and storytelling will become far more important. He says transformative abilities like empathy and creativity are not so easily outsourced and will be key employability factors.

The talents, experiences, attitudes and skills women bring with them are precisely those needed in what Seth Godin calls the 'connection economy'. According to Sally Helgesen, author of *The Female Advantage,* this confluence of abilities and required leadership capacities is creating unprecedented opportunities for women to play a vital role in leading transformational change in organisations and communities. Management and training consultant Mary Farmer notes that women are better at seeing the human side, quicker to cut through competitive distinctions of hierarchy and ranking, and impatient with cumbersome protocols.

Mary goes on to say that bestselling author Esther Wachs Book, who wrote *Why the Best Man for the Job is a Woman,* defines 'new paradigm leaders' as those who combine many of the managerial talents traditionally attributed to men with many of the stereotypically 'weaker' female skills. In detailed interviews with 14 of the top female managers in the USA, Book concluded that new paradigm leaders achieve success for three main reasons:

a. Self-assurance compels new paradigm leaders to stay motivated and take risks.
b. An obsession with customer service helps them anticipate market changes.
c. New paradigm leaders use 'feminine' traits to their advantage.

Manage your Expectations

Transitions involving career changes and physical relocations can often have an impact you weren't expecting. Uninformed and unrealistic expectations are one of our greatest sources of discontent. Manage your expectations appropriately. For example, don't assume your transition to another culture will be easy. Anticipate challenges and even temporary setbacks. The better you prepare beforehand the more easily you'll make the move into your new environment. When I (Colleen) moved to the Netherlands a friend told me that studies say it takes seven years to become fluent in a language. This information helped me be realistic about developing my ability to communicate in the local language, and pleasantly surprised when I was able to work in the local language providing career development training within two years. However, I was surprised and unnerved when after 20 years of driving experience I had to retake my driving theory and practical exam. That was something I wasn't expecting!

Find out what opportunities may be available to somebody with your talents, skills and training. Through a buddy or mentor or online, try to discover what kind of activities - paid or volunteer - other people in your situation are doing.

Access the support of your friends, family and new acquaintances to help you make sense of the transition you are going through. A UK study publicised in 2005 in the *Calgary Herald* noted that with eighteen friends people are able to successfully negotiate change and transition. Here 'friends' can range from people you have recently met to those you have known for a very long time. This reinforces the importance of being conscious of your need to connect with others during this transition, and taking action to make this happen, even before you have made your first choices about what to do. Don't follow your usual rules of how many times you need to see someone before you exchange contact information or arrange to meet. More information is available in *Chapter 8 — For the Journey*.

Before you make any choices or plans check them thoroughly. Any time you spend on research and planning will not be wasted. Find out in advance whether your brilliant idea is viable in your new location, or anywhere else. This includes checking the availability of affordable childcare, good Internet connections and reliable transportation. Plan it out, imagine you have the career of your dreams and live with it for a few days. See if you still consider it to be ideal after a few days. It's always wise to look at your idea from all angles and do thorough investigation before committing to it and spending any money. Get a grounded idea of what to expect so you won't be setting yourself up for unnecessary disappointment.

'If you don't like what you are doing, where you are, or if you can't get a job where you are, you also know that it won't last and you'll have another chance in another country.

'Finding a job in Nigeria when everyone had said it was impossible [was my greatest moment]. I was, at the time, the only expatriate wife in full-time employment.'
Els, Dutch in Oman, *www.careerinyoursuitcase.com*

Cultural Considerations

Operating in a new culture asks two different things of a person:

- Respect for other cultures is absolutely essential
- Insight into your own culture and how that influences your behaviour and expectations of others

Take some time to assess your own culture to become aware of how it influences your behaviour, and explore where you would be willing to adapt and be flexible in order to be successful in another culture. For example, in order to be successful as a woman working in a male-dominated business sector in Southeast Asia are you, like Hilary Corna, winner of the *Expat Women's Career Success Abroad* prize, willing to adjust? Would you adjust your style of dress and the way you cross your feet? Would you also help the other women clean up after a business event, while the male employees of same the function and status as yourself return to their desks? Becoming aware of your preferences and needs here will help you choose a good match for your next experience. Where are you willing to be flexible to open yourself up to new experiences?

Cultural values: Check those that apply to you.

10 mins

- ☐ Punctuality
- ☐ Direct communication
- ☐ Equality of gender (specify: _____)
- ☐ Efficiency
- ☐ Family honor
- ☐ Good name
- ☐ Hierarchy
- ☐ Honesty
- ☐ Ethics (specify: _____)
- ☐ Friendliness
- ☐ Family ties (specify: _____)
- ☐ Acceptance of and respect for individual differences
- ☐ Organisation
- ☐ Rules
- ☐ Status
- ☐ Structure
- ☐ Safety

☐ Eye contact
☐ Handshaking
☐ Public order
☐ Language – being able to communicate and be understood
☐ Style of dress

_____

_____

_____

_____

Cultural values common to my potential and preferred destination(s):

_____

_____

_____

_____

What types of cultural frustration can you expect to experience based on the above, and how can you prepare yourself to deal effectively with them? For example, if men in the culture where you are living will not shake hands with you, what will you do? Will you choose to feel unacknowledged and undervalued, or will you collaborate with them to find a way to acknowledge them that still respects their values along with yours?

_____

_____

_____

_____

'The greatest expat lesson I learned was from my son Alex, when he was five, in a French ski resort. One evening after dinner the kids went sledding, and I watched from a distance as Alex dragged his sled up the hill, alongside an older boy, and they seemed to be having a conversation. I later asked him what language the boy was speaking, and Alex admitted French. I asked if he understood what the boy was saying, and he said no, not really. "Sometimes, when I don't understand what people are saying; I just nod and say oui." That's the lesson: nod and say yes.'

Chris Pavone, Author of the novel *Expats*

Influencing Factors

These things are so important to your wellbeing that without them you could not consider a position, even if it is based on your passions and uses your top skills. For example, if you love to dance and your top talent is performing in public then you may think a job in an international dance troupe is heaven sent. Only if you hate working at night, long distance travel or long periods away from your family, this would not be such a good fit for you.

Think of the list below as your 'job filters'. Once you have compiled a list of the things you cannot live without, run any potential job ideas you have generated so far through your list and check they also match your values.

When developing a portable career, many of the options will involve differing levels of self-employment. Before you make a choice about what to do and how to do it, it's a good idea to ask yourself what you need from your work and what will provide a framework for your choices. Sometimes it can be easy to embark on something new as a knee-jerk reaction to the negatives of your past freelance or corporate career. Starting something new as a way of running away from previous issues is no recipe for success. You may find the old problems were actually *your* problems and travelled with you!

'It is never easy re-establishing a career after a move, but I enjoy the social aspect of working, as well as the money. No, it is not easy, but as I said before I am very motivated and like to have some financial independence as well as a professional identity.'

Sue B, British, *www.careerinyoursuitcase.com*

Let's explore now what factors are of key consideration when preparing to choose your career direction.

HOW DO YOU WANT TO LIVE?

Do you want the neat packaging of a prescribed job description, or do you want the choices to be yours alone? This can be a double-edged sword. As a freelancer or entrepreneur, you're not bound by company-determined starting times and schedules.

On the other hand, you'll decide your own hours based on the needs of your work. These needs often acquire a life of their own. Like the broomsticks in *The Sorcerer's Apprentice* in the Disney movie *Fantasia* – they keep multiplying. When you have your own business, sometimes it seems that everywhere you turn there's a 'broomstick' (i.e. a problem with a life of its own that quickly multiplies into other problems).

This can create difficulties for both you and your family. Many people complain their spouse is married to their work and seems to be more attentive to its needs than to the spouse's. And the child of one entrepreneur announced one night that she'd like to be one of Daddy's clients, 'because he's always with the clients and then I'd get to see him more often'.

As an entrepreneur, the more successful you are, the more your work's needs and demands on your time can grow. You will need to institute policies much like those you find in a larger organisation. For instance, you might declare yourself off limits to family until a specified time, but also make a commitment to keep work off-limits after that time. You may need to refuse to answer the phone at a certain hour, letting the calls go to voice mail no matter how seemingly important. You might have to turn off your mobile phone or turn on its voice mail feature. You may need to force yourself to take lunch hours, small breaks and even holidays (even if only for a long weekend); no one's going to give them to you but yourself.

You're likely to get the most family support if you commit to reasonably predictable rules and guidelines which give them reliable access to you. They will resent you and your work less, and they'll be more likely to respect your work time if they know they will have access to you soon after.

HOW DO YOU WANT TO WORK?

Is it important for you to have time for your family, that school holidays are kept free and you have time to show your guests the local sights when they visit? Do you have the space and the discipline to work from home? Would you rather work with people in a formal office or through an informal office share? Is it important for you to use all your skills and passions, or would you be happy only using a few of them? Do you still want time for yourself and your hobbies? Do you want to work from nine to five, five days a week? Do you want a busy office or do you prefer to work alone? Do you want a management position, to work in a team? Which job would match your values and passions? Do you crave variety or routine?

At a more practical level, do you want to be dealing with tax and Value Added Tax (VAT) returns? Do you want to employ staff formally and be responsible for their tax and benefits? Your goal may be to earn just enough to keep you away from having to pay any tax at all, or enough to keep you away from paying high level tax. In England, for example, if you form a Limited Company you need to employ an accountant and have your books audited. So think seriously about how large or small you want your business to be.

And how about the work conditions? You may know of a job you think you'll love. But are you willing to work the 70-hour weeks it takes to be successful in it, or to commit three out of every four weeks to the necessary travel?

WHAT DO YOU NEED FROM YOUR CAREER?

In *Chapter 2 — Find Your Passion* you created a list of values. There are also some things you may express as 'needs' in your work.

Tick the needs below that are important enough to form the basis of your decision to accept a job offer or start a business.

15 mins

- ☐ Frequent interaction with others
- ☐ Opportunity for personal growth
- ☐ High financial reward
- ☐ Being in charge
- ☐ Challenged to expand professional competence
- ☐ Constant variety
- ☐ See a tangible result or final product
- ☐ Contribute to the well being of others
- ☐ Use analytical and problem solving skills
- ☐ Well-defined and routine responsibilities
- ☐ Freedom from rules and procedures
- ☐ Recognition of achievements by others
- ☐ Authority to make final decision
- ☐ Work that requires solitary concentration
- ☐ Mental challenge and stimulation
- ☐ Always something new and different
- ☐ Job security
- ☐ Opportunity to influence the ideas and values of others

- ☐ Low level of stress
- ☐ A stable work schedule
- ☐ No spillover of work into personal and family life
- ☐ Freedom (from measurement relative to others)
- ☐ Ability to move physically from place to place
- ☐ A short (no longer than 30 minutes) commute
- ☐ Plenty of opportunity for advancement
- ☐ Build friendships and attachments with colleagues
- ☐ Opportunities for dealing with differences and conflicts
- ☐ Work with a spiritual (not religious, necessarily) dimension
- ☐ Environment that fosters close relationships
- ☐ Competitive environment
- ☐ Always know what to expect in your day

Write down any more that apply to you and that were missing from the list, here:

_____

_____

The second step in this exercise is to identify the five most important items from those you ticked.

Most important:

1. _____
2. _____
3. _____
4. _____
5. _____

After doing this, review the entire list again and select the five items that are least important to your professional satisfaction.

Least important:

1. _____
2. _____
3. _____
4. _____
5. _____

There are no magic formulas, but here is a guideline: if the work option features any fewer than four of your most important needs, or any more than one of your least important, then you need to think long and hard about accepting it.

Purposes

Be aware of the purposes your career will serve. They can be economic and relate to having the money to do what you want, when you want, providing security for the future and evidence of success. They could be social and a way to connect with others and feel needed and valued by others. Finally, they could be psychological and give you a feeling of mastery or control, and support and shape your identity. Here are some examples:

* Supporting family
* Learning
* Being free of children
* Being there for husband
* Being busy
* Working on repatriation
* Leaving a legacy

What purposes are you aware of that your career serves for you?

1. What are your purposes?

_____

_____

_____

_____

_____

2. What is success to you? How will you know when you've succeeded?

_____

_____

_____

_____

_____

15
mins

3. What level of financial remuneration will you need to earn in order to achieve these purposes and live out your vision and mission?

_____

_____

_____

_____

DO YOU LIKE TO BE ALONE?

Most people tend to think of themselves as either an introvert or an extrovert. If you did the MBTI as an assessment tool in *Chapter 2 - Find Your Passion* you will have new insights into this for yourself. In fact, very few people are all one or all the other - most of us are a mixture of both. When I (Jo) analysed my typical working day I realised I work best alone, not only by myself in an office, but in a whole building. I like to work from home or a small office, but only when no one else is there either, as I do not like being interrupted. Yet I do need daily social input in order to redress the balance. Working alone as I do, I still need time to brainstorm with others, preferably face to face. So I belong to a women's business network and try to plan a few lunch or coffee meetings each month. I also run writing and career workshops and have a busy speaking career, as this gets me among people. As an authors' mentor and publisher, I encourage face-to-face meetings rather than by email or Skype, as I need the energy from being in a room with other people. I also need to get away from my normal environment regularly, and enjoy time at conferences and speaking and teaching tours abroad to recharge my batteries with concentrated interaction and learning.

For an example of just how tailored you can make your work schedule, consider my (Colleen's) friend Heather who wakes up at 6 a.m. with the means to make tea next to her in bed and then works for four hours in bed. She then gets on with the rest of her day with all her administrative, email and writing tasks completed. Winston Churchill also spent the first part of his workday working from his bed. Visit *http://dailyroutines.typepad.com/daily_routines* to see the variety of ways accomplished people have structured their work life.

Think about your ideal working environment. Do you like time alone, with people, or a mix of the two? Like me (Jo), do you need to do one sort of task completely alone (writing, editing and preparation) and another which allows you to be with people (teaching, speaking and consultancy)? Would you like to work with people, but spend your leisure time alone? What's worked for you in the past? What hasn't?

10 mins

Describe your ideal alone/ with others and work/ life balance:

_____

_____

_____

_____

_____

ORGANISED TOUR OR SPONTANEOUS ADVENTURE

In order to pinpoint the most suitable portable career for you, identify some more of your personal preferences and attributes. For example, you can work formally for an organisation, or you can venture off on your own and do your own thing. Each of these approaches is more suited to a particular personality type than another.

What are your work style preferences? Circle the word that describes you most accurately.

Risk taker	or	Security seeker
Routine	or	Variety
Work from home	or	Work in an office
Set hours	or	Flexible hours
With others	or	Alone
Lots of responsibility	or	Little responsibility
Low stress	or	High stress
Predictable	or	Unpredictable
Direct supervision	or	Work independently
Benefits package	or	No benefits package
Long hours	or	Short days
Doer	or	Thinker
Competitive	or	Collaborative
Driven	or	Externally motivated
Goal oriented	or	Go with the flow
Decisive	or	Indecisive
Emotionally resilient	or	Emotionally vulnerable
Results oriented	or	Relationship oriented
Creative	or	Structured
Optimistic	or	Pessimistic
Self-disciplined	or	Unstructured

10 mins

135

Self-employment and contract work generally fit someone who is open to taking risks, likes variety, responsibility and unpredictability. They are willing to work longer hours but can structure their work and are self-disciplined to set their own hours and create their own boundaries around work.

More traditional forms of employment, like full time and part time work provide structure and routine and perceived sense of security. They tend to be more predictable, more often involve working with others in an office and come with a benefits package.

Each different way of working provides a different mix of these elements. What is your ideal mix?

_____

_____

_____

_____

_____

Your Career Evolution

What you based your first career choices on may have shifted in the past number of years. Take time to consider the evolution that has taken place in your career.

1. What has changed in the world and for you personally since you made your first leap into the world of work and adult choices? Think about the evolution and influence of technology, demand for certain skills in different parts of the world, demographical shifts (e.g. aging baby boomers), cultural changes and economic shifts. Think as well about your personal shifts: what role does work play in your life now?

    _____

    _____

    _____

    _____

    _____

    _____

    _____

30
mins

2. Who do you know who is now working in a 'non-traditional' way? Describe how they are working.

    _____
    _____
    _____
    _____
    _____
    _____

3. What do you dislike about this way of working?

    _____
    _____
    _____
    _____
    _____

4. What do you like about this way of working?

    _____
    _____
    _____
    _____
    _____

5. What do these insights mean for your current career options?

    _____
    _____
    _____
    _____
    _____

Getting Ideas

There is no denying it can be soul-destroying to have spent years training for one occupation only to find you cannot practise it in your new environment or learn that a career break doesn't lend itself to re-entering this field. You are going to have to be flexible. Sure, you trained to be a nurse and that is what you want to do, what you are good at and where your passion lies. But if the language barrier is insurmountable, you may have to make changes. Think about how you can transfer or 'morph' your skills to fit the realities and needs in your new environment. Maybe you could offer English language classes to pregnant women? Or you could offer to go in and visit new mothers in their homes soon after the birth? Perhaps you could write a handbook on common childhood ailments, or run first aid classes?

Where there are problems there are also opportunities. If you are flexible and open to change then you may stumble upon a new career that is more fun and rewarding than you thought it might be.

The following are some suggestions to generate ideas and be adaptable to finding new ways to apply your skills in your current and future locations.

> 'I took a part-time position as an admin assistant to get my foot in the door at a hotel management company here in downtown Denver and within 4 weeks I had been promoted to Corporate Accountant. I busted my backside but I had to prove a point. The owner of the company loves me, he knows that I am proving that point and he gets a full day's work out of me.'
>
> **Lizzy, British in America, *www.expatwomen.com***

Think laterally

Wikipedia defines Lateral Thinking as 'solving problems through an indirect and creative approach, using reasoning that is not immediately obvious and involving ideas that may not be obtainable by using only traditional step-by-step logic.' Some people think creatively by nature, but others are not so adept and can use some of the following techniques to break out of their boxed thinking.

'In pottery, there will always be clay wherever you go in the world. There will always be things you can do if you apply yourself. You can take courses when possible and subscribe to international magazines. So many careers are open to the artist. You can teach, you can become a tour guide of artistic areas and even charge more because of that expertise. You can write about your work or local traditions. Of course you can produce your art and sell it too, and most expatriate locations have several annual craft fairs, it is a marvellous career. My father says that you can never have too much education, and by that he means that knowledge and experience are totally portable. My kiln may not fit in my suitcase but my knowledge weighs nothing.'

Cheryl, American in Vietnam, *www.careerinyoursuitcase.com*

MIND MAPPING

Described in Tony Buzan's books *Use Your Head* and *The Mind Map*, mind mapping is a playful but serious way to get your creative juices flowing. Begin by writing down in the middle of a blank piece of paper a couple of words that describe one of your passions. Now think of all the permutations of this word or phrase, and write them down on a line radiating from the centre of the page. As you come up with ideas related to others already there, link them up, in the fashion of an 'organogram'.

Buzan recommends you use colours and illustrations to bring your mind maps to life; you can see examples at *www.mind-map.com.*

Using your notebook, produce a mind map for each of your passions and see what ideas flow out of these exercises. Once you've created several mind maps to learn this skill, start a new one with the words 'my career' in the centre and, using your best ideas, see what feasible possibilities are revealed. See Jo's example on the next page to see how it works.

20
mins

My Mind Map

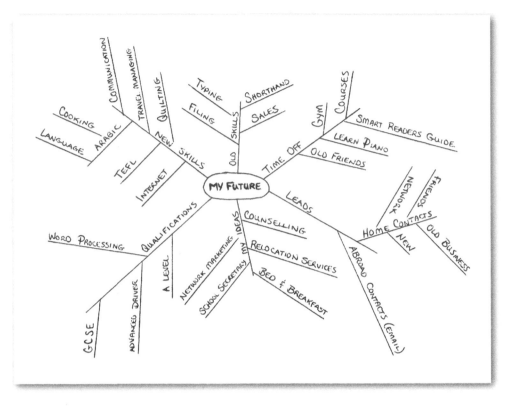

25 career ideas

I (Jo) have used this exercise many times with my students, and it always creates up to 25 separate job ideas.

10 mins

Write down a list of five things you love to do across the top of the grid below. These will comprise the main subject areas and should be nouns - such as cookery, art, sailing and computers.

Now write down another list of the five things you enjoy and do well in the left hand column under 'I am good at'. These words should be doing words, or gerunds, that end in *-ing*.

Finally, you need to pair up the words on the vertical axis with the words on the horizontal axis. If you look at the filled in example on the next page you'll get an idea

140

of how your grid should look. You will have 25 pairs of words that should inspire your thinking towards possible career options. There is an example of my (Jo's) completed grid on the next page.

I LOVE					

(left axis label: I AM GOOD AT)

In Jo's example here you'll see 'cooking art'. If you think laterally then this leads to possibilities like food styling, painting still life food, designing cookery book covers, cake decorating and many other options. You now know the source of Jo's 'book cook' idea!

		I LOVE				
		ART	COOKERY	SAILING	COMPUTERS	GARDENING
	COOKING	Cooking art	Cooking cookery	Cooking sailing	Cooking computers	Cooking gardening
	ORGANISING	Organising art	Organising cookery	Organising sailing	Organising computers	Organising gardening
	MARKETING	Marketing art	Marketing cookery	Marketing sailing	Marketing computers	Marketing gardening
	DRAWING	Drawing art	Drawing cookery	Drawing sailing	Drawing computers	Drawing gardening
	ACCOUNTING	Accounting art	Accounting cookery	Accounting sailing	Accounting computers	Accounting gardening

(left axis label: I AM GOOD AT)

Connect

Connect with people in every way you can, both formally and informally. Join networks, use the Internet, become a member of professional associations. Keep yourself informed of upcoming local and international conferences, workshops, seminars and professional development possibilities. These gatherings offer superb opportunities for making new contacts, for both present and future use. Try to assess the merits of women-only versus more general events; there is a great deal to be said for both.

One of the best ways to come up with innovative ideas is talking informally with other people. If your own thinking hits a brick wall, get together with some people to brainstorm ideas. If you haven't already done so as suggested in *Chapter 2 — Find Your Passion,* form your own group of people who are also in transition and share ideas with each other. One key purpose of these groups is to extrapolate possibilities from your known interests and talents. Often it is easier to help another than it is to figure it out for yourself. Someone else may be able to provide the needed trigger to get you thinking along a whole different line that will lead you to the opportunities you seek.

Another place to find possible ways to connect is to go to the library or supermarket and see what is being advertised on the notice boards, and which local amenities have placed their brochures there. You may notice a service missing in this community you'd taken for granted elsewhere.

Read local news

Oliver Segovia, on the *Harvard Business Review Blog*, finds too much navel gazing and trying to find your passion can be detrimental to your sense of happiness and wellbeing. He suggests it may be better to take your focus outside yourself and look for problems that speak to you; problems you want to be a part of the solution for. In addition to joining networks and meeting people, reading the local paper, with the help of a dictionary if you don't speak the language, to see what people are doing, what the local issues are, what advertisements are posted and what people are asking for in the 'wanted' sections will give you insights as to how to apply your values and apply your skills. Learning the names of local companies who are advertising or written about, and further researching these companies on the Internet and LinkedIn, can help spark more ideas. Not only will this give you an idea of where you can look for work or contracts, but you will also become acquainted with your local labour market.

I (Colleen) found the first step in my effort to work in my field in a new language, by reading the local paper. I read an article about a new charity whose purpose connected with my values and passions. There were looking for volunteers and, after meeting with me decided to design the perfect volunteer role for my skills, instead of filling one of their standing vacancies. This gave me the opportunity to network on a new level and that led a few steps later to my first paid contract in the Netherlands. Learning about what is of interest, concern and importance locally can give you insight into what is needed in the community. Perhaps these needs will inspire you to come up with a great idea and solution for the situation.

THAT'S NEWS

Read the news (local, regional and world) and notice which headlines catch your attention. Usually headlines are negatively worded, so when you read them ask yourself where the opportunities are that are being created by this event. Think it through in terms of all industry sectors. What is needed to create the elements needed for this event to take place? What will be the ripple effects of this event? What needs to happen simultaneously for this event to take place? Use the following worksheets to practice this way of processing the news you hear every day and develop your skill to uncover new opportunities for yourself. Find five headlines which interest you and go to it. Have a little fun and be creative with your answers. The first time I (Colleen) did this exercise developed by Dave Redekopp of Life-Role Development Group, it was based on an announcement related to Viagra. You can imagine some of the fun we had with our answers! A playful attitude can help you uncover some hidden gems you might otherwise have been too serious to find.

Example:

Headline: The world will end on 21-12-2012.

Background: Mayan calendar ends on this day. Theories related to UFO's, interplanetary collision, too much sun and a great deal of media hype.

Needed to make it happen: Forces beyond our understanding and knowledge.

Will happen simultaneously: Mass panic and unrest. Purchasing of products and supplies to survive the end of the world.

Will happen as a result: The end. Or a whole bunch of people feeling as silly as they did at Y2K when all the computers in the world were supposed to crash.

Opportunities created:

- Consultants and futurists sought for their expert opinions
- Travel experts to make travel arrangements to Bugarach, France
- Calendar developers to create alternative calendars
- Space travel for those wanting to leave earth to survive
- Products: 'End of the world' survival kits, End of the World Confessions website, greeting cards, survivor t-shirts and mugs
- Theme parties
- Journalists to cover the event from all corners of the world, live, recording it in pictures for the inevitable book
- Intercultural therapists for relationships between aliens and humans
- Therapists to restore relationships for those who confessed something and now have to deal with the consequences
- Sun specialists to devise a way to reduce the impact of the sun and global warming

Now it's your turn:

1. Headline:
_____
_____
_____

2. Background:
_____
_____
_____

3. Needed to make it happen:
_____
_____
_____

4. Will happen simultaneously:

_____

_____

_____

_____

5. Will happen as a result:

_____

_____

_____

_____

6. Opportunities created:

_____

_____

_____

_____

Listen to people

One of the best ways of finding what goods and services people in a given area need and want is to go out among the local community. Be open about being new in town and demonstrate your interest in knowing more about where you are living and the people around you. Chat with people who have been around for a while and listen for what problems they are complaining about. In my (Jo's) village in England people were always wishing they could find reliable babysitters, gardeners, house cleaners and window cleaners. Here in the Netherlands people moan about not speaking Dutch, not understanding the administration procedures, finding good schools and so on. While you yourself may have no desire to babysit, garden or clean, you might like to manage a team of other people to do such jobs. Problems are opportunities in disguise, so find out what gaps exist in the local market and think laterally about how you might be able to fill them using your skill set.

It was only when I realised that people, including myself, were frustrated about not having a portable career, and not knowing how to create their own career on the move, that I came up with the idea for *A Career in Your Suitcase*. Make sure to use this griping about problems as a window to finding opportunities, and don't get sucked into the negative cycle yourself. Remember to focus on the opportunities this griping points to.

> 'Somebody asked me to go out with them because they were a foreigner here and always buying the wrong thing. Spending money, coming home with the wrong thing and then not having the courage to go back and tell the shop.'
>
> **Belinda, Dutch and now in Holland, The Expatriate Archive, OAC5/3/3**

Problems that exist here and have caught my attention:

_____

_____

_____

Keep your eyes open

It's important you don't set your mind on one option and close it to other possibilities. New ideas, while initially daunting, can also be energising. Try not to keep your eyes so firmly on your chosen path that you miss other opportunities. Instead, think positively about turning the challenging circumstances of life into opportunities, and be alert to life's happy accidents.

In Muscat several years ago, I (Jo) was sitting outside having dinner with a group of friends one evening. It was dark and the slim date palm trees were silhouetted against a navy blue sky.

'I wish someone would write a cookery book about dates,' said Susie.
'I have written a cookery book before,' I joined in, 'and I'm sure I know enough about publishing to be able to self-publish this time.'
'With my food science knowledge and love of cookery I'm sure I could create some great recipes,' said Sue.
'I already have some great recipes,' added Susie.

Nine months later *Dates* was produced and published by Sue and myself, with contributions from Susie. It sold 4,500 copies in the first year.

John Krumboltz in his book, *Luck is No Accident* advises people to stay open to options and develop the skills that set you up to recognise and accept opportunity when it comes knocking. He says most things that happen in life are unplanned and unpredictable. Take a look at your own life and see where what he calls 'happenstance' has played a role in how your life and career have unfolded so far. Then make room for it to happen again!

Every time an idea pops into your head write it down in your notebook, think about it, mind map it, and whatever you do don't forget about it! If you hear someone say, 'I wish we had… here,' then log that idea too.

'I am registered with the consultancy bureau of the university here. Every two to three months they have people that are going to Malaysia for a business trip or people from the foreign office who are going to work there. They call me to give lessons in our language… usually 20 to 30 hours or so.'

Zohra, Malaysian in Holland, The Expatriate Archive, OAC5/3/3

Look on the Internet

Many country or city-focused websites advertise local information and job opportunities. Reading these can be a way to inspire ideas of different options. If none of this interests you, ask yourself what you would like to have found. You may be able to find your own creative niche, originate an innovative pricing structure, or target a different kind of client.

If you subscribe to *www.going-there.com* you'll find local job opportunities are advertised on their website.

Volunteer

Volunteer activities are an excellent way to come in contact with new people, information and experiences. These will undoubtedly feed your idea generation process and perhaps lead you in a direction that otherwise would not have been discovered by you or even been available to you. Some locations will have an organised volunteer centre where you can look through available volunteer positions just like a job centre. In other locations you will need contact organisations directly in search of voluntary opportunities.

Blue sky dreams

From the moment you picked up this book you have shown your interest in finding the perfect portable career. The blue sky featured on the book's cover is no accident. We all need to dream and to find the blue sky of open possibilities.

A dream is more likely to come true when you give it voice and write it down. When you first have a dream you create it in your mind; when you write it down you give it life; and every time you talk about it you give it more power. So as you share your dreams with friends and others whom you trust, the idea grows, problems are addressed and solutions are found. At each stage your blue sky dream takes on a more concrete shape and fills out with the particular steps to be taken and tasks to be addressed which will translate the dream from the sky to its real, earthly incarnation. Remember you can go from 'blue sky' to 'the sky's the limit'.

BLUE SKY PARTY

This is a brainstorming activity to help you 'take your own weather with you'. The basic rules are to stay positive, be proactive, talk about dreams, share dreams with others, allow others to join us and inspire us to make our dreams come true. Underlying this activity is a belief that there is always blue sky around the corner.

4
hours

You can choose to host a party and do this collaboratively.

Who to invite (seven friends for a two-hour party means 15 minutes Blue Sky per person):

_____

_____

What to serve (think Blue Sky!):

_____

_____

_____

When:

_____

_____

_____

Ways of Working

In addition to thinking creatively about how you will mix your skills and passion to create opportunities as you have just done, there are also many diverse ways of applying them in the work world. The industrial age is really when the 'job' as we know it with a set job description and task responsibilities evolved. Now with the Internet and globalisation, the sky really is the limit when it comes to the shapes work can take. Following are some of the current ways of working.

Concurrent careers

Many people pursue two or more careers simultaneously. One career may be a full time job while the other occupies evenings or weekends. Or a person may have two or more part time careers, with each job expressing a vocational interest or passion. These jobs may complement one another or be in entirely unrelated fields. It's not uncommon for a board level director to work for separate companies on different days of the week, some of which may be voluntary.

Whenever we run Career in Your Suitcase workshops we can guarantee that someone always asks this question:

'It's all very well, this idea of finding a career based on your passion. I need to work and earn money and what I do right now is not based on my passion, so how can I start this great new career and put bread on the table?'

We understand this issue completely. In 1997 I (Jo) moved back to England after ten years abroad and I had to earn proper money for the family. Determined not to compromise my belief in working with passion, I decided I would have to run two types of jobs concurrently. I would do the work I termed 'job' because it brought in the most money and I would make time for the work I called 'career' too. For me, as I mentioned in my introduction to this book, the thing that earned the most money was journalism. And though I love to write, churning out articles week after week and constantly coming up with new ideas under pressure and to deadline was not all fun. I set myself a target of eight articles a month and then spent the rest of my time building my Career in Your Suitcase business. Over time, as my business grew, I could earn more money from my 'career' and could ease off on the 'job'. Eventually, I was in a position, as I am today, to follow my 'career' alone.

Eclectic careers

Similarly, the eclectic career takes the concurrent career one step further and is increasingly popular as people take on a variety of work roles rather than only one. Some people choose to take on one or more better-paying roles to further their career ambitions. Rather as an artist contains many samples of work in one portfolio, this kind of career appeals to those who enjoy a varied work life, based on a combination of activities.

In this case the career portfolio may contain some work roles that are related or have a common theme, and others that do not. They can include an assortment of child rearing, part time paid employment, entrepreneurial endeavours, volunteer work, community activities and hobbies. This combo-career offers a mix of activities able to satisfy a person's wide range of needs for fulfilment, purpose and variety. When I (Jo) lived in Muscat, Oman, I had a portfolio of careers. I taught desktop publishing and creative writing, ran a CV-writing service, did some journalism, sold books via a party plan scheme, made and sold date chutney, ran a take-away service for my Indian maid and even made Christmas tree decorations to sell at festive bazaars. That kept me busy, and the variety of so many different projects at once was exhilarating.

Temporary work

Consider doing temporary work, which ironically can sometimes last longer than one would expect. This can tide you over while you continue researching options or prepare for a longer term work opportunity to arise. These temporary contracts can be a source of fulfilment and continuation of your professional identity during a time of transition.

Temporary placements can present an ongoing variety of experiences and a way to test out different career ideas. In fact, some people work on a virtually permanent basis for temporary agencies. Others in recognition of their ability and performance are subsequently hired as full time employees.

Temporary workers are currently found in many sectors of the labour market, with more and more temporary placements being made in the professional, medical and technical/ IT sectors. Often employers will use temporary placements as a way to get to know a person and their skills before they commit to a longer term contract, and temporary workers provide the workforce flexibility an employer needs in today's rapidly changing world. At the very least, temping presents a wonderful opportunity to expand your network.

Job sharing

In a job sharing arrangement, two people collaborate to perform the duties of a single, usually full time, position. Some companies hire new employees who are looking for part time work into positions they can share with another employee. And if a job is not advertised as a job share you can always explore the idea.

Compressed work week

Another popular option is compressing the 40-hour week into four or even three days. A number of US hospitals pay nurses for a 40-hour week to work three 12-hour days. Federal and state governments in the USA also offer this arrangement to some of their employees. Some couples with children work three-day compressed schedules so there is only one day a week when both parents are out of the house.

Pro-rated contracts

In some countries, such as Norway, it's normal for an employee to negotiate pro-rated pay for a reduced working week. Some employees are able to work a four-day week, others do this during term time only. Employers are becoming increasingly flexible about this kind of arrangement in order to retain key staff, particularly mothers returning to work.

Telecommuting

Many companies now attract desirable employees with telecommuting arrangements that allow them to perform many, most or all of their duties from their home office. The telecommuter may work at home several days a week, or alternate between a week at home and a week in the office. In this way many employees find themselves spending their work week in another country or city. Companies tend to be reluctant to employ people who work full time in a different location than their colleagues for fear that they may grow too detached from the organisation.

It's worth noting that human nature causes us to crave community, and anyone who embarks on a virtual telecommuting career may need to be creative to find a way to balance working alone with time with people. Nevertheless, for some, this is a perfect solution.

Work virtually

Consider setting up a business that allows you to work by computer or telephone from home, anywhere in the world. Website design, coaching, writing, editing, marketing, market research, accounts, virtual assistance, teaching and many other businesses can be successfully run on this basis. Some companies, particularly those requiring people to run a telephone based enquiry service or telesales office, recruit freelance staff to work from home.

In addition, many careers are becoming Internet based. You can now mentor, coach, teach or provide therapy by email or webcam, using a service such as Skype. You can also conduct teleseminars or video conferences from wherever you live and talk to huge numbers of students based all over the world. While nothing can beat personal contact, there are lots of opportunities for teleworking.

In fact, running a business from your computer, thanks to the marvels of broadband and the Internet, means you can create a virtual business that is also a global business. And when your clients are global you can take them with you. I will be writing more about establishing a mobile client base in *Chapter 5 — Networking.*

Some elements of my (Jo's) business are now global and virtual. I speak with clients all over the world, using my webcam and Skype and have face to face meetings. I run occasional teleclasses, host an online radio program and, because I have an international client base and keep in touch with them through an email newsletter, my publishing clients are based worldwide too. Every now and again we talk via Skype, but in between we use email to send documents back and forth between each other. I live in Holland and use a large freelance staff of editors, proofreaders and designers, based as far afield as South Africa, Canada and Qatar. And, thanks to my global network, when I arrived here in Holland, instead of being invisible as I was when I moved back to the UK in 1997, plenty of people already knew me and greeted me like an old friend.

The disadvantage of working virtually and from home, however, is that you may find yourself starved of human contact. If you are an introvert and happy with your own company (not me!) then this may be perfect for you. But for me, needing to be with people on a daily basis is important for my happiness. The only way I can cope with extended periods alone is to make time in my agenda to see at least one other person, face to face, every day. Running workshops and making an effort to meet consultancy clients personally whenever possible is of great help. Some people believe we only get energy from being in the same room with someone and that email conversations, Internet chats and video links are not the same. Others find these means sufficient for their human contact needs. Consider your own needs before you decide to work virtually.

'When we lived in Sweden, I worked from home, online for an American organisation that provided their clients with "outsourced" expat support.'

Victoria, New Zealander now in India, *www.expatwomen.com*

Flexitime

This is a boon to parents who want to be home when their children go to school, or ready to greet them at the other end of the day. Flexitime is also an attractive option for people who want to arrange their hours around what would be an otherwise unbearable commute. Some flexworkers may put in a standard five day, 40 hour workweek, but shift the hours during which they work towards the earlier or later part of the day. Others may work flexitime yet also have a reduced workweek - so they are effectively able to spread out three or four days' work over the five-day week.

Volunteer

It's always worth considering voluntary work, particularly if it is in line with your interests and passions. Regardless of how you approach volunteering, using your time meaningfully and constructively will improve your employability.

Volunteer work can often give you additional insight into a specific field and introduce you to contacts who can give you valuable advice about how to pursue your interests. I (Colleen) took on a volunteer role as my first step towards working in the Netherlands. I approached a service organisation dedicated to helping people in the areas of societal and community participation, integration and emancipation. This connected with my values and was something I was happy to give my time and energy to. It will add to your people skills, skills for working with teams, organising, administration and other areas. There is no reason why something that begins as a voluntary project can't eventually grow into or lead to a paid work opportunity.

Working without pay can make business sense too, says Mary Farmer of Global TMC. Volunteer work can offer satisfaction, connections and intrinsic rewards that are at least as valuable as monetary compensation. An added bonus of volunteerism in foreign countries is that it can be excellent cultural adjustment therapy.

'Service work, like volunteering a few hours a week at a children's hospital or just helping someone in need, is much more important to our mental health than we think,' reports Dr Kirsten Thogersen, a psychotherapist based in Beijing. 'One of the reasons people in transition often suffer is because they feel disconnected from their surroundings. To be connected with someone else, by giving them some of your time and energy, is the best possible protection against depression and other psychological reactions experienced by those living outside their passport country or place of origin.'

Expatriate spouse expert Robin Pascoe says, 'Many expatriate women's organisations in foreign countries organise welfare committees to allow members to channel energy, money and resources into local causes in a way that won't overwhelm them. Frontline volunteering is not for everyone.'

Two other benefits of volunteering are making lasting friendships (often with locals) and having the opportunity to practice and use the language on a regular basis and in a meaningful way.

Self-employment

In the last two decades we have seen the rise of a new kind of entrepreneur, the self-employed company of one – the sole trader. It's interesting to note that an increasing number of women choose to work for themselves rather than advance their careers into management in large companies.

It appears women opt for self-employment because they crave the flexibility and independence it provides. There is no doubt working for yourself allows you to create the career that suits you, with the hours, environment and personnel you choose. It's common for this type of entrepreneur to develop consulting businesses in areas of specialisation they've honed through their work with previous employers. Others capitalise on speciality markets perfect for the small company, such as catering, party/event planning and website design.

There are different kinds of self-employment, and many people who work for themselves work alone, or with a team of similarly freelance associates, rather than building a staff. Whether you fancy being freelance, an entrepreneur or a small business owner, self-employment can be highly portable.

BECOMING A CONSULTANT, INDEPENDENT CONTRACTOR OR FREELANCER

This option is often the best for people who have a specific expertise which can be sold to individuals and companies. It has the advantage of low capital outlay, scheduling flexibility, variety and autonomy. But you also need to be realistic about the downside or challenge of consulting - the lean periods, the need to sell yourself constantly and the intermittent (or frequent) feelings of isolation.

ENTREPRENEURS

These are simply people who work for themselves. The word 'entrepreneur' may sound daunting but it's an umbrella term referring to someone who is self-employed, freelance, an independent consultant or a small business owner, even someone who runs a kitchen table business. As an entrepreneur you could buy an existing business or a franchise. You could call yourself a 'creative entrepreneur' and make your work an expression of who you are. All of these are entrepreneurs.

Depending on the amount of personal control, investment of time, budget, marketing effort, risk, innovation or the number of staff you desire, you may consider your own case to be closer to the 'freelance' end of the spectrum than 'small business owner'.

If this sounds like something for you, you can read more about it in *Chapter 7 — Working for Yourself,* in Jo's book, *Expat Entrepreneur,* or *Laptop Entrepreneur* by Nick Snelling and Graham Hunt.

Researching Options

It is important to also look at the different occupations that exist in order to spur yourself to uncover new ways of using your skills. Perhaps you will find a role tailor-made for your skill set, passion, values and current reality!

Researching occupations

There are thousands of websites where you can do career and work related research, so at the outset it is valuable to know what information you are seeking. All the effort you have put into the previous chapters should have given you some ideas to start this research with. This will help prevent you from fitting yourself into the information, rather fitting the information to you. Take a moment to ask yourself what questions you want answers for. What key information do you need to know in order to make some choices? Most of us can name just the tip of the iceberg when it comes to the amount of different occupations there are in the world. Galen Tinder of REA says one of the most complete and reliable sources of information about occupations is the United States government, specifically the US Department of Labor and Bureau of Labor Statistics *www.bls.gov*. This website's *Occupational Outlook Handbook*, breaks the world of work down into industries and occupations. Its discussion of each occupation usually features nine headings.

- Nature of the Work
- Training, Other Qualifications, and Advancement
- Employment
- Job Outlook
- Projections Data
- Earnings
- OES Data
- Related Occupations
- Sources of Additional Information

On a neighbouring site you can find more detailed information about the economic outlook expected to affect any specific kind of work in the years to come. While this information is obviously US-centric, the vocational and professional information has broad applicability to many other parts of the world and can help you fill in some of the blanks about your current ideas for your portable career.

156

You can check to see if the country you are currently in has also developed this information, like Canada's National Occupational Classification (NOC) with over 40,000 occupational profiles in 500 occupational groups. As the sheer number of occupations in these lists can be overwhelming, be sure to use the 'related occupations' section of the occupational profiles to help you navigate your way from one option to another related one. Consider it a voyage of discovery and remember that because of technology and globalisation among other things, there are new work roles being created every day. Maybe you will create the next one!

There are thousands of websites which feature or include career resources and lists of career destinations. Among the private sites here are several good places recommended by Galen to begin — quintessential careers *(www.quintcareers. com)*, careeronestop *(www.careeronestop.org)*, its cousin site *(www.acinet.org)* and Jobweb *(www.jobweb.com)*. Publicly funded sites also worth visiting include *www.alis.alberta.ca* (click career explorers or job seekers) or visit CAREERinsite at *www.alis.alberta.ca/careerinsite*.

Researching companies

Once you have a pretty good idea of what kind of work you are looking for, the next subject of research may be the companies in which such work is found. The three sites listed above are good places at which to begin. Having a company website is indispensable in today's world and so nearly all medium to large sized companies have websites and depending on what part of the world you are in, most smaller ones do too. Visit these websites and read their news updates, annual reports and gather as much insight into the company as you can through their web presence.

An excellent new source of company information is LinkedIn. Once you have created your LinkedIn profile (see *Chapter 5 — Networking* and *Chapter 6 — Marketing Your Skills)*, you will have access to the plethora of information available here. Click on the 'companies' tab and select 'search companies'. Enter the name of a company you are interested in learning more about. LinkedIn will provide you with amazing summarised information including:

• Where current employees worked before joining the company
• Where employees went after leaving the company
• Where the employees are living in the world
• The most common skills of employees

- What types of functions the company has (e.g. sales and marketing, executive leadership, R&D)
- The years of experience employees have
- The level of education employees have and where they were educated
- The rate of occupational title change within the company as compared to other similar companies

Because LinkedIn is a living network, the information gathered is up to date. However, its accuracy depends on how completely the employees at a given company have built their LinkedIn profiles.

The purpose of company research is not only to identify promising organisations of potential interest. It is also critical to your success when you get to the point of marketing your skills. Conducting company research will provide you with the information you need to target your marketing materials. Read more about this in *Chapter 6 — Marketing Your Skills.*

Researching the big picture

The winds of change that influence work formation and shifts are economic, demographic, technological, social, cultural and societal. It could be there is a regional mini-baby boom creating needs right where you are planning to locate. It could also be a new technological development that creates opportunities. I (Colleen) recently read about new kinds of work being created. One person calls himself an 'idea DJ' and he streams sound and visuals inspired by what's being said during a conference, onto the big screens and speakers in the conference hall. Another new occupation similarly created by these changes is the 'Social Media Director'. And yet another is the 'Vertical Gardener'. It has been said that for children currently 12 years of age, there is a 50% likelihood their future work role has not yet been invented. This gives you a sense of the rate of change in the way occupations and jobs are evolving.

Harness the winds of change for yourself and use them to sail to your next career destination! The previous exercises will have helped you gather information you need. Now think about this information from a trends and demographics or big picture perspective. You may have an 'aha' moment and gain some insights that could help you find your unique portable career niche.

Evaluate Your Options

One way to consider what style of working will fit your situation best and what option looks like it has the most potential for your portable career is to do what is called a SWOT analysis. Mary Farmer suggests performing a ruthless assessment of the Strengths, Weaknesses, Opportunities and Threats is always revealing, and very often provides us with key answers.

Ask yourself some soul-searching questions:

Strengths:
How does this option use my best skills?
What are my strengths?
What do I like doing?

Weaknesses:
What skills do I need to update in order to stay current?
How sustainable is this option?

Opportunities:
What are the local/global trends for this option?
Can I relocate/travel more easily now (for instance, than when the kids were younger)?
What kind of work would I prefer: how much of a commitment do I want?
Can I work on a contract/interim/consulting basis?
How does success with this option fit with the changing needs/roles in the rest of my life?

Threats:
What are the obstacles I can foresee to developing a (new or different) career for myself at this point in time?
What is happening in the economy?
What are the laws and regulations that have impact on me right now?

Try to pry the lid off the box, as Mary calls it, the one that was the 'old you' and get outside it. There are many paths, and you just might discover a brand new you. You can find an example of a SWOT analysis applied to career planning on *www.quintcareers.com/SWOT_Analysis.html*. Use the grid on the next page to record your analysis.

Strengths	Weaknesses
Opportunities	Threats

Don't be afraid to ask for help. See *Part 10, Talking to a Professional.* Barbara Sher, bestselling author of *I Could Do Anything If I Only Knew What it Was,* advises, 'Failure to achieve our career ambitions does not result from a lousy attitude; rather from isolation.' Norm Amundson calls a career crisis really a crisis of imagination — not being able to imagine any other possible alternatives. You can't be expected to have all the answers at your fingertips. Go out, connect with people, collect new experiences and find your answers.

Complete the *Summing up Your Options* worksheet in *Your Career Passport.*

Living Your Mission

Setting goals

Anthony Robbins, author of *Unlimited Power,* says, 'The greatest achievers in the world all started by setting a goal.'

Gail MacIndoe says goals are what motivate us and give direction to our life.

The reason most people do not set goals or follow through with achieving them is because they think they will fail. They don't realise progress towards a goal can only be made one step at a time. Each little success will provide a boost of confidence and a sense of accomplishment that will help to keep you motivated.

For example, if you wanted to write a 300-page book but had never written anything of significant length before, the task would be daunting. However, if you were to write two pages a day for 150 days the goal would seem much more realistic and achievable.

Remember goals are not written in stone and you can adapt them as life evolves. However, with a written goal you have a benchmark to rate progress against and somewhere to check in to see if you are on track with living out your values.

STATE YOUR MISSION

It's not enough to know that you have goals; they need to be written down and clearly thought out. Stephen Covey also recommends identifying your mission statement as a starting point for setting your goals. You will have started this in *Chapter 2 — Find Your Passion* and in this section we give more detail as a foundation for writing your goals. Covey was perhaps best known for his book, *The Seven Habits of Highly Effective People,* in which he suggested we 'begin with the end in mind'. He recommended developing a personal mission statement as it focuses you on what you want to be and do, based on your values. He compared the process to the construction of a house: no one would start building without first having a design and construction plans. Use the carpenter's rule: 'measure twice and cut once'. Begin with the end in mind — clearly define what you want beforehand.

As you are discovering, a mission statement isn't something you write overnight. It takes careful analysis and deep introspection, and could take several weeks or months to get it to be a complete concise expression of your innermost values and directions. You may need to review it regularly and make changes as required, depending on your experiences and circumstances.

Once you have that vision and have established your values, you have the basis upon which to set long and short-term goals. Having a vision/mission allows you to judge every major decision you make and prioritise your activities according to what is important - hence making more effective use of your time and energies.

Continue to refine the mission statement you started in *Chapter 3 — What Can You Do,* and incorporate the influencing information you have uncovered through these last exercises.

Think of your mission statement as a North Star to guide you and help you focus your energy and activities. Write the current working version of your mission statement here:

_____

_____

_____

'It's easy to get overwhelmed by the big picture. The way that works best for me is breaking a large goal down to smaller more manageable chunks. Like if you need to lose 10lb and you say instead that you'll lose 1lb a week for ten weeks – it's much more do-able. Translated into business goals, I start with a sheet of paper and brainstorm all the elements of the particular project. Then I prioritise them into a timeline to visually show what has to be done by when. Then each step is broken down into mini-brainstorms and lists of tasks. This was the way we worked when we were setting up the business. Nowadays it is less necessary as the pressure has reduced somewhat.'

Diane, Canadian in England, *www.expatwomen.com*

'[I believe in] making plans, which set goals and objectives to be achieved within specified time periods. As an example, I may decide that within one month I will initiate 8 new contacts or attend 5 networking events with the goal to expand my network of contacts at a factor of "x" per function. I do the same in business by setting a realistic goal although one that will also stretch me.'

Carol, American in Saudi Arabia, *http://delhi4cats.wordpress.com*

'I work with a team that is scattered at the four corners of the world and there are moments where losing the plot is too easy. A way to gather momentum and spring forward is achieved by setting short term targets, where everyone has to pitch in, in order to complete a goal. The breaking down of any objective in digestible pieces is for us all the key to overcome the discouragement that might set in when you look how distant in the future is the achieving of your goal. A concept based on the old Chinese saying "even the hardest journey begins with a small step".'

Patrizia, Italian in France, *www.paguro.net*

'What we get in life is a result of the choices we make and the actions that we take on a day-to-day basis. Hence, I achieve goals by identifying, prioritizing, scheduling and doing my best to stick to that schedule. I adjust my schedule as needed and incorporate as many things as I need to keep me on track and motivated. I keep enough flexibility in my schedule to allow for "life to happen" (I do live in Italy and so the idea of time can be relative!)'

Megan, American in Italy, *www.careerbychoice.com*

'The first week of each year, I look back at the last year and think of situations both good and bad and decide how to handle future dilemmas. Then I set my goals, personal, work and spiritual.'

Lizzy, British in America, *www.expatwomen.com*

'I really struggled giving up my work, identity and financial independence in Shanghai to move to Russia with my boyfriend. I suddenly became a 'nobody' in a very small expat community and a very un-dynamic city, which was a very big blow to my self-esteem and my motivation. I decided I needed to feel like I achieved something at the end of each day, no matter how small and so started writing a list of things I would do tomorrow - things as simple as do the washing, buy dinner (a challenge in Russia!!), read another chapter of my book, go for a walk and file the credit card statements, but at the end of the day I could tick those off which made me feel in control of something and that I too achieved something today. Three years later and I feel much more confident and in control of who I am (an extremely steep learning curve that a job does not define who I am), but I still plan what I'm going to achieve tomorrow, the night before.'

Victoria, New Zealander, now in India, *www.expatwomen.com*

Now you will develop more specifics for your mission statement.

STATE YOUR GOALS

Determine the reasons why you want what you want. If they are big and compelling enough you will always figure out how to achieve them. As Daniel Burnham, American architect and urban planner said, 'Make no little plans — they have no magic to stir your blood to action. Make big plans, aim high in work and hope.'

Goals need to happen in our minds before they happen in reality. The unconscious mind does not differentiate between what is imagined and what is real. The brain always strives to help us achieve what we focus on, so make sure you focus on what you want and not on what you do not want.

Gail MacIndoe believes all things are created twice; first there is the mental vision and then the physical creation. If you think about what you want to achieve and visualise it, and then you write it down, you will have created the goal twice. When the goal is achieved, you will have created it three times.

'Set a goal to achieve something that is so big, so exhilarating that it excites you and scares you at the same time. It must be a goal that is so appealing, so much in line with your spiritual core, that you can't get it out of your mind. If you do not get chills when you set a goal, you're not setting big enough goals.'

Bob Proctor

If your mission statement is the North Star guiding your journey, then the goals are the points on the star that define it and give it more shape. Goals serve your purpose and passion and express them in concrete actions. They lead towards your vision and mission in one way or another.

Your list of goals can answer some of the following questions:

- How will you achieve this?
  - What are the sub-steps of this?
- How and what will you need to research? What pieces of information are you missing at this point?
- Who do I want to meet and add to my network?
- Where can you find your clients/potential employers?
- Where can you network?

164

- Where will you advertise/post your CV?
- What will you do for free to reach this goal?
- What will you need to do/produce first?
- How will you find out what to charge/what salary to ask?

What are some goals that will allow you to express more of your values and passion in your everyday life, leading you in the direction of your portable career and fulfilling your mission?

20 mins

1. _____
2. _____
3. _____
4. _____
5. _____
6. _____

MAKE A ROUTE MAP

It can help to list the steps from the last to the first that you can start today. Think of the song that goes, 'one thing... leads to another' and use this graphic. Start at the top with your 'North Star' and mission and work downwards. Or start at the bottom of the stairs and work up. Or start in the middle and work outwards like you did with your mindmap. Look at the two graphics that follow and choose whichever approach helps you to get some steps on paper and start forming your route map. Be open to following needed detours and pit stops while staying focussed on your north star for guidance.

For example:

North Star: I will provide relocation services to newcomers by pointing them to appropriate local resources and providing them with a warm personal (and virtual) connection upon arrival.

Objectives:
1. Three international companies will contract my services with two-year agreements.
2. Clients will refer me 90% of the time to at least one person in their network because I treated them as people and not numbers.

3. I will maintain ties with my former clients by including them (with their permission) on my mailing list for 'tip of the month for living in X'.

Route Map:

*   I will network with people from international companies and express genuine interest in their relocation experiences
*   I will join clubs and groups and contributing to their success where I can
*   I will offer free support to 4 people making international moves in exchange for a recommendation on LinkedIn and a quote for my website
*   I will join related LinkedIn groups, share what I know and learn from the experiences of others

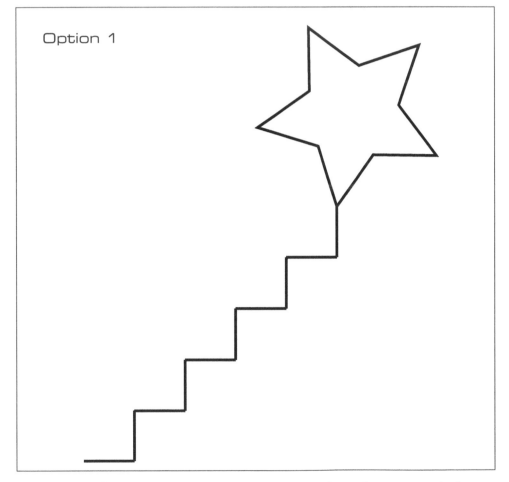

Option 1

This process of creating a route map is not meant to limit the ways in which your vision can be realised. Often your vision will be achieved through serendipitous moments where planning and actions meet unplanned opportunity.

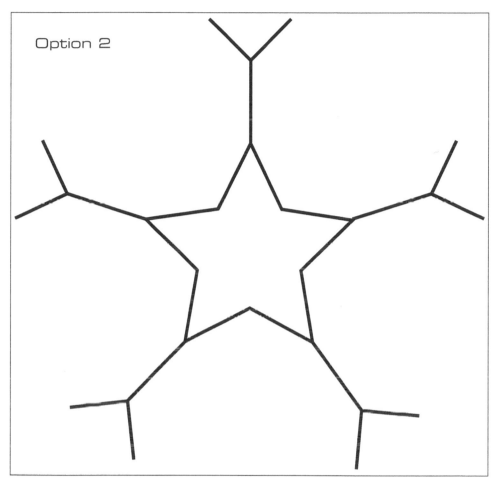

Option 2

Keep the door open for serendipity

The beautiful thing about making plans is that they are made to be changed! Life has a great way of introducing curves in the road where none were expected. Some of these curves give way to opportunities that are serendipitous. John Krumboltz says serendipity happens when planning meets opportunity. Don't become so fixated on carrying out your action plan that you miss the scenery and the opportunity for serendipity to play a role in your journey. Leave room for serendipitous side-stops, detours or re-routing on your journey. This is also a form of flexibility expressed by the term career resilience.

Recognise when you have arrived

What will it feel like? Describe the emotions you expect to feel. What will you hear? Will you hear people congratulating you and if so what will they be saying? What will your success look like? What will be happening when you achieve your goals, where will you be, who else will be there? The more vivid you are in making the picture and including all the senses, the more realistic and achievable the goal becomes. Remember what we said earlier: your unconscious mind does not know the difference between imaginary and real. Visualisation is something we all do, but we don't do it regularly enough. The more vividly you can imagine the outcome the more your unconscious mind believes it has already happened. You need to ensure you include the sound and feeling too. Then you will begin to feel as if you have achieved your goal and you will start to act as if you have - resulting in the likelihood that you will achieve it. Successful people and athletes spend a lot of time imagining themselves winning.

Recognise what your current state does for you

We all get some kind of benefit from our current state or otherwise we would not bother to maintain it. Imagine you were a smoker. By smoking at work you would probably get a few minutes' break and the opportunity to chat with colleagues. Stopping smoking would remove these benefits. It's important to consider these needs and imagine, if you decided to become a non-smoker, how you could address the need for a break and developing social contacts in a new way. Add these elements to your route map.

The same applies for living out your mission and vision. What are some of the changes and potential investments you will need to make? Your mission needs to inspire you to go beyond the inconvenience of some of these changes and continue to make the investments over the long term. If needed make some revisions to your mission to ensure that the inspiration you need is there.

SCENARIO BUILDING

The ability to think of a variety of different scenarios that could arise and preparing a rough plan of action for them will help you to respond to the way things unfold in a proactive and productive way without losing as much of your momentum. Anticipating and rehearsing a potential situation will help you respond in a way that supports the expression of your mission and purpose. Scenario building helps you

30 mins

take a step back from your initial response and think of alternative responses so that you choose the one you think fits best, as opposed to going with your first, often emotional, response. These scenarios can be referred to as Plan B, C and so on.

What are some of the things that can get in the way of your Plan A which you worked out on the previous pages?

1. _____
2. _____
3. _____

Taking these into account, create some alternative scenarios to address them on the following worksheets.

Plan B

Situation

_____
_____
_____

Head (thoughts)

_____
_____
_____

Heart (feelings)

_____
_____
_____

Actions

_____
_____

Results

_____
_____
_____

Plan C

Situation

_____

_____

_____

Head (thoughts)

_____

_____

_____

Heart (feelings)

_____

_____

_____

Actions

_____

_____

_____

Results

_____

_____

_____

This chapter has given you the chance to actively and creatively look at ways of applying your skills and expressing your talents in the world of work. You have also been able to continue to develop your mission statement and create scenarios that will support you to live your mission.

Fill as much as you can in the _Summing Up Your Options_ worksheet in _Your Career Passport_. This will help you clarify what you still need to research and learn.

The next chapter focuses on building the relationships that will help you fill in some of this missing information and continue to support the expression of your passion and mission through your portable career.

Chapter 4: Resources for Creating Your Career

B Sher, *I Could Do Anything I Wanted if Only I Knew What it Was,* Hodder and Stoughton

BR Anchor: *Home Away from Home, Relocation 101, Let's Make a Move,* and other books

C Eikleberry, *The Career Guide for Creative and Unconventional People,* Ten Speed Press

C McConnell, *Soultrader,* Momentum

C Sangster, *Brilliant Future,* Momentum

Culture Shock!: Culture Shock! Venezuela, Culture Shock! Austria, Culture Shock! Japan, Culture Shock! Norway, How to Succeed in Business in Thailand, How to Succeed in Business in India, Global Customs and *Etiquette guides,* and many other country specific titles, Kuperard

D Foster, *The Global Etiquette Guide to Asia, The Global Etiquette Guide to Europe,* and other country specific titles, John Wiley and Sons

D Freemantle, *How to Choose,* Momentum

Edited by AM Boels, *The Insider's Guide to Working in Europe,* Benefactum

E Wachs Book, *Why the Best Man for the Job is a Woman,* Harper Collins

G Pyke, & S Neath, *Be Your Own Careers Consultant,* Momentum

Government of Alberta, Human Services, Advanced Techniques for Work Search, *www.alis.alberta.ca/publications*

H Gelatt & C Gelatt, *Creative Decision Making,* Crisp

H Ibarra, *Working Identity: Unconventional Strategies for Reinventing Your Career,* Harvard Business School Press

J Clark, *The Money or Your Life,* Century

J Krumboltz & A Levin, *Luck is No Accident,* Impact Publishers

J Mole, *Mind Your Manners,* Nicholas Brealey Publishing

J Parfitt, *Expat Entrepreneur,* Summertime Publishing??

Living and Working in Britain, Living and Working in America, Living and Working France, Living and Working in Spain, and many other country specific titles, Survival Books

L MacKinnon, *Cosmic Coaching,* Ryder

M Buckingham, *Go Put Your Strengths to Work,* Free Press

M Malewski, *Generation Xpat,* Nicholas Brealey

M Sinetar, *Do What You Love and The Money Follows,* Dell Trade Paperback

ME Gerber, *The Emyth,* Harper Collins

N Amundson, S Niles & R Neault, *Career Flow*, Pearson

N Amundson, *The Physics of Living*, Ergon Communications

N Snelling and G Hunt, *Laptop Entrepreneur*, Summertime Publishing

N Williams, *The Work We Were Born to Do*, Element Books

P McGraw, *Life Strategies*, Vermilion

P McGraw, *Self Matters*, Simon and Schuster

R Nelson Bolles, *How to Find Your Mission in Life*, gift edition, Ten Speed Press

R Nelson Bolles, *What Color Is Your Parachute Workbook: How to Create a Picture of your Ideal Job or Next Career*, Ten Speed Press

R Nelson Bolles, *What Color is Your Parachute?*, Ten Speed Press

S Griffith, *Work Your Way Around the World*, Vacation Work Crimson Publishing

S Helgesen, *The Female Advantage*, Doubleday

S Longman, *Choosing a Career*, The Times with Kogan-Page

T Buzan, *The Mind Map*, BBC Active

T Buzan, *Use Your Head*, BBC Active

Vacation Work: *Health Professional Abroad, The Good Cook's Guide to Working Worldwide, Working with the Environment, Working with Animals,* and many other career specific titles

'All things being equal, people will do business with, and refer business to, those people they know, like and trust.

Bob Burg

Chapter FIVE

Networking

The Importance of Relationships

Dr Anne Copeland, director of The Interchange Institute in Brookline MA, has conducted a series of studies into the happiness of accompanying partners. Copeland has discovered that it's not the women who maintain close contact with their friends and family back home who adjust best, nor is it those who have a strong family unit with them on assignment. It's the women who make new friendships who adjust most easily to their new environments. And the way we make friends is by networking.

'Research has shown that women with strong social networks are usually physically and emotionally healthier than those who are isolated,' she says. 'But when a woman moves half way round the world she is hit triply hard. Firstly, she needs the support of friends more than ever because of all the changes she encounters. Secondly, she's now far away from those who know her best. And thirdly, she faces language and cultural barriers to making new friends.'

When you're trying to create work opportunities as well as a social life, nothing can kick start your career better than networking. In a new location, you can start networking straight away, if not before you arrive, by making contact with people to whom you have been referred by your contacts in the previous location. You can also use a search engine to discover other expats through their blogs and online activities. Statistics say that 65 to 75 percent of work opportunities are found through networking rather than through things like recruitment agencies, advertised vacancies and Internet postings.

We like people who are like us. We buy from people we like. How are we ever going to let people find out whether they are like us or they like us if we don't get out there and network? And no, networking is not about handing out business cards, it is about being nice to people, sharing and making friends. Stephanie Ward of Firefly Coaching defines networking as 'building relationships over time'. Read on to find out more.

The importance of networking

Did you know advertised vacancies are often filled by networkers, before or while the advertisement appears? Indeed, 50 to 80 percent of the positions that interest you will be filled at the 'hidden job market' level?

These jobs are snatched up by people who are not necessarily better qualified than you, but who are better connected. People get these jobs by networking or by being part of an already existing network. Networking gives you the best chance of knowing the right person in the right place at the right time. Studies of networking have demonstrated this 'right person' is rarely a close friend – or even a friend at all. She's more likely to be the acquaintance of a friend, or the friend of an acquaintance. So your chances of getting your desired position increase in proportion to the number of people you know and their networks.

Over the years we have come across countless examples of people who found work through the hidden job market. One of my (Jo's) friends, newly arrived in Dubai, found herself a job as a secretary for an airline company by chatting to someone at a drinks party. I started working for an employment agency writing CVs, because my husband had told someone he'd met in a bar that his wife had arrived in town and was looking for work. I once ran a writing workshop for a large ferry company because I met someone who worked there at a wine tasting event. And I found a publisher because I got chatting to the man sitting next to me on a ten-minute train ride. He was that publisher.

My commissions at *The Independent* came about because one of the members of our local writing circle did some sub-editing for them. At least two career consultants hired by Ricklin-Echikson Associates (REA) were recruited as the result of an email I received from them when I was editor at *Woman Abroad* magazine asking if I could recommend anyone suitable.

A four stage event

A work opportunity has four stages. The first is when there is nothing available. The second is when it is recognised the amount of work is more than can be managed with the current resources. The third stage is when it's agreed new skills or more resources are required and informal enquiries are made to find these. The fourth stage is when the opportunity is made public and advertised in the usual ways. Most opportunities will be filled at stage two or three as it is more efficient for the employer. A formal recruitment process costs an employer time and money. The more people you know and who are aware of what you can do and are looking for, the more likely you are that when the opportunity comes up, you will know about it before it is advertised.

Building Your Network

Networking builds a web of contacts and associations. It is from your network you will most often find your next work opportunity. Learning how to network is essential to creating a portable career.

Like a spider, you cannot build your whole web instantly. It begins with the people you know - relatives, close friends, casual acquaintances and people you haven't seen for some time. Don't forget to include people you see regularly and those you must make a special effort to reach.

Your network is made up of all these people:

- Family
- Friends
- Neighbours (past and present)
- Business colleagues and co-workers (past and present)
- Social acquaintances (golf, tennis and other sports/recreation players, social club members, members of the community met through social or civic activities)
- Professional acquaintances (people with whom you have interacted in present or past jobs)
- Former classmates, teachers and college alumni
- Mentors
- Relatives
- Priests, ministers, rabbis and other religious leaders
- Members of any professional, religious, or leisure organisation to which you belong
- People met at a course or conference
- People in your town and area with whom you have a friendly relationship (local business owner, hairstylist, bank tellers, your estate agent, supermarket cashier)
- Internet network on LinkedIn, Facebook or Twitter and so on

Once you have established your own first level network, you will discover that the people who belong in other people's networks find their way into yours. Like an elastic band your network can always expand to fit in more people.

But how do you find your way into the networks that belong to your networks? You ask. You ask a specific question based on your need. We are sure you are used to doing this in your daily life. You need a plumber but you are new in town and know very few people. You are desperate and so you ask the only person you do know, the lady at the reception desk at the school where your children go. She has been there a few years and has no difficulty giving you a few names and numbers. Easily, her network becomes yours. Networking is a normal human activity. You need to normalize it for your search for work opportunities as well as a plumber.

Networking etiquette

Mention the word 'networking' and many people raise their eyes to the ceiling as they conjure up pictures of brash, aggressive types, thrusting business cards into the palms of complete strangers. It should not be like that, particularly if it's to produce the desired outcome. We could just as easily call the subject of this chapter 'relationship building', 'connecting' or 'making new friends'. Networking is taking a method you use naturally on a personal level and using it to form relationships and exchange information with people with whom you share vocational and professional interests. Donna Messer built her business out of networking. A regular on the international speakers' circuit at conferences and for corporations, her business, Connect Us Canada, facilitates connections between people and businesses. Donna has a training suite at her offices in Ontario. She starts many of her presentations with the words 'Hello, my name is Donna Messer, how may I help you?' Because helping is what she does so well.

'Networking is not about handing out business cards,' she says. 'If you build the relationship first, get to know someone, and they like you, then they will *ask* you for your card. That's much better.'

Donna believes the secret of good relationship-building is to give presents. And she doesn't mean presents which cost money. The nicest present you can give someone is the name of someone else who might be able to help them. For the newcomer to a community, the name of a recruitment agency, someone who has lived and worked in the community, or a cheap stationer may be the most welcome gift of all.

When you give someone something they need, even if it is just the number of a plumber, as seen in the example earlier, you are giving them a *present*. The recipient of the phone number feels pleased with the outcome. The person who gave the gift feels of value too and, at the same time, a relationship starts to form between the giver and receiver of the gift. These relationships are the foundation of business. We do business with people we like and so the giving and receiving of a simple phone number may have far-reaching benefits.

Do not expect that if you give a 'present' to one person they will give you one right back. You give randomly and receive randomly. Thomas Power, founder of Ecademy, has calculated he has to give 98 presents in order to receive two back in return. However, those presents he receives are of such value it makes it all worthwhile. This is the abundance mentality at work.

Where to network?

Of course we don't need to join a professional organisation in order to start networking. It's just as easy to make contacts in the school playground or supermarket queue. But sometimes we need a little help.

For those like me who want to work while they are abroad, the best kind of networking starts with getting to know people of all kinds in all places. In time those people can become friends. If you're as passionate about your business as you are about making friends, then those often friends become your clients too.

> 'I make my own business cards and spread the word. I join professional and other groups and network as much as I can.'
>
> **Kitty, American in Norway, *www.careerinyoursuitcase.com***

CLUBS

All over the world the American Women's Clubs thrive on helping newcomers to make friends - and while many of their meetings do involve cups of coffee and sticky cakes, they provide a service that is second to none. Many have offshoot groups for working women, local history or travel. The umbrella organisation, the Federation of American Women's Clubs Overseas (FAWCO), is now in its 82nd year and the number of associate member groups is growing.

I (Jo) remember, back in the early nineties, living in Dubai with two young children and an oft-absent husband made the days seemed endless. It was then I joined a group called Mother to Mother. Back then I didn't class this volunteer group as a network, but that's exactly what it was. The monthly coffee mornings became a lifeline to me. There were lots of toys for the children and the chance for some adult conversation for me. But this group offered much more besides. There was a library of child related books and videos available, as well as offshoot groups that concentrated on, say, breastfeeding or twins, and a series of grown-ups only events. I soon found myself editing the monthly newsletter, which led me to make new friends with those involved in editorial, events or photocopying. But it also led me to perfect my desktop publishing skills. When the children were less dependent I found myself teaching desktop publishing. The added value of such an organisation was clear.

In 1996 when my family moved to Stavanger in Norway I experienced the benefits of networks within a day of arriving. My husband was working for Schlumberger, a large oilfield services provider, and their spouses' association (SSA) is run on a voluntary basis by the spouses themselves. There are now around 100 active chapters worldwide. Shell Global Outpost has its own similar worldwide network, which currently is available in 50 locations.

It was January. Ian had gone to work and I was alone in our temporary apartment with the boys. Snow was falling outside the vast windows. Coming from the Middle East we were not equipped with snowsuits and boots so we couldn't venture out to play. With only *Cartoon Network* for company, the day ahead looked bleak, until Ian would return with the company car and we could go and hunt for schools, somewhere to live and fur-lined clothing. Then I received a phone call from Maureen who introduced herself as my appointed welcomer from the SSA. The next day she visited me in person, armed with flowers and a welcome basket. Inside I found a local street map, newsletters from various local networks and information about pre-schools. I also had the luxury of a real live adult to bombard with questions about living in snowy Scandinavia. Importantly, I also received an invitation and the offer of a lift to the next SSA coffee morning. Despite having already spent ten years with Schlumberger in two different countries, this was the first time I'd ever been able to meet up with the spouses of other employees. It was only a matter of time before I found myself working as their newsletter editor, and ultimately arranging seminars.

I was determined to make my first outing to the local FAWCO club too. It was there I re ceived the extra gifts I needed to make my life more contented. Within five minutes I had the number of a babysitter and discovered how good Norwegian pastries were. I also received a calendar of events for the year ahead and found out how to advertise in their monthly newsletter, the creative writing classes I hoped to run. My first course was soon fully booked.

PROFESSIONAL NETWORKS AND ASSOCIATIONS

My professional life has always been important to me, of course, and so I (Jo) also joined a group for working women that called itself Women's International Network (WIN). I don't mind admitting it took me almost five months to pluck up the courage to go along. When I arrived I could not have met a nicer, more helpful bunch of people. Here I was able to attend a series of fascinating seminars, meet women who shared my passion for maintaining a portable career, and learn new skills. In the true spirit of abundance I was soon giving my time back to the group producing the newsletter. I also met Elizabeth Douet, who helped me with the first *Career in Your Suitcase* and its associated seminar, joined a group that taught me how to present, and found more students for my creative writing classes.

When I returned to England in 1997 I had a tough time repatriating my career, but it was harder still to repatriate my identity. After nine months of feeling I did not belong, I decided to start a women's professional network of my own. Four years later, I was still on the committee of Women Connecting Women (WcW) with a database of 200 regulars. Find out how I set it up later in this chapter.

In the Netherlands, becoming a board member of Connecting Women was the first thing on my agenda. In fact I was their speaker at my very first meeting. Six months later I grabbed the opportunity to be on the board. This was a wise decision and helped me to make firmer friends and a stronger network. It also gave me the opportunity to stand up and speak at the monthly meetings about my role as workshop co-ordinator, which raised my profile in the local community. Volunteering to do something which benefited my business directly was a bonus: while I organised the promotion of the group's workshops I could also promote my own.

Similarly, I (Colleen) joined the Dutch Association for Career Professionals (NOLOC) as one of my first steps towards developing the local network I need to create and sustain my career here. Often referred to as 'The old school tie network' or the 'old boys network', professional associations are a frequent source of business. Clients are often referred to you and you can engage in projects with fellow members of the association. I (Colleen) attended a meeting of NOLOC while my Dutch was still very rudimentary. It was very intimidating but I challenged myself to share at the meeting, in Dutch, at that meeting. Sharing on the night's topic of core values, I said my goal was to remain authentic to who I am as I strived to adapt and fit in in a new country, language and culture. Because I shared at the meeting, I was approached afterwards by Arnold Veenhof, a then starting coach, who offered me some free coaching sessions to help me get started.

I also met Geraldine Sinnema of *Een wereld van verschil* (A World of Difference) and she later connected me to someone who referred me a number of clients. Even later she and I partnered up to develop a series of career workshops for parents of school-age children. They were the only two people I met at that meeting, but they turned out to be key members of my new local professional network and have definitely made a world of difference for my career.

'For the first month I could not cope. I could not face going out because I couldn't communicate in Norwegian. I sat at home and read most of the time. It was so demoralising. After visiting a couple of shops I was exhausted and had to come home again. The *Petroleum Wives Club* and the *Women's International Network (WIN)* became my lifeline. I soon took on board positions for both. I also took any substitute teaching I could find at the International School. It took six months to settle down.'

Penny, British in Norway, *www.careerinyoursuitcase.com*

THE INTERNET

This is another source of new friends. Find sites which appeal to you whether they focus on your specialist area, your hobby, where you are living, or are more general in focus. Many will have chat groups you can join, Facebook pages and blogs you can follow and 'like' or comment on, or electronic newsletters (ezines) such as Jo's called *The Inspirer*. All will be a source of contacts, inspiration and information to share with others in your networking.

Take a look at a website, find out the contact details of the organisers, or click through to the sites of those who are featured there, and get in touch.

Expat sites

Sites such as:

www.expatexchange.com
www.expatwomen.com
www.expatica.com
www.paguro.net

To help you to connect with other expatriates in your new location before you arrive. Try *www.newcomersclub.com* to find out about existing networking groups.

Online networks

Of course, there are plenty of networks out there that exist solely online. Ecademy *(www.ecademy.com)* has hundreds of thousands of members worldwide and real time meetings. Members can post their profile, join forums and search for and connect with other Ecademists.

LinkedIn *(www.linkedin.com)* is growing exponentially. At the end of September 2012 the LinkedIn network was growing by two new members per second and more than 64% of its 200+ million members were located outside the United States. Here, you do not make connections with strangers right away like at Ecademy. Instead, you invite people you already know to link with you and then you can look at their links. Clicking on your company of interest can help you work backwards through their current employees to your own network. LinkedIn has more than one million user groups you can join to contribute to discussions and share information. Find the groups that relate to your passion and career direction and get to know some of the key people in your chosen area. By doing this you can also keep ties with the network you already have.

I (Colleen) notice that in groups which connect strongly with my values and passion I want to contribute what I know to a discussion. By sharing on LinkedIn you will be able to profile your knowledge and expertise and create the opportunity to build your professional connections. If you blog, connect your blogging activity to your LinkedIn profile. As small business coach Stephanie Ward suggests and does herself, when you notice you are in several similar groups and have a number of contacts in common with someone you can send them an invitation to link noting these similarities.

Facebook *(www.facebook.com)* is also being used professionally. You can visit and link to business pages of companies. This allows you to be kept up to date on their news. You can also 'like' some of their activities and initiatives as well as comment on them. If you find a company that connects with your passion, you can connect with them virtually and become a supporter or follower, thanking them for and appreciating their efforts, offering useful and relevant information and tips, and perhaps this will resonate at the right level and result in the creation of a work opportunity.

Both of these are great ways to grow a client-base out of your current personal network. Accept it is not possible to keep your professional and personal networks separate in this age of social media and that people want to do business with other people. It is about building authentic relationships. Take the time to build an online profile or brand consistent with your career goals and objectives. Revise your already existing profiles to bring them in line with your current direction. On your LinkedIn profile make sure you check you are interested in being contacted for work opportunities and by recruiters if that is a fit for you. See more about the type of content needed for your online profile and personal branding in *Chapter 6 - Marketing your Skills.*

Twitter *(www.twitter.com)* is another place to connect with people. You can follow anyone who interests you, even famous authors and professionals in your field. See what others are Tweeting, find what you consider to be effective Tweets and choose how you want to use this for yourself. Give yourself some time for the learning curve of Tweeting effectively for networking purposes and finding your own Tweeting style. There are many apps and tools available to help manage your Tweets effectively. Your Twitter account can be connected to your LinkedIn and Facebook profiles.

Pinterest *(www.pinterest.com)* is a very popular newcomer to the social networking scene, seeking to connect people through their common interests. It is helpful for people who are visual or work in visual ways. Like Facebook, you build a profile, but this time a visual one, of things you like that express who you are. If you like something you can 'like' it, 'pin' it on your own bulletin board and/or make a comment. It is another way to communicate who you are and what is important to you and find other like-minded people. Its value as a career development tool is becoming more recognised as it is similar to creating a collage of images to help you gain insight into yourself, determine your passion and can also help recruiters and HR people learn more about you.

Whatever you do, use these online networking tools consistently and with integrity and authenticity: you are building your online identity or brand. Make sure it is accurate and reflects who you are professionally. Use the appropriate settings to keep your personal online activities personal. Be creative and find ways to connect online regularly in helpful and generous ways, building trust and credibility, and your network will solidify as well as grow.

'I have found online networking to be an excellent tool – especially the site *www.linkedin.com*. This is a professional networking site and the more information one is willing to share about themselves the better results received. Through LinkedIn networking I was contacted by an international American firm to assist with a detailed marketing research project in Saudi Arabia, which in turn led to additional contacts and opportunities.'

Carol, American in Saudi Arabia, *http://delhi4cats.wordpress.com*

BLOGGING AND NEWSLETTERS

Maintaining and expanding your network is also possible through blogging and newsletters to which people can subscribe or follow. Find a number of good ones to follow and you will receive a constant stream of information and insights, See *Chapter 7 — Starting for Yourself* for more information on developing your own blogs and newsletters.

PUBLICATIONS

Several years ago, when I (Jo) was living in Norway, I subscribed to Writers News magazine. One day I spotted a small feature about a lady called Bobby Meyer, who had started an enterprising new publication called Dual Career Network. I was so inspired by her initiative I got in touch. On my next trip to England we met up and Bobby and I have been firm friends ever since. She helped to proofread the first version of *A Career in Your Suitcase,* wrote a chapter for it and later joined with me to create a website. We've run seminars together and continue to connect with each other and support each other's work as often as we can.

If you see an article that appeals to you in a magazine, newspaper, newsletter, blog or website, ask the editor to connect you with the author or search for them online yourself. The editor will be delighted to get some feedback and know the articles are of interest. Magazines such as *Transitions Abroad, American in Britain* and *Global Living Magazine* tend to be written by and for expatriates. If you want to make new friends, try contacting the people who write or feature in these and other similar magazines, blogs and newsletters.

Remember, you can write to magazines and websites requesting people contact you to help you with your career research. This can be very productive.

And why not write to authors too? One of my (Jo's) closest friends met me that way. She read a copy of the second edition of *A Career in Your Suitcase* when in Australia, found my phone number in the book and gave me a call. Soon she was in London and attending my first ever Release the Book Within seminar. It was Jacinta Noonan who invited me to speak at that first Connecting Women event in The Hague, because she was living in the Netherlands too. Jacinta and I developed and ran a workshop called Find Your Passion as a result of that phone call. She then moved to Singapore, and ran our workshop there.

Making contact with others who are writing, publishing and contributing content to the Internet is a wonderful way to expand your network.

GLOBAL OR LOCAL?

We believe for a portable career to be sustainable and productive you should develop both local and global networks. We need global networks so that our clients are not reliant on the place in which we live.

When I (Jo) lived in Dubai, Oman and Norway, before the Internet, I lost my clients with every move and had to begin again elsewhere. Now, thanks to cyberspace, my clients come from all over the world. I can build an online network of mentors, mentees, clients, potential clients and information sources that grows with every passing year. If I look at the invoices I sent out during the past year, I see that less than 20% of my income is generated from within the Netherlands. Having a global network has allowed me to create a business that actually continues growing no matter how often I move.

So, why do we need a *local* network? We need a local network because working alone in a home office can be dull and lonely. As a writer and poet I (Jo) need to get out there among real people to get inspired. I crave real time, face-to-face, contact. While I acknowledge that I am able to make friends via cyberspace and forge quality relationships, local contact is much more emotionally rewarding.

Like I said earlier, I need a balance of extrovert and introvert activity. I am lucky to have been able to create a career that allows me to do both. This is why I belong to local networks, attend local events, talk to local groups and teach workshops to local folk. This is where I get my energy.

If you remember, we said earlier in this book that we do business with people we like. We believe that we get a much better idea of whether we click with another person when we meet them in the flesh. Most of our clients come via referral, so it is important that we build quality relationships with those referrers in real time. We believe that it is the people we meet locally who go out and tell their friends, either in this country, or in the place they move to next, about us.

Simply put, we believe that both local and global networks are essential to a portable career and we need to make an effort to grow and nurture them both.

Global networks

A global network can be established in two ways:

- Connecting with people when you are overseas and adding them to your database or LinkedIn network
- Connecting with people you have not met previously through the Internet or publications and adding them to your database

Now you have these global connections in your database or in your LinkedIn or Facebook contact lists - and a name, email address and record of where they live is enough - you need to keep in touch with them virtually by email newsletters, online postings to their profile, following them on Twitter and keeping your online profiles active and up to date.

It is no good meeting someone once, taking their details and then never contacting them again. You need to keep each other in mind.

It is said you do not buy from someone until you have 'connected with them six times. So, in order to connect with someone you could send them an email, a card, or give them a phone call now and again. I (Jo) do not have the time to connect with the thousands in my database individually, so I find the easiest method of 'touching' is to send them my monthly email newsletter, *The Inspirer*. Even if they do not read the newsletter itself, they see my name pop up in their inbox. I do not add people to my database at random: I always ask them first as is legally required. Here are the ways I add people to my list:

- I invite workshop and keynote attendees to give me their contact details if they want to receive notes afterwards and sign up to *The Inspirer* at the same time
- I have a sign up box on my websites
- I have a line in my email signature inviting people to sign up and receive a free gift
- I make sure that my newsletter is of value, and fill it with inspiring words, tips, news and connections
- I mention *The Inspirer* in my publications
- I suggest that all those who contact me for any reason might like to sign up to *The Inspirer* too
- I have three websites
- I blog regularly and encourage people to follow my blog.
- I Tweet about my newsletter, blog, radio program and other professional activities
- I give articles to websites and publications read by my target market. I do not charge for the piece if I am able to promote myself at the end of the article
- I share relevant information with targeted sub-groups of my mailing lists

You do not need to issue a newsletter in order to stay in touch with your network. You may prefer a more personal approach, contacting a small number of people individually. I attempt to do both and tend to stay in closest contact with those with whom I have a special connection or those I realise do more work with me than others. In other words I stay in touch most with my 'connectors'.

It is only by establishing a global network that you can have a global presence and a reputation all over the world. Then, when you are next on the move the chances are you will know someone when you arrive. Seth Godin's *Tribes* is about our ability to create and lead global communities through the technology available today. Take a look at *www.globalniche.com* for one example. Is there a tribe you can start?

'I have always maintained all my contacts and networked like crazy. In fact the only reason I found a job in BP was because I met up with an old friend who mentioned a rumour that EDS [my former employer when I had lived in Houston] were putting together a proposal with BP in Stavanger. I made sure I was at the first meeting. In fact, as my old company, Britoil, were bought by BP, I had a hunch that I would know someone at that meeting. Not only did I know three people round that table, but one of them later showed me a photograph in his office of his team from 20 years earlier. I was in that photograph.'

Alice, British in Norway, *www.careerinyoursuitcase.com*

Local networks

As I (Jo) said earlier, I need to be with people regularly and cannot work alone all the time. It is important to me that I have a reputation in the location in which I live and so I work hard to establish a local network too.

Being on the board of Connecting Women in The Hague really helped here. I need a local network in order to ensure enough people know about my regular workshops and my publishing service and to have customers for my books.

Here are some of the ways that I achieve this:

- I attend meetings of local networks, both social and professional.
- I belong to a local business club
- I write for local magazines and websites, ensuring my name and contact details appear at the end
- I offer to speak at local club meetings and events, often for free.
- I take a table at newcomers' and other events where there will be lots of expats present
- I place my books for sale in suitable outlets and leave my flyers and adverts in places frequented by expats
- I offer everyone the chance to sign up to *The Inspirer* newsletter
- I give prizes based on my business (free books or places in my workshops) to raffles

- I have business cards, a bookmark with my details on and a free tips book to give people so they have something to take away that will remind them of me
- Whenever I speak I suggest people sign up to receive the notes and *The Inspirer* and make a separate list for those who live locally. Then I can send them specific information pertaining to where they are living, like details of a play, a visiting speaker or special event

Growing a local database takes a little effort but is well worth it. If you want to grow your work or business where you are living you need to ensure people know about you and that they tell their friends, so you need to make it easy for them to do that.

'I put out a newsletter called Paris Gourmet every three months that also lists cooking classes and weekend gastronomy tips. I also network within the many English-speaking interest and study groups in Paris.'

Sue Y, English in France, *www.careerinyoursuitcase.com*

Breakfast clubs

If you prefer the idea of making networking part of your routine and timetabling it for a set day and time every week, then you may like to try joining a breakfast club. Business Networking International *www.bni.com* (BNI) has been around for more than 25 years and now has chapters in 57 countries worldwide. Members pay an annual fee and are then obliged to attend weekly meetings, which are designed to help you gain referrals for yourself and find them for others too. If this kind of networking appeals to you, then you would do well to check into your local option and visit the clubs as a guest first of all.

In their book, *Building a Business on Bacon and Eggs*, authors, Stephen Harvard Davis, Andy Lopata and Terence P O'Halloran, have grown their own businesses through the breakfast club and believe that it holds the key to business success, whether you attend or lead the meetings. Adhering to a set agenda, members all have their chance to share with the group, ask for advice and promote their businesses. Further, they all gain valuable experience in speaking in front of a group.

'Networking is about sharing our individual resources,' they write. This is what makes the business networking format so successful — groups of business skills are brought together for the benefit of all. Members are expected to give to the group and know it is their giving that will make it succeed.'

Men and networks

Dr Copeland's research proved without doubt that local friendships are of vital importance on overseas assignment, particularly for the accompanying partner. Women are largely conditioned to accept that coffee mornings are an inevitable part of expat life. Although women who don't have children comment that they feel uneasy in this environment, men feel even less comfortable. It can be difficult for a man to feel relaxed in such a group, particularly if he's the only male in sight. Many of these great organisations, such as Petroleum Wives, The British Society, American Women's Clubs and so on are non-profit and run by volunteers. Not only are these clubs the traditional bastion of females, but not all men will be happy to run bake sales or serve teas. Ask a man to run the local Boy Scouts or junior football club and he's likely to be much more at ease.

'There is therefore the problem that though the group may accept the men, the men do not always want to be accepted, as they would prefer to do 'men's stuff'.'

Huw Francis, Author of *Live and Work Abroad: A Guide for Modern Nomads*

'Many of the problems men encounter are not dissimilar to those experienced by women,' says expatriate Australian Leonie Elphinstone, who conducted a survey into the male accompanying partner. 'What makes the difference is that men are brought up to be the breadwinners and when things go wrong they find they have further to fall.' While men need to make new friends on location as much as women, they appear to feel happiest when their involvement is not too far removed from their 'comfort zone'. Often the local squash club or playing in a local band will be the best place for them. Other networking options men might enjoy include starting a book club reading professional books or a cycling club.

Employees need networks too

Networks are vital for business, which is why large multinational corporations and even government ministries are offering networking workshops to their employees. A growing number of companies encourage networking among their own employees; Sony Semiconductors runs monthly networking lunches with a visiting speaker. With the retention of key staff a major objective for the employer, it makes sense to facilitate relationship building and true friendships between colleagues. This influences staff motivation and morale, and ultimately the bottom line.

Because of the increased use of short term contracts employers are finding it beneficial if the people currently there can network effectively. A short term contract in one department can lead to another in a different department if you network and that is more effective for both you and the employer.

You can have the best product or experience in the world, but if you want to maximise potential you need to be seen by your clients or the people who can offer you work. Relationship building is key to this. Below are some of the key skills you need to network and build relationships effectively.

Networking Skills

Connecting

It is said most people have a personal network of 250. As mentioned earlier, each of those contacts will, in turn, have his or her own contacts. Ask your contacts to connect you with someone in their network. Check if they have a LinkedIn profile, a newsletter, blog, Facebook page or Twitter account and suggest to people in your network that they may find it good to connect with another person in your network. The best networkers, as we said earlier, like to give presents - and giving a connection or tip is a great gift. Whenever we are told about a great seminar, new book, or exciting conference we email the information to any of our contacts we think may be interested. Sometimes this generates new and beneficial relationships between contacts of mine who were previously unknown to one another. The strength of your network depends on the connections made between your contacts.

Alternatively you may want to introduce two people to each other because you know they will benefit from knowing one another. You will soon discover some people are much better at connecting you with others. In fact, they offer to connect you before you have even asked. It is worth nurturing contact with these valuable people. In his book, *The Tipping Point,* author Malcolm Gladwell calls these connecting people 'mavens' because of their knowledge, connections and ability to influence their network.

A solid foundation for a relationship is usually created if you start off with being connected by a mutual friend. In this way, your initial conversation is not a *cold* call. Instead it begins in a much *warmer* place. If you can, be introduced to someone at a party or network event, but many such connections are initiated online. When we make Internet connections for our friends we tend to send an email to both the people we want to introduce, and say something along the lines of 'Jane meet Sue, Sue meet Jane. Jane is an interior designer who has worked on some of the great stately homes of England. Sue works at Highview House and is looking to turn it into a hotel'.

I (Colleen) am not a natural networker. Networking is a skill I have learned and have come to really enjoy. I find that when networking is more about someone other than me I can do it very well. So I take the focus off of myself and enjoy learning about other people. When I see someone standing alone and I have also attended the event alone, I will approach them and start by discussing something general about the event. If I learned something about them that connects them with someone else I have just met, then I will share that information with them, encourage them to approach that person too or introduce them myself. I get a real buzz from connecting people with other people and other resources, although I am nowhere near a 'maven'. And the bonus is that, without much work, I am also networking effectively for myself!

Abundance

We mentioned the abundance mentality a little earlier. Let's go into it in more detail now. The law is, 'share abundantly there will be lots for everyone'. It can be difficult to keep the faith with this, when you start to count up that you have given out 25 contacts to the people you have met and only received three in return. But the whole point of approaching life and work from a place of abundance is you need not expect to receive directly from those to whom you have given, nor on the same day, or in the same way, nor in the same circumstances. Instead, imagine all your gifts are invested in a huge universal bank, and your returns will be given out at random.

I (Jo) remember once that I became disillusioned with practising abundance and decided to stop being so nice. I stopped connecting people and I stopped answering people's questions and being nice to them for free. Not only did I soon start to dislike myself, but I also noticed I was no longer receiving abundantly. As soon as I went back to giving, the rewards flooded back in.

Passion, presents and persistence

Here we are again, back with one of our favourite words. Passion can make all the difference to networking. I (Jo) have even run a networking seminar called 'Passion, Presents and Persistence'. I expect you are beginning to understand how the name came about! We've talked about presents already, but it pays to repeat it here as we believe that presents are an aspect of networking people easily forget.

PASSION

Remember when networking we want to stop focussing on how many business cards of our own still linger untouched in our jacket pocket. We want to build authentic connections. And there is no better way to do this than to talk about something you have in common, not related to business.

When you meet someone new it's tempting to talk about what you do for a living first. But consider what a difference it would make if you asked, instead, what they like to do with their time off, who their heroes are or where they buy their shoes. When you are with your real friends you don't spend all the time talking about work, do you? Build new relationships by leaving work until last. Once you've found out more about someone as a human being, rather than a potential work source, you will find the work talk comes naturally if there's a fit.

Remember, people like people who are like them and do business with people they like. Have you ever noticed how you tend to like people who like the same things as you? Maybe even those who share your passions? This is why people often end up doing business with those they meet in their recreational pursuits - on the golf course, at amateur dramatic clubs and so on.

PRESENTS

You can invest in a new relationship by giving. Give connections, give answers, give help, give support, give tips, give a free gift, a memorable promotional item, the copy of a useful article, the name of a website, the list is endless. Listen to what people say and consider what gifts you could give them as they talk. If they are complaining that they need a language teacher, make them a recommendation. If they say they need clients, tell them about networking groups and so on. Find out what they are passionate about and offer presents based on that passion. So, if someone says they love climbing, tell them about a mountain climbing society, magazine or enthusiast they might like to meet. Presents, particularly when they relate to passion, can be the greatest gifts of all - and they cost nothing.

PERSISTENCE

If you attend a networking event or club only once or twice you are not likely to make friends or business contacts, nor are you likely to sign up new clients. Friendship and trust are built up over time. Many people attend just one meeting at Connecting Women and then never return. No one should expect to get lucky the first time they go along. Over time, as friendships form and you are seen to be dependable, people will begin to trust you and want to do business with you. Remember that while the attendees may not directly be of use to your business or work search, they may well have contacts who could be. Don't give up. Be persistent. Remember people tend to buy when they have 'touched' you six times, so try to go to six meetings. It is hard to create a relationship with someone when you have only met once. The more often you attend a meeting, the more faces will become familiar and soon you will feel you belong. It's normal not to feel you belong at your very first meeting.

In the four years that I (Jo) attended Women Connecting Women in England, I can claim to have bought magnetic insoles from Jill, who sells magnotherapy products, been colour-me-beautifulled by Carolyn, bought make-up from Jane, found Fiona to edit my books and Nadine to design my marketing materials and seen countless members on my writing courses. I have also been inspired by the stories of so many of the members I have written articles about them and given them much-needed publicity. The list is much longer, but you get the idea.

Thank you

Remember the mavens we mentioned earlier? The people in your network who are particularly good at referring you to new clients or giving you presents? Saying thank you to these people may seem an obvious thing to do, but you'd be surprised how many people fail to do this simple act. You don't need to buy flowers, take them to lunch or give them tickets to the next Olympics. An email of thanks is enough. To send a card through the post is also effective and maybe a bottle of wine if they were particularly kind. You can, of course, reciprocate in kind by giving them referrals and leads.

Thank everyone who gives you presents, keep them posted if things go well with these new clients and chances are these great connectors will continue to be generous.

Building rapport

Rapport happens when there is a connection formed on an intuitive and subconscious level believes Mary Farmer. As mentioned earlier, we are more likely to buy from, agree with and support someone we can relate to than someone we can't. Learning how to build rapport is an essential component of networking and building relationships.

Mary says rapport is about being on the same wavelength and appreciating each other's feelings. It is the ability to connect with someone's world and make him or her feel you understand them, and that you have a common bond. It's a means of creating trust and understanding and being able to see each other's point of view (though not necessarily agreeing to it). Building rapport is fundamental to creating connections, communicating effectively with others, negotiating, teaching or introducing change.

Neuro Linguistic Programming (NLP) studied skilled communicators and influencers to understand how to build rapport. They found people in rapport will often unconsciously 'match' or 'mirror' each other; they adopt similar body gestures, posture, and rhythm in speech and movement. NLP found that when we adopt the same physical posture as someone else we experience similar feelings and start to think alike. This is rapport.

Networking and establishing rapport then are much more than what you say. Research has shown that:

- 7 percent of our communication is through words
- 38 percent comes from voice tonality, range, rhythm and volume
- 55 percent is physiology, or body language

The three steps to creating rapport with another person or a group are:

1. Mirroring

In order to build initial rapport NLP recommends starting with assuming the other person's physical posture, voice tone and words. Adopt their posture, gestures, facial expressions, blinking patterns and breathing. When in rapport, this happens naturally a number of seconds after the other does it. If you do it too soon, it feels wrong and can seem fake. You can 'cross mirror', which is to do the same movement as they are doing but with another part of the body. So while one person is tapping his foot, you can tap your fingers, but using the same rhythm. Mirroring occurs naturally with people we like, so pay attention and see if you can catch yourself doing it already. Practice with your friends and family to become more conscious of how you are already doing it, how it works and to be able to do it 'naturally' when networking professionally.

2. Voice

Match their voice as soon as possible by mirroring the pitch, tempo and range of their voice. I (Colleen) often find myself mimicking the accent of another unconsciously. I didn't understand why I did this until I studied NLP and realised I was mirroring voices and seeking to establish rapport.

3. Words

Listen to the key words used frequently by the other person and then use them yourself. Try to find common experiences and associations. Use the same kind of predicates they use too. These are their preferred verbs and give insight into the level at which they process information. A visual person will say things like 'I see' a lot, while an auditory person will say 'I hear' and a kinaesthetic person will say 'I feel'. Another verbal element of creating rapport is through matching the size of their sentences, notice whether they are long or short.

WHEN YOU ARE IN RAPPORT

When you have achieved rapport you should feel warm inside and both your faces will heighten in colour. Sometimes you'll find yourself suggesting you have met before or have a third party in common. If you shift your position, the other person will unconsciously start to mirror you.

The skill is to build and maintain this rapport beyond the level of body language. To do this you need to really listen with your whole body, be curious about them and give your total attention. Don't sweep away their concerns or try and impose your solutions. Rather acknowledge them and find out how to meet their needs. You are not being a hypocrite or giving up your identity when you match someone. You are being flexible and honouring them. When you are matching them you are getting more insight into their feelings, experiences and thoughts.

The real key to establishing rapport is flexibility, genuine interest in another and not assuming everyone has the same map of the world as we do. Using rapport as a networking skill will be most effective when it comes from a genuine interest in the other.

Presenting

Public speaking and giving presentations, workshops and seminars can give your work or business the edge. We think it is the most productive form of networking one can do. How else can you attend a meeting of some kind and ensure every single person in that room goes home knowing who you are and what you can offer?

I (Jo) learned to present in an unthreatening and wholly supportive environment back in 1996. Since then I've never looked back. In Stavanger, Norway, I belonged to the women's networking group, WIN. Today I give credit to WIN for much of what I have achieved. Not only were there monthly meetings with a motivational speaker, but a number of sub-groups for WIN members to join. No fee was charged and members met once a month, informally in each other's homes. I joined the group which called itself 'Presenters'.

HOW WE LEARNED TO PRESENT

There were usually only four or five people at 'Presenters'. At each session we would write down a couple of topics on scraps of paper and put them into a hat. As the hat went round we each picked a random topic. We allowed ourselves 15 minutes to prepare our speech and then five minutes to give it. The topics could be as crazy as 'lost socks,' as fascinating as 'dreams' or as unusual as 'ferret farming'. One of the other members was chosen to be the heckler, another to be over-enthusiastic, another to be bored, and this audience would listen to each talk and give constructive criticism later. The results were dramatic, humorous and immensely useful. Six months later I (Jo) found myself being the guest speaker at a WIN meeting, talking about my pet subject: portable careers. Three months later I was paid to develop and present a three-hour workshop on the same subject to a group of about 20 expatriate women. A year later I presented the same workshop to more than 100 people at the 1998 *Women on the Move* Conference in Paris. Since then I have offered keynotes, seminars or workshops to networking groups, companies and conference delegates all over the world.

I (Colleen) gave my first presentation as part of my work as a Recreation Therapist to people who had been diagnosed as obese. I was also a certified fitness instructor so it related to my values and interests and I really enjoyed giving the monthly talks. As part of my work role I also found myself addressing larger groups when introducing guest performers as well as leading activities. As my career progressed I continually found myself put into positions where speaking was part of the role. I have addressed groups as large as 750 speaking as the president of a provincial professional association and have also provided keynotes and conference sessions. One of my more recent experiences was presenting at an *International Day* networking event for the Undutchables employment agency.

THE POWER OF PUBLIC SPEAKING

It was after the Paris presentation I (Jo) came to realise the power of public speaking. My workshop had lasted over two hours, but the queue of people who wanted to buy my book, ask additional questions or exchange business cards, lasted a further hour. There were several hundred delegates at the conference and it would have been impossible for me to meet them all at the various break times. Now, after giving this presentation, I could be identified by more than a third of the attendees. Thanks to the copious handouts I had passed around they also knew my contact details.

When I returned home I made the effort to contact every single person who had given me his or her card. I wrote a short note to thank them for attending and to suggest they could contact me again at any time if they had further questions.

'I give talks but usually on a voluntary basis. I earn a good fee though when I speak to the homeopathy schools. Sometimes I teach foot zone therapy to small groups. I believe that you should always be prepared to do some things for nothing. When I give a free talk on, say, health, homeopathy or foot zone I always end up acquiring a handful of new patients from the audience.'

Angelika, German in Norway, *www.careerinyoursuitcase.com*

Today, as I said earlier, I have learned to ask for those who would like to receive my email newsletter, *The Inspirer,* and extra notes from my presentation, to sign up there and then at the conference. In this way I add to my contact base every single time I speak in public.

CONFERENCE SPEAKING

Before you race off to learn presentation skills and begin to count the money you will make from conferences, you need to know that conference speakers are not always paid a fee. Often though, the conference fees and a hotel room for a night or two may be underwritten by the organisers. Those speakers with a service or product to sell are often happy to fund their own travel expenses for the opportunity of showing their face and addressing a captive audience. There are many ways to be paid for speaking to audiences, but this section is about networking and so we will concentrate on the *pro bono* variety.

Many of the conference delegates will have arrived alone. Whilst talking to total strangers can be daunting, striking up a conversation with the speaker you have just heard is much easier. Similarly, speakers find it as easy to start chatting to someone they have seen in their session as to a fellow presenter. Networking can be much simpler and more productive at a conference. After half an hour or so presenting, you are more likely to be remembered than if you had merely chatted to someone for a few minutes during a coffee break.

Since that first presentation at WIN I (Jo) have now spoken to organisations and corporations all over the world. A month doesn't pass when I don't speak to my target market. Usually I am paid to speak. But one thing that does not change is the networking potential of these engagements. When *Woman Abroad* magazine was first launched on the international market, we decided to market it by giving away up to 20,000 copies of each issue. In order to do this many publishers often buy numerous databases of potential customers. We bought none. Thanks to the exponential effect of contacting all the people I've met along the way and asking them to tap into their own networks, we accessed hundreds of thousands worldwide.

JOIN OR START A GROUP

You may not have a 'Presenters' group near you to kick start your own speaking career, but you can always start one. Go on a short course, buy a book or practise on your own in front of your video camera or webcam. The Toastmasters organisation offers training in a non-threatening environment in many countries worldwide. This is a great place to start. Go to *www.toastmasters.org* to find them. If you already have some experience and want to hone your skills and learn from some of the most generous and highly paid speakers in the business, look no further than the US-based National Speakers Association (NSA) at *www.nsaspeaker.org* and UK-based Professional Speakers Association (PSA) at *www.professionalspeaking.biz* and their sister groups. Membership will provide you with regular meetings, conferences, a newsletter and audio CDs. If there is no group near you and you don't want to start your own, watch the numerous excellent presentations by renowned speakers available on TED Talks *(www.ted.com).* Never underestimate the power of public presentation.

SEVEN STEPS FOR PREPARING POWERFUL PRESENTATIONS

After several years of presenting I (Jo) decided to call in an expert to assess what I'd been doing and to see if she could improve on my work. Christine Searancke runs a consultancy called Be Clear and specialises in writing presentations for people; she also runs an affordable assessment service and has written a valuable book called *How to Write Winning Presentations.* You can find out more at *www.beclear.co.uk.*

As a presenter Christine believes it is her job to 'paint pictures with words' and well-told anecdotes stay in the mind of the audience. Here are her steps to a powerful presentation:

Step one
State the objectives and write them down:
At the end of the presentation I want the audience to think…
I want them to do… I want them to say… I want them to feel…

Step two
Answer the basic questions:
Why am I making the presentation?
What am I going to say?
Who is the audience?
What does the audience want to hear?
Where will I be talking?

Step three
Use a clear and logical structure:
Break your material into manageable chunks like the chapters in a book. Share the structure with your audience. It will help them as well as you

Step four
Tell the audience what they want to hear, nothing more:
They don't want to hear everything you know, or have done. They want to hear the parts that are relevant to them

Step five
Think of your presentation as telling a story:
There should be a beginning, middle and an end. Each part should flow logically from the previous part and it should be told in your natural style of speech

Step six
Spend time on the opening words of the presentation:
You need to grab the audience's attention while you have the chance; once you've lost their attention it is very hard to get it back

Step seven
Rehearse with someone who doesn't know the subject:
They can tell you whether or not it is clear, whether you've left something out and more importantly whether it will meet the objectives from step one

MAKE IT MEMORABLE

In February 2007, I heard a presentation by Nick Oulton, who runs a presentation company called M62 *(www.m62.net)*. He told us people attend a presentation for one of three reasons:

- To buy something
- To learn something
- To modify their behaviour

It is worth knowing that those people who attend will only remember around five things from your presentation, so it is important they remember the five things you want them to recall.

'If you give people information without pausing and giving them time to process it, they will have a very low retention rate,' says Oulton.

The memory is such that people only remember 50% of what they heard on the day of the presentation, and only 50% of *that* the following day and so on. The more people can remember the day after your presentation the better.

A stream of slides covered in text and bullet points is not easy to remember. However, if you combine pictures with text you will help the audience to have a much better chance of remembering than if you have text alone. According to creativity facilitator Helen Kuyper, for the most effective presentation use pictures with a maximum of one word to give your message. This gives you the flexibility to adapt your content to the audience and keeps the audience engaged. Helen says decisions are made on emotion, not information. It is therefore important to focus on the emotion of the stories or anecdotes you provide and how they flow together and not the details. Based on current research, she recommends injecting emotion into the presentation every seven and a half minutes and making sure you always end with the emotion you want to leave people with.

Topics I can present on:

_____

_____

20
mins

_____

_____

Places I can present:

_____

_____

_____

_____

How to create a formal network

Before I (Jo) learned how profitable existing networks could be, I had inadvertently been creating my own wherever I had been living. Writing was my passion and I needed to be around other creative people in order to feel fulfilled. When I arrived in Dubai I decided to set up a Writers' Circle. Getting started only involved writing a simple notice, pinning this up on a few noticeboards, and asking people who might be interested to give me a call. We held monthly meetings in each other's homes, kept things informal, charged nothing, took it in turns to make a cake and made great friends. As often happens with network groups like this, some of them became my closest friends - and ultimately clients because as soon as I decided to offer a short creative writing course they all signed up.

After creating a Writers' Circle in Dubai, I created one in Muscat and then in Stavanger — but by the time we repatriated to England in 1997 I was more interested in business. So I set up the women's business group, Women Connecting Women. In four years it went from strength to strength, and while I only ran it myself for the first year, I loved attending every meeting.

Here in the Netherlands I focused first on joining the board of Connecting Women. Not long after, I realised that the companionship of my writers' circle was essential for me overseas. I immediately started one and now rarely miss a meeting.

CREATING A NETWORKING GROUP

To create a local networking group, start off by determining the group's focus and target market. When I (Jo) formed Women Connecting Women I decided I wanted to create a place where women would feel supported, make friends, learn, develop their careers and their sense of self, and would be affordable. I wanted to appeal to women who work for themselves, who want to return to work, or who are already employed.

I decided to hire a room in a local arts centre and placed a few small announcements in the local press and on the radio, stating that a new group was starting and people were invited to attend the inaugural meeting. I organised a photographer from the local paper and press-ganged all my friends to come along and swell the numbers this first time. I promised I wouldn't expect them to attend again unless they wanted to. We had 50 at that first meeting, and from my friends I found three people who would do a short talk on the value of networking.

Next we held a discussion on how everyone wanted to proceed and chose to hold monthly meetings on a weekday evening. For the first year we had about 13 regulars, the next year about 20, and ultimately most meetings were attended by 30 or more. Each year we changed the committee, one person was responsible for sending out press releases regarding the next meeting, and another for writing a meeting report which we circulated to everyone on the mailing list.

We found a local sponsor who paid for the design of our annual program, another who printed it, and another who gave us free use of the restaurant adjoining his public house for our meetings. We charged an annual fee for membership, which entitled members to attend all the meetings, advertise their business at the meetings, receive a printed newsletter, obtain discounts for extraordinary events, for purchases at participating retail outlets and for a host of other benefits. Not all groups operate this way. Some groups charge a separate fee for individual meetings, some provide coffee, and others provide wine and even food. It's not uncommon for attendees to be obliged to pay for annual membership after attending two or three meetings.

Mentoring

None of us is really out there alone. We all make connections and contacts along the way. We meet people who inspire us and teach us. We also meet people who we can teach and inspire in return. A mentor can open doors for you, as well as inspire you to learn, grow and be your best. Identifying mentors for your career journey can help you in countless ways. Many larger organisations run formal mentoring programs to foster this within the organisation. As an individual you can connect in person, or virtually, with someone you identify yourself with, and who you want to learn from. You don't have to scare someone by saying you want them to be your mentor. Flatter your potential mentor by telling them you like what they do, or how they do it, and would love to talk to them more about it, or have the opportunity to have them teach it to you or let you watch them at work. Reading biographies of people who inspire you is another way to learn from others and allow them to mentor you.

Identify five people who have been or currently are role models and mentors to you on your career journey. They can be someone you know personally or have read about. Write their name and why you consider them a role model or mentor for you.

Name: _____

I appreciate this person because:

_____
_____
_____
_____
_____
_____

Note the reasons you have written down why this person is a mentor or role model for you. Is there consistency and a pattern between these elements? Do you recognise some of those elements as the ones you have written down as your values and what is important to you to accomplish? It is encouraging to note that if you can spot a characteristic in someone else, then you possess it to a certain extent already yourself, even if you weren't really aware of it!

It is also important to share what you have learned with others, to be a mentor yourself. This can give you insights into your current level of competency instead of taking for granted all that you've learned. As well, it can help keep you actively engaged using your skills while you are looking for opportunities.

How are you a mentor to others?

_____
_____
_____
_____
_____
_____
_____

What kind of mentor would best be able to support you on your journey at this point?

_____
_____
_____
_____
_____
_____
_____

Information interviews

A more targeted level of networking is arranging information interviews. This is when you organise a meeting with someone, not to ask for a job, but to research information about the company, a field of work or career. This will take the company and occupational research you have already done in *Chapter 4 — Creating Your*

Career to the next level and help you be able to make informed choices about which career direction to pursue.

First review your current network to see any of them are working in the area or company of interest to you. You can broaden this search by posting it in a LinkedIn or Facebook status update. If no one you know has the direct information you are looking for, ask if one of them can refer you to someone who can. Use the company search feature on LinkedIn to see how the company is linked to your network. If you are still unable to identify a suitable person to interview, then you can use local business directories and contact information on company websites to find the person you want to interview. A personal connection can really warm up the whole process so first try to find someone via your network. You will be surprised at the people your network can put you in touch with.

An information interview will usually begin with a telephone call to ask a few questions or to arrange a time to meet. Always check you have called at a convenient time for them. If needed you can always call back at a time that works better for them. Your questions in the telephone call are first targeted at making sure you are talking with the person who has the information you need and then arranging a meeting time. Alternatively you may choose to begin with an email. If you choose this option, let them know when you will follow-up so that you are not left waiting indefinitely for a response.

The information interview itself will usually be half an hour or so and is designed so you can find out more about the area of work or company which interests you. Most of the people you choose to talk to will feel flattered you considered them knowledgeable about their field, and will be happy to talk to you.

You can also use this meeting to ask about opportunities in general, not necessarily with that specific company, and to see if you can obtain the names of some more people you could contact who may also have additional further information. You should always dress for such a meeting as if you were going to an interview, and take along your CV just in case. You can ask for feedback on your CV or marketing materials, so you are better able to target these when you do start actively searching. You never know, you may be offered a job or contract on the spot, but let that be on their initiative.

EIGHT TIPS FOR INFORMATION INTERVIEWS

1. Prepare a script for your information interview, including a very brief introduction of yourself. Adapt your elevator pitch for the purpose of this meeting.

2. Identify the purpose of the meeting and why you have chosen to meet with them. Tell them who referred you to them.

3. Clarify that you have no hidden agenda or want to use this interview to have them offer you work.

4. Let them know what questions you plan to ask so that they see you are prepared and know what is expected.

5. Use the networking skills described earlier in this chapter and share information you have that may be of interest to them.

6. During the course of the interview, provide additional detail about yourself — your experience, competencies and corroborating examples.

7. Sample questions for an information interview:
   a. Please describe your career path for me — your qualifications and experience in this field.
   b. What are some of the changes you have seen in this field over the course of your career?
   c. In your opinion, what qualifications does one need to enter this field today?
   d. What are some of the challenges you see in this field of work today? For the future?
   e. Where are the opportunities developing in this field?
   f. Can you recommend anyone I should contact for more information? For example a colleague or professional association.

8. Say a sincere thank you for their time and make sure you have their contact information. Follow-up immediately with a thank you note or email in which you restate the key information for you from the meeting. Stay in touch to let them know what you have done with the information they provided and how they have helped you. Through these appropriate continued contact points they can become part of your network.

Preparing for your information interviews

30 mins

What key information would you like to gather from people in the field?

_____
_____
_____
_____
_____
_____

Who do you need to talk to? If you don't know names, describe the person you need to meet and include the people you identified as potential mentors in the section on mentoring.

_____
_____
_____
_____
_____
_____

What will you say about yourself? Tailor your elevator pitch (see a few pages further in this chapter) to the purpose of an information interview.

_____
_____
_____
_____
_____
_____

What key relevant points about yourself will you include in your personal presentation?

_____
_____
_____
_____
_____

What kind of information from your own research and experience to date do you have which may be of interest to people you interview?

_____

_____

_____

_____

_____

_____

Make a list of your potential questions

1. _____
2. _____
3. _____
4. _____
5. _____

What are some of the ways you feel comfortable to follow up after the interview? Make sure you have what you need on hand so you can send it within a day or two of the information interview.

_____

_____

_____

_____

_____

Use this information interview sheet to prepare for specific interviews and record the results.

Information Interview Record Sheet

Information Interview with: _____

Date and time: _____ Location: _____

1. Introduction

2. Reason for meeting: _____

3. Set tone

4. Agenda: _____

5. Personal Presentation (key points for this particular interview)

a. _____

b. _____

c. _____

6. Questions

a. _____

b. _____

c. _____

d. _____

e. _____

f. _____

7. Referral (write down the referrals shared)

Name: _____

Contact information: _____

8. Conclusion

Notes: _____
_____
_____

Additional copies of this form are available for download at *www.careerinyoursuitcase.com*

Fear of networking

People who are naturally outgoing may feel more comfortable with networking than their more reserved counterparts, but this does not necessarily mean they are better at it. Introverts usually have valuable gifts on which they can capitalise - the capacity to listen attentively, ask thoughtful questions and execute thorough follow-up.

And networking gets easier once you take the plunge. Like other mentally and emotionally challenging tasks, it resembles the lift-off of a rocket. It takes the most energy at the beginning — making your first couple of telephone calls and setting out on your first meeting or two. As you gather momentum and develop these skills, it gets easier. Before every contact remind yourself that networking is the standard way of doing business and finding employment in much of the world.

Still, however much you know you need to network, it can be a daunting prospect. Do you remember, I (Jo) told you how long it took me to pluck up courage to attend that first WIN networking meeting in Stavanger? And I would say I'm fairly extroverted. Going up to complete strangers is difficult, but usually more so when you expect to be tongue-tied. It's normal to feel nervous talking to new people, even if they are just other mothers in the school playground. Going along to a coffee morning full of strangers or attending a new class can be daunting. Even so, I'll wager most people feel less scared at the thought of a playground or a watercolour class than something that brands itself as a professional network. It's all a question of perception. There is little difference between them.

You join a network because you want to meet people with whom you have something in common, or who can teach you something. You join a network because you feel you may have something to offer the members. There is no difference between joining the school parent teachers' association and a professional network. If anything, at a professional network you're likely to meet far more people with whom you have something in common.

I (Jo) know my greatest fear is not the walking into a room filled with strangers, but that I will walk into the room alone, and no one will talk to me. However, once I arrive it only takes one person to exchange a few words with me, or to tell me where to find the coffee, and I feel much better. Perhaps you could persuade a friend to accompany you on your first visit? This might allay your fear of going alone. However, you should not fall into the trap of spending the whole evening with your friend, and missing out on meeting new people - otherwise you will feel just as daunted the next time you attend.

Make contact with the meeting coordinator beforehand and ask her to make herself known to you when you arrive. This will make you feel welcome, and will give you the purpose of finding a familiar name in the crowd. You could even ask your contact to introduce you to someone as soon as you arrive.

When you attend this kind of event, begin by introducing yourself to some people you may know vaguely, reminding yourself that they were strangers once. If you stand around waiting for your nervousness to evaporate, you may grow more scared. Take it from untold numbers of the formerly networking phobic — the fear of networking is far worse than the networking itself. So the sooner you swing into action the sooner you'll feel better.

Attending a conference alone can be even more daunting. Focusing on helping others to connect and feel comfortable will take the focus off of yourself and make you seem like a super-networker to others. Of course, you will find all the people in the room will be more than happy to talk about themselves — so if you do find yourself faced with no one talk to, you can confidently approach a stranger and ask them why they came, what they do, or if it's their first time too. Using the rapport building skills described earlier in this chapter will help networking feel more comfortable for you.

Will Kintish is a networking expert based in the UK who runs Kintish *www.kintish.co.uk.* I (Jo) attended one of his workshops at a Professional Speakers Association conference *www.professionalspeaking.biz.* He recommends that it is best to make a beeline for someone else who is standing alone, and to introduce yourself to them. However, if everyone appears to already be in conversations look out for those who are in 'open groups' and there is a gap in the circle of those who are chatting, leaving a space for you to slip into the group and then the conversation. Groups of two, where both parties look deep in conversation can be the hardest to gain access to.

Andy Lopata, *www.lopata.co.uk,* speaks and writes about networking strategy. In his book, *And Death Came Third,* he recommends the best way to make conversation with a stranger is to ask open questions, those questions that do not expect a simple 'yes' or 'no' answer, and to listen more than you talk.

'The key to good conversation is listening effectively and if you are listening effectively, you ask the right questions,' he writes. 'Ask questions that show you are listening, questions based on what the other person has just said and questions likely to draw out the conversation. Ask them to tell you more. Don't spend the time when they are speaking coming up with your own story to match or one-up theirs.

Sometimes the simplest methods can be the most effective. A few years ago, I (Jo) found myself at a social gathering where the only people I knew were the host and hostess. As I stood there scanning the faces of everyone else in the room I saw how they all seemed deep in conversation with people they clearly knew well. As I pondered how to break into a conversation someone thrust his right hand at me.

'I'm Dave,' he said.
'I'm Jo,' I replied.
'Where do you live?' he asked.
I told him. 'And you?' I asked.
'Oh, I flew over from England,' he said.

The conversation had begun. Neither of us felt awkward or threatened. Over the course of the next few minutes we discovered we both shared a passion for theatre and that Dave was a communications expert. I moved on to offer to connect him with a friend of mine, who was also in his field and looking to combine theatre and corporate communication. We soon swapped cards.

As we talked I made a mental note to write about that en route. As you can see, not all opening lines need a complicated script.

Elevator pitches

Inevitably, during my conversation with Dave, he asked me what I did for a living. 'I'm a writer and publisher,' I said. 'And help people to write books.'

This way of describing what you do in such a way that the other person is likely to want to know more, is called the *elevator pitch*. The term came about to describe how you might tell someone what you do when asked in an elevator and you only have the time it takes to reach the next floor to answer in a compelling way.

The elevator pitch I used failed to describe every aspect of my work and did not mention I specialised in expat issues. It did pique Dave's interest enough for him to say:

'Oh! What sort of books?'

'Living abroad, mainly. Stuff like transition, portable careers, identity, Third Culture Kids..."

'Third Culture Kids? What's that?'

... and so on. You see. The best kind of elevator pitches are so compelling the stranger in the lift would prefer to miss his floor and stay talking to you than to leave you not knowing.

It is important your own elevator pitch is short and raises curiosity. But it is also important you are clear about your target market. The reason for this is you want the person who is asking you to identify right away whether he may need your services, or just as importantly, he may know someone else who does. If possible create a pitch which clearly shows the benefits of your business too.

An elevator pitch can serve you socially as well as professionally.

Chris Pavone, author of the bestselling novel *Expats*, says his answer to the 'what do you do' questions encountered at parties was, "I take care of the children, and the house, and I try not to go insane." While this wouldn't have opened doors professionally it certainly lowered the barriers socially with others experiencing the same things. You don't need to be working in order to have an elevator pitch that captures what you find meaningful in your life at that moment.

My (Jo's) own elevator pitch is short and sweet, but it has been designed to ensure that the person to whom I am talking keeps wanting to know more. When you are talking to a group, giving a workshop or presentation for example, there will be no opportunity to take questions. In this case you may need to work a little harder at your pitch, in order to make it memorable. When I am in this situation I tend to tailor what I say to the audience. So, if I am speaking to expatriates I may say something like:

'I inspire and help people to write books about their life abroad.'

Yet, if I am speaking to writers I may say:

'I am the author of 30 books and now Summertime Publishing where I help people to write books about life abroad.'

The ultimate goal is that on hearing your pitch the person asks, "How do you do that?" This is your invitation to explain what you do in greater detail. However, if you are speaking in front of a group and people don't have a chance to ask how you do it, it is important you describe what you do in a memorable way that means they do not feel they need to ask you for more information.

Elevator Pitch examples:

Financial Planner: 'I work with professional women who want high returns on their investments.'

Life Coach: 'I help busy doctors find more time to spend with their families.'

Massage Therapist: 'I help stay-at-home moms feel pampered and relaxed.'

Personal Chef: 'I create delicious, healthy meals for busy executives that have no time to cook.'

Computer Technician: 'I rescue stressed out business owners when their computers crash.'

Professional Organiser: 'You know how sometimes mothers have so much going on that they can't find anything? Well that's what I do, I help busy moms get rid of clutter and find what they need fast.'

Stephanie Ward, *www.fireflycoaching.com*

Stephanie Ward, the source of the examples above, explains a three step approach to your elevator pitch or answering the 'what do you do' question: "I work with (your niche or ideal clients) who are having trouble with (problems your ideal clients face) and who want (what they want to see happen, the result)." Alternatively, you can relate your elevator pitch or answer to a common problem or situation they can relate to.

It can take some time to create your own set of elevator pitches which will work well for you in the situations you most commonly find yourself. Practise on your friends and get their feedback, then try them out and see which work best when you are with complete strangers. And just as you may keep changing your location or what you do, remember you may need to change your elevator pitch too.

Try out a few elevator pitches in the space here:

20
mins

_____
_____
_____
_____
_____
_____
_____
_____
_____
_____
_____
_____
_____
_____
_____
_____
_____
_____

Follow up

If you find yourself networking consciously or unconsciously as much as we do, it can be hard to keep track of the new contacts you make. You can never hope to remember everyone you meet, or to keep in touch with them all. Inviting them to join your network on LinkedIn or Facebook will allow you to keep in touch with them through your status updates. If you are keeping business cards, write a few notes about each person on the back of their business card. Those notes will help you remember your contact with the person better. However, in some cultures this may be considered disrespectful, so perhaps write your notes immediately following the event if you suspect there are cultural sensitivities.

Ways to keep track of contacts:

- maintain a database
- use a card scanner
- LinkedIn, Facebook and other social media
- make a point of emailing soon after the event to say how much you enjoyed meeting them. This will enter their email address into your contacts. After a few email exchanges you are more likely to really remember them and vice versa

Once a year it's a good idea to remember all the people you have met over the last 12 months, with either a Christmas card, e-card or a short email. Try to keep yourself in the minds of those contacts, and at the same time to remind yourself of them too. Put it in your agenda.

I (Jo) try to categorise the people I meet into, say, media, human resources, entrepreneurs and writers. I put their email addresses into separate groups in my email program and then when I get useful snippets of information I think could be of interest to a group I send out an email to them or Tweet to my followers. LinkedIn, Facebook and Twitter allow you to develop specific lists through labelling. As I mentioned earlier, I have a database of local people for this same reason. This allows me to keep on giving them 'presents' and it keeps me in their minds. What categories of people can your network members be divided into and what types of information or 'presents' can you share with them?

Equip yourself so you can keep track of all these contacts, and try to keep contact details updated as people often move or change email addresses. This is where online networking tools like LinkedIn and Facebook are handy as people update their profiles and contact information themselves. Every now and again, flick back through these records to remind yourself just how many people you know and who you have met over the years.

Chapter 5: Resources for Networking

A Lopata & P Roper, *And Death Came Third*, Lean Marketing Press

C Searancke, *How to Write Winning Presentations*, Stanley's Books Limited

D Darling, *The Networking Survival Guide*, McGraw Hill

E Schalks, *Networking – a tool to achieve your goals*, (ebook) *www.ande.nl*

J Parfitt & J Tillyard, *Grow Your Own Networks*, Summertime Publishing

M Gladwell, *The Tipping Point*, Little Brown Book Group

N Boothman, *How to Connect in Business in 90 Seconds or Less*, Workman Publishing

N Boothman, *How to Make Someone Like You in 90 Seconds or Less*, Workman Publishing

S Godin, *Tribes*, Little Brown Book Group

S Harvard Davis & TP O'Halloran, *Building a Business on Bacon and Eggs*, Life Publications Limited

S Knight, *NLP at Work*, Nicholas Brealey

S Ward, *No Sweat Networking – Simple Solutions to Overcome Networking Obstacles*, (ebook) *www.fireflycoaching.com*

T Power, *Networking for Life*, Ecademy Press

Part 3 Putting it together

'Go confidently in the direction of your dreams.
Life the life you have imagined.'

Henry David Thoreau

Chapter SIX

Marketing Your Skills

Finding Opportunities

Regardless of what type of opportunity you are looking for, you will need to market your skills. There are occasions when you will need to submit your CV on its own or as part of a proposal. As well you will need to write cover letters and emails.

Jo has been freelance for more than 25 years now and Colleen for 15 years. We tend to think that, while we never apply for a single full-time, salaried position, we have to apply for many more and repeatedly. When you are freelance you are constantly looking for your next source of work. Whether we are applying for a short term contract, a one day training job, and part time work over an extended period, or persuading a client to buy our work, many of the same principles apply. We need to make a proposal face to face and/or on paper. We need to be interviewed as well, though this can be a formal or informal process. Additionally, because we also offer consultancy services, opportunities arise regularly when we find ourselves in a position to promote ourselves. Running our own businesses means it is vital we are always positive about our work, that our passion for what we do is palpable and our enthusiasm persuades others to hire us. These same skills are required to find any kind of opportunity.

Marketing your skills will require you to prepare a summary of your skills, accomplishments and qualifications, otherwise known as a CV or resume. You will need to write a cover letter or email to accompany and introduce a CV or proposal. Few jobs and contracts are offered until at least one, often face-to-face, interview has taken place. Even if you are offered a position through your networking efforts, you will probably still need to supply the required documentation to meet some procedural requirements. The society in which we now look for work is more competitive, complicated and confusing than a generation ago. Much of this has to do with the accelerated pace of change — and, of course, the impact of the Internet on our economy and society. The CV today will most likely be a digital one sent with an email cover-letter and you may be interviewed using Skype, but the key basic elements are still the same. Below you will find some helpful guidelines.

Your successful search strategy

GETTING AND STAYING ORGANISED

Conducting a focused work search requires a method of organising the information you're collecting, and of recording the concrete steps — such as information interviews and sending out CVs — that you have taken. Getting and staying organised has several advantages over just trying to remember what you've learned and done. Unless your search is short, or you are blessed with an extraordinary memory, you won't remember everything.

A nearly universal curse of looking for work, especially if you have just moved to a new location and are unemployed, is the sense of not being in control. Staying organised with notebooks, folders, files, forms or computerised tracking systems will help you feel on top of what you are doing. Most work searches last from three to six months in the western world and longer if you are highly specialised and/or making an international move on top of this. Prepare yourself accordingly. Approach work search as your 'work' until you find your next opportunity.

Keeping orderly records helps you to internalise and track the information you have learned and actions you have taken. This helps to build your self-confidence, sense of purpose, and to maintain momentum, and all of these impact your ability to present yourself.

How to get organised

The goal of organisation is to achieve order and clarity with the least complicated arrangements possible. To organise your job search you may need the following supplies:

- A calendar or agenda that provides plenty of room to record appointments, action steps and in which to make notes
- An opportunities binder, alphabetical filing system or online document access like Google docs in which to keep track of all the companies you research and the vacancies you find and to which you apply. Keep a copy of the vacancy, the targeted CV itself, to whom and how you sent your CV, and when you sent it. Keep track of when you called to ensure the CV was received and to whom you spoke. This is an essential opportunity to use 'charming persistence' and to monitor progress of the process

- Copies of all your credentials including certified copies of official university transcripts, as these are often required when looking for opportunities in a new country
- Forms with which to record and monitor your goals, research, actions, results and follow-up plans. Consider generating an Excel spreadsheet that will provide an overview of your worksearch activities and their progress. See *www.careerinyoursuitcase.com* for examples of these forms
- A street map to familiarise yourself with the area
- A professional looking email address which you use exclusively for the purpose of work search and make sure you check it daily. Once your work search is over, you can forward this address to the email you use personally. It allows you to separate your personal email time from your work search email time
- Set detailed goals and implementation plans for every week and break them down into daily chunks. Write down these goals and plans on paper and share them with other people, for example your Blue Sky Team, to help keep yourself committed and accountable. Don't try to plan too much work search per day and make sure also to schedule in exercise, learning and social activities

STAYING MOTIVATED

Most work searches lasting any longer than a month or two hit 'dry stretches' during which it feels as though nothing positive is being achieved. When you hit a patch like this, don't permit yourself to wallow in self-pity or negative thinking. Few people go through a work search without going through times of discouragement and low morale; it is a normal part of this process and ultimately will help you focus in on what you really want. Continue to believe in yourself and your goals. Remind yourself that feelings are not facts and their main source of power comes from whatever energy you give them yourself. Sign up for a daily or weekly free email message to help you. I (Colleen) really like Mike Dooley's positive and humorous *Note from the Universe* available for free at TUT's Adventurer's Club, *www.tut.com*. Their slogan is 'Thoughts become things. Choose the good ones' and the Notes definitely help me to do this. Reward yourself along the way for successes, such as getting an interview, and for achieving goals you have established for yourself. This is essential for maintaining your energy and pacing yourself well.

Read more about staying positive and dealing with transition in *Chapter 8 — For the Journey.*

Finding out about opportunities

There are many ways to find out what career opportunities are waiting to be discovered by you. Even though most people get their jobs through networking, it is important to support this with good research. For example, finding out which skills seem to be in demand, and how frequently certain companies appear to be hiring, can provide you with information regarding the stability or growth of a business. John Krumboltz says, 'luck happens when planning and preparation meet opportunity'. This research will prepare you for the unexpected moment when you are in the right place at the right time talking to the right person. Set yourself up to be 'one of the lucky ones'. Maybe you want to choose this as the theme song, as mentioned in *Chapter 7 — Working for Yourself,* for this chapter of your life. You will find many of these sources are similar to the ones you used when generating work ideas in *Chapter 4 — Creating Your Career.*

NEWSPAPERS AND MAGAZINES

Take a look at the recruitment or want ads of both national, local and industry publications. Remember, many publications are also available online and vacancies appear here too.

Read the headlines and see what announcements are being made. Then think laterally using the 'That's News' approach described in *Chapter 4 — Creating Your Career.* This will generate insights into what this means for potential opportunities and work for you.

COMPANY WEBSITES

Company websites most often have a tab or button for people looking to work for them. Look for the names of companies operating in your area and visit their websites to research what kinds of positions are currently available. Even if the kind of work you want is not currently advertised, you can contact them for a networking or information interview or submit an open application, in person if possible, so you are already in their database if that position does become available.

NEWSLETTERS

Often the free newsletters produced by businesses, local networks and clubs are a source of information about work opportunities. Some may be voluntary positions, but don't disregard unpaid work as it can provide valuable and meaningful experience as well as a stepping-stone to paid opportunities. Don't forget to read the headlines watching for potential ways you can network your way into a position before it is advertised.

JOB LISTS AND CLUBS

Keep an eye out for organisations that seek out locally available vacancies and then compile an email or online list of vacancies for you to view. Some of the Shell Outpost networks available to Shell spouses create such a list and distribute it by email. Often you will find a local organisation or website specialising in newcomer services will compile a similar list. There may also be a government website and service that lists work opportunities. At the least, these resources should be able to inform where you can find listings. Where there is no compilation of vacancies perhaps you will find a real-time job club where you can meet other job seekers and share leads with each other. Connecting Women in The Hague has a free group like this called *Connect with your Dream Job*. This can be a good source of information about vacancies, a support group and a network builder. If none of these exist where you are, then maybe it's an opportunity for you to create one.

NOTICEBOARDS

Sometimes you'll find opportunities advertised on noticeboards at libraries, in supermarkets or at community centres. Keep your eyes open for potential work everywhere you go and you will be amazed at what you can discover.

CONTRACT OPPORTUNITIES

Those looking to get started in a new field of work or wanting short term work can consider subscribing to sites offering contract opportunities such as *www.ceweekly. com, www.smarterwork.com, www.odesk.com* and *www.elance.com*. Search online for the websites specific to your field. For example, if you are a journalist, you can find information on projects around the globe through email bulletins such as 'Jobs for Journalists' from the European Journalist Network at *www.ejc.nl* and at *www.freelance.com*.

A criticism of this type of website expressed by Nick Usborne, as quoted in *Future Expat's* online book *Untether Yourself,* is that it turns your service or skill into a commodity where the level of competition is the price alone and not your talents. Don't underestimate the value of the specific knowledge, experience and skills you have. Always use your network and previous clients to keep contracts coming your way. Offer your services for free at first to build up a source of referrals. More on this is available in *Chapter 7 —Working for Yourself.*

EMPLOYMENT AGENCIES

Companies pay employment agencies to send them qualified candidates. In rare cases the job seeker may be charged for this. Most employment agencies are honest and reliable - but you must bear in mind their client is the company, not you. Be sure not to sign any contracts without taking at least 24 hours to examine and evaluate them. Read every word of small print and think through the implications.

Employment agencies will usually submit the names of as many qualified persons as possible for each available position. So if you use an agency, you may find yourself going through two screenings, one by the agency and the second by the company itself.

In the last decade, an increasing number of agencies have specialised in particular industries. They are placing people in positions which require a high level of skill and training as well as support positions. You will enhance your chances of success with an agency if you use one specialising in the field in which you're looking for employment.

Don't overlook agencies that specialise in temporary or contract placements, even if your goal is full time employment. It's not unusual for temporary placements to be extended for longer periods of time or to develop into permanent positions. An agency will sometimes offer a low risk (for them) temporary contract to you, often in a position that doesn't fully use your skills, before sending you to one of their high risk (for them) preferred positions and clients.

Call or email weekly with your contact person at the agency to let them know you are still actively looking for opportunities. In that way you will stay top of mind (and on top of the pile). Some people register and don't keep the agency informed when they do find an opportunity elsewhere. See contacting them as providing a service to the agency so they know you are still available for opportunities. You can also communicate respect for the service provided by the agency through keeping regular contact and building your relationship with your contact person.

There tends to be a rhythm to how these agencies work, so find out when most of the new positions are submitted each week and plan your weekly contact strategically.

EXECUTIVE MANAGEMENT FIRMS

This type of organisation offers a blend of recruiting and career management services for a price which, in this case, you will pay. Their goal is to form long term relationships with established and upwardly mobile managers and executives who either command, or can be expected soon to command, salaries approaching and exceeding $100,000. These firms promote their ongoing relationships with major companies and may appear to function like recruiters. Beware of firms who promote their special access to the decision makers in companies, but are vague about whose door they will usher you through. You can end up paying $10,000 for little more than basic career counselling in lush, dark wood-panelled offices.

See *Chapter 8 — For the Journey* for more information about evaluating and choosing a company or coach to work with you during your search for opportunities.

PROFESSIONAL ASSOCIATIONS

Joining a related professional association can also be a source of leads. I (Colleen) often receive vacancy notices through the Dutch Association for Career Professionals (NOLOC).

JOB AND CAREER FAIRS

Job fairs are places to make contacts with companies in person and often combine group and employer presentations with individual booths. If you go to a job fair, plan to take in both - not only for the exposure to potential employers, but also to gather information about companies who are hiring and to learn from their expertise. During my search for opportunities in the Netherlands, I (Colleen) attended an HR job fair and really enjoyed the stimulation of the workshops (which were free). Afterwards I had the opportunity to meet the presenter and ask a question and thank them. Saying thank you is a great way to open a conversation, especially if this type of networking doesn't come naturally for you.

We suggest you use these fairs primarily as a networking and information gathering opportunity. Don't expect an immediate job offer to result. With good preparation beforehand, a career fair can be enjoyable and interesting. Bring your networking CV, your business cards (ones you have made up specifically for your work search) and a notepad and pen. Dress as if you were attending an interview. Research in advance the websites of the companies who will be hosting a booth. You can use some of the same questions you prepared for your information interviews in *Chapter 5 — Networking* to help you gather information. Be prepared to tell people about yourself and prepare in advance a one-minute self-introduction or elevator pitch targeted at some of the companies who will be there. See *Chapter 5 — Networking* for more on elevator pitches.

A more recent development in this avenue of finding opportunities is the virtual job fair. Search online for these events.

VOLUNTARY WORK

Perhaps a volunteer opportunity fits best at this time. In addition to contacting local charities or learning if your local community has a voluntary work information centre, you can find out about voluntary positions at *www.workingabroad.com* which is an information portal for environmental and humanitarian voluntary projects. The *www.transitionsabroad.com* website also has information about voluntary opportunities. Because these can lead to other (paid) work, don't disregard something voluntary which grabs your interest and looks like a good option to get you started.

THE INTERNET

The growth of the Internet has produced marked changes in how most of us live, work and connect with information and other people. The rate of change online is unprecedented and what follows may be out of date already by the time of printing. To access the most up to date information about using the Internet for work search, read the most recent annual *Quintessential Careers Report on the State of Internet Job-Hunting* at *www.quintcareers.com*. Below are tips on using what are currently the most standard tools for online work search.

New to the Internet

If you are not yet familiar with or adept in using the Internet, you will be glad to know there are numerous free introductions to the basics available. Three excellent ones are cited by Richard Bolles on his website, *www.jobhuntersbible.com:*

- Primer to Using the Internet *www.cameratim.com/computing/Internet-primer*
- Your Internet Guides, *www.thirteen.org/edonline/primer*
- Basic Web Lessons *www.aarp.org/learntech/computers*

Social media

Social Media is revolutionizing the world and the way we connect with each other. This includes how we are networking and finding out about work opportunities. Do not underestimate the value of these tools for finding opportunities in today's labour market. Online work search today is more than posting your CV on a website or reviewing job listings. It is about developing a relationship with your potential employer's recruiter and developing trust. A 2011 US survey from Jobvite reports nearly two-thirds of the 800 employers surveyed had used social media in their recruiting; 55 percent of these were expected to increase their budgets for social recruiting in 2012. According to the Society for Human Resource Management survey *(www.shrm.org/research),* the social networking websites used most often by organisations for recruitment in 2011 are: LinkedIn–95%; Facebook–58%; Twitter–42%. More and more work searchers are leveraging their online social networks to find job referrals. Here are some of the most commonly used social media networks:

LinkedIn

LinkedIn is a key location to search for work opportunities. Connect with your network here to let them know you are interested in working with a certain company or looking for a specific opportunity. That way you will be one of the first to be informed when something becomes available.

Research company profiles on LinkedIn and see how your network connects you to them. Approach these contacts to share information and network your way closer to the company itself. Join LinkedIn groups where you can participate in discussions with these contacts.

Potential employers can also find you here, based on the skills in your profile. Make sure to click that you are open to being approached for opportunities at the bottom of your profile. Recruiters troll LinkedIn profiles to find passive candidates who are open to opportunity but not actively searching. Passive candidates are the people many recruiters are looking for. Some companies and recruiters start LinkedIn groups in their area of interest and then approach potential candidates who join the group and demonstrate the competencies and knowledge required. To stay up-to-date on developments at LinkedIn join their blog and try out all the different features for yourself.

Facebook

Facebook is another key social media site. Use the timeline feature of Facebook to create an online CV-like profile. Facebook has a number of related apps for work search available including 'the who button' and 'BeKnown'. Another way to use Facebook for your work search is to follow their job hunting and careers pages. The Branchout app has over three million jobs and 20,000 internships and can be used to leverage your Facebook network and strategically get introduced to others *(http://branchout.com)*.

Keep in mind the personal branding principles described later in this chapter and the privacy issues which may arise with posting your information online this way, and balance this with the fact that many recruiters are searching LinkedIn and Facebook to find their candidates. A LinkedIn profile at the very least is a required online professional work search tool these days.

Twitter

Twitter is another way to communicate your perspectives and expertise to your network as well as let them know about what specific kind of opportunities you are looking for. You can Tweet about information and opportunities you hear about that you want to pass along to your network. Tweeting with a recruiter can help them get to know you and allow you to demonstrate your capabilities, authenticity and enthusiasm for your field of expertise.

Others

You may be a member of other similar sites like Pinterest, which is gaining momentum, or sites that are more targeted to your specific work or location. Explore how you can use them effectively and ethically to network for work search purposes.

Of all the methods to find opportunities, social media tools most closely align with some of the benefits of in person networking and may end up being much more effective for the work searcher than the first wave of Internet work search tools has been.

Interestingly research is showing that the brain often fails to differentiate between virtual and real experiences.

Source: *Virtual Reality and Social Networks Will Be a Powerful Combination,* Jeremy N. Bailenson, Jim Blascovich (accessed 22-12-2012at *http://spectrum.ieee.org*). See their *Infinite Reality* book trailer at *www.infinitereality.org*.

While this claim challenges some of our strongest beliefs about networking, I do find that having a picture beside the comment of the person in my LinkedIn groups helps me (Colleen) feel like I know or am getting to know the different members when we are contributing to discussions. Use these social media sites to actively network your way to work as described in *Chapter 5 — Networking*.

'I found my current job on CareerBuilder and signed up for the company job alerts directly. These email notifications let me know of openings in the company. Ultimately I got my 'in' because the recruiter was Irish.'

Lizzy, British in America, *www.expatwomen.com*

'I found the Internet an invaluable tool for job related information either directly or by finding a contact and then contacting them directly. I have had two experiences of using the Internet to find employment. I subscribe to a few expat/HR type online newsletters and within my first week of being in Mumbai came across an advertisement from an American intercultural consulting company looking for representatives in Mumbai. I got that job.'

Victoria, New Zealander in India, *www.expatwomen.com*

Online job listings

According to the *2011 QuintCareers Annual Report on the State of Internet Job Search,* the future trends in job boards as noted by experts include: growth in mobile applications, the possibility of job boards 'in the cloud', and increasing importance of boards that feature freelance opportunities since the weak economy has pushed so many job-seekers into working for themselves. Indeed, there is more work available in smaller packages for freelancers these days and less often a full time job with benefits.

Galen Tinder of REA notes that the majority of job openings are posted online; 80 percent of job openings are never advertised elsewhere.

Five levels of job listing websites

There are roughly five different levels of online job listing websites: generic, affinity or specialist, niche, geographical and aggregator.

1. Generic sites are the big all encompassing sites like *www.monster.com*
2. Affinity or Specialist sites are geared toward a particular segment of the job seeking public, such as teens, women, disabled people, professionals making over $100,000 a year, graduates of particular institutions, association members, freelancers, expats and so on. Affinity site *www.expatica.com* may have a list of vacancies for your current location.
3. Niche sites specialise in particular industries or vocations. These are often more effective for people in that industry than the generic sites.
4. Geographical sites focus on a particular region or location in the world.
5. 'Aggregators' (also known as job search engines), search a large number of job sites to find postings matching your criteria and can save you a great deal of time. Indeed, *www.indeed.com,* and SimplyHired, *www.simplyhired.com,* are aggregator sites.

Evaluate before committing

Spend some time 'playing around' - trying a number of different sites and following a series of links to see where they take you. This will help you to clarify exactly what kind of information you're looking for and which sites will serve you best. To make the best use of Internet job postings you should decide on a list of sites you will check regularly — at least every other day. And don't forget the sites of specific companies you wish to target.

Evaluate and compare the different sites, asking:

1. How long has the site been in business?
2. How many employers use the site for recruitment?
3. How many individuals have been using the database as a resource as well as how many employers are members?
4. Which organisations endorse the site? The best sites are not necessarily the oldest or the biggest.
5. Ask what information is provided on generic sites. Better sites will provide the job title, company name, a description of the qualifications required and salary information
6. Does it provide searchability options using criteria such as geography, company name, industry, position, discipline and specialist area?

To help you evaluate which employment websites to use, Galen suggests you visit the International Association of Employment Web Sites and use ones which are members. Evaluate non-member websites against those that are members to ensure there are no unethical gaps in their practice before deciding to use that site.

'I found work on *www.craigslist.org*. The only recommendation I have is to follow up with a letter in the mail. If you are close to the company, hand deliver a resume. Online companies receive hundreds of resumes. Stand out with a well-printed resume.'

Ursula, South African in America, *www.marketingmentorexpert.com* and *www.expatwomen.com*

Here are two sources of online job postings for portable careers:

Partnerjob

If you are a supporting spouse and your partner's company is a member of Partnerjob, you will be able to post your CV on a member site for viewing by all other member companies. In addition you will be able to search for vacancies. This site is designed to offer the kind of short-term contract work perfect for mobile spouses. Find it at *www.partnerjob.com*.

PassportCareer.com

This website provides support on four levels, one of which is the individual work searcher. They provide insights into and support for work search in more than 75 different countries around the world.

Online CV databases

Just as you can search the Internet to find out what jobs are available, hiring employers can search the Internet themselves to find potential candidates to fill their available positions too. Online databases offer you, the job seeker, a 'billboard' on which to advertise your credentials and your interest in finding a new position. Hundreds of CV databases are online today, each offering different services. You'll need to understand the various features and then decide which arrangement will best suit your needs. A few sites charge a fee to show your CV, but most are free for the job seeker. All-encompassing websites like *www.monster.com* have different versions for different countries, include tips and guidance for work search, and of course provide a list of vacancies.

> 'I found a job listing, applied with my CV, was asked for an interview and secured the job. I have secured four jobs this way. Having worked in career and professional development for many years, I probably have more knowledge than most about how to create strong career marketing materials and present a compelling case in the interview. However, as a career coach, I do not recommend that my clients depend on job listings to find a job, as many jobs are never published.'
>
> **Megan, American in Italy, *www.careerbychoice.com***

Depending on the job you are looking for, it may be worth using a fee-based posting site. When a fee is involved, the site managers should be able to tell you roughly what sorts of companies use it to locate candidates and what their success rates are.

They should also have a privacy policy for what happens with your CV when you are finished your work search.

Online privacy

According to Richard Bolles, once your CV is posted it is almost impossible to completely remove it and he quotes an estimated 40,000,000 lost CVs floating around in cyberspace.

Decide what level of privacy you feel comfortable with before you post your information anywhere. Read current articles about what is happening with online privacy by doing some related online searches. Then you will be able make informed choices based on current information.

Be aware that potential employers are also using social media to access your network and perform 'back door' reference checks. Make sure your online image is clean and consistent with your desired work. Remember you can use this same technique to research the potential employer yourself.

Tips for using online work search tools

You will need to bring a measure of organisation and discipline to your efforts in order to target, structure, focus and limit your Internet work search. Here is Galen's suggested approach to doing so:

1. Determine in advance the job sites you will focus on for at least a week at a time and don't deviate from this list. If you run across other interesting sites, note the URL and incorporate it into your next weekly round.
2. Have in front of you a job description that represents what you are looking for, and keep to this description. It is not true that casting a wide net affords the best prospects of success. A lack of focus dissipates energy. If you are responding to positions in both accounting and the zoo management of chimpanzees, your likelihood of success plummets and so does your sense of purpose and mission as you try to fit yourself into many different moulds at the same time.
3. Once a week or so re-evaluate your site selection, dropping and adding appropriately.
4. Plan to get on the phone and out of the house at least once a day. There is no substitute for meeting people face-to-face.

Relative effectiveness of work search methods

Internet job posting boards can be seen as a passive form of work search. You feel you are busy and you spend as much time as you can searching through many opportunities and sending applications out. But you don't necessarily get back what you put in. Most applications are never responded to or acknowledged unless you get invited for an interview. This makes this type of work search a very one-sided experience that can drain your energy. Richard Bolles, author of *What Color is Your Parachute,* rates Internet work search as the number one worst way to find work! The top five ways to find work according to Bolles all involve actively making contact with people:

1. Referrals from family, friends, people in community (33% success rate).
2. Knocking on the door of any employer (47% success rate).
3. Researching and contacting or visiting the companies directly yourself (65% success rate).
4. Forming a job club or, as we call it, Blue Sky Team (70% success rate).
5. Doing an inventory of yourself, what you did in *Chapters 2 and 3* of this book (86% success rate).

According to Bolles, the most successful approach brings you in contact with yourself — who you are, what type of work environment helps you to thrive and making a plan to create this for *yourself.* All of these are contained in this book!

Make sure to balance out your more passive Internet activities with a number of active networking and in person activities.

Creating Your Own Opportunities

Brand you

Personal branding has become a common element of marketing your skills in order to find opportunities and to be successful.

So how do you go about establishing yourself as a brand? The first step is to identify what type of person you are and how you want to be perceived. Mary Spillane, in her book *Branding Yourself,* suggests Brand You is a combination of three factors — your assets, your values and your image. In *Chapter 2 — Find Your Passion,* you already have made a good start. Here we will look at each area in more detail with an eye to creating your own brand statement identifying who you are, the essence of your achievements and what you have to offer.

Before that we'll examine the characteristics and activities of successful brands so you can learn and use these to your benefit when creating what Tom Peters coined *Brand You.*

CHARACTERISTICS OF A SUCCESSFUL BRAND

Gail MacIndoe, learning and development specialist, lists the following characteristics of successful brands and how you can apply these to building your own:

Be congruent and have integrity — how you look, act and talk must be in line with your values; people are quick to sense when you are not being congruent. Research is showing this congruence is also a key to personal happiness. All your activities in person and online need to be congruent

Show yourself in the best light and appeal to all the senses — your brand is mainly communicated through the non-verbal impact you make and your ability to connect on a feeling and sensing level

Adapt to the times without sacrificing your identity — you must keep reassessing your skills to make sure they are relevant to the market place - but not at the cost of sacrificing your values

Be easy to find — don't expect a job or business to come looking for you. Make sure you get your website, brochure, CV or your product/service details out to as many potential customers as possible. Have a business name that communicates your service or product clearly

Be easy to understand — be clear about who you are, what you do, what you stand for and what you offer. Simplify your message and focus/highlight your core strengths/features so as to be able to drive it into the minds of potential customers. State what problem you solve for customers

Stand out from the crowd — distinguish yourself from the rest, sell your uniqueness, what you do best, and capitalise on the differences

Meet market demands — there's no point having a great product, service or skill if people don't need it. That is not to say you can't identify or even create a need

Reduce perceived risk — the simpler it is for people to understand what it is that you offer, the easier it becomes for them to decide whether they want it or not. If you're a known quantity with a good or trustworthy reputation then people will find it easier to buy 'you'

Provide value and satisfy needs — unless you provide a real benefit for the employer/purchaser there will be no need to buy 'you'. Make sure you add value, know and communicate what that is

Think global — think global but act local; bear in mind cultural differences. This is sometimes called 'glocalisation'

Remember psychological rewards try and define what psychological benefit people will get as a result of hiring/buying you, and play on that

Sample activities of great brands

Brands spend a lot of time and money undertaking a number of activities in order to launch, establish and sustain themselves, such as:

Vision — begin with the end in mind - determine what business you are in, what your offering is and what you are working towards in the long term

Market analysis — unless you know what the market needs/wants and what the competition is doing, you are shooting in the dark. Start out by looking at the political situation, the economic climate, finding out what advances or changes there are in technology and any social trends. This may give you an insight into possible gaps and opportunities. Consider the 'barriers to entry' in your market, the threats, potential new entrants, what buyers require, the nature of your competition and what it offers, and other possible substitute products/services

Constantly reassess your values and identity to make sure they are still relevant to the market — do a SWOT analysis (see *Chapter 4 — Creating Your Career*)

Invest in research and development, allow yourself to evolve and introduce improvements — employers no longer manage our careers for us, so it is up to you to develop yourself and add new skills. Become a lifelong learner

Build relationships — make connections with your clients on different levels and in such a way they feel they know you and are important to you. Build a 'tribe' as Seth Godin would call it

Market yourself — even if you are employed keep your ears to the ground and network, promote, advertise and sell yourself and your skills. This is even more applicable when you are in a new market

Take advantage of opportunities — network, be proactive, take opportunities as they arise, make things happen

Assets

You need to establish what makes you special. Value your background, experiences, achievements and capabilities. To determine your assets make a list of your skills, your education and your experience. Highlight your achievements, focusing on things which differentiate you particularly in three keys areas - where you have saved money, made money and saved time.

Chapter 3 — What Can You Do? concentrates on analysing your skills or assets, but it's worth noting again that we easily discount our own key strengths because they come naturally.

Your Assets

Think about your Shining Moments Stories in *Chapter 2 — Find Your Passion*. Where in these stories have you saved money, made money or saved time? Where did you increase efficiency, organise effectively or produce something of value? These are assets of your brand.

20 mins

1. _____
   _____
2. _____
   _____
3. _____
   _____

Values

Only by knowing, understanding and living your values can you create your life's direction and ultimate destination. It is vital you define your values; they are your foundation and essential to successful branding.

Your unique promise of value

What are your values and what does that mean to your client? Review your values (from *Chapter 2 — Find Your Passion*) and link them together in a sentence which clearly communicates your values to your clients or contract providers.

_____
_____
_____
_____
_____
_____

How are you different from the competition? It could be your love of pets which leads you to your niche market. Or it could be a 'weakness' that provides your unique selling point. Management speaker and author Jos Burgers gives the example of marketing yourself as a 'consultant without paperwork' if writing reports is not a strength and there is also demand for this type of consulting. If you don't already know who your competition is, get to know them so you can answer this question effectively (See the *Chapter 7 — Working For Yourself* section on market research).

_____
_____
_____
_____

What potential market do your passions, values and hobbies point you towards?

_____
_____
_____

Learn more about your niche market through *search.twitter.com* (advanced search) and Google blog search.

Image

As previously mentioned, you have 30 seconds to make an impression and 93 percent of what you will be judged on has nothing to do with what you say. You need to be analytical and establish how you are going to live your brand. What image do you want to project? What should your voice sound like, what kind of appearance is suitable? How are you going to manage yourself, and how will you conduct yourself?

Remember, whatever you are feeling you will project. If you are feeling negative or lacking in confidence people will sense this. Try to visualise how you act when you are at your best. Think of a time when you were successful. What were you wearing?

How did you present yourself? What made you different that day? What thoughts and messages did you give yourself? Get yourself into a positive frame of mind, think about what your body posture would be like and then adopt that pose. Your physical state has a great influence on your mind. It's more difficult to feel down if you get your body into a 'positive' posture. What physical posture communicates feeling happy and successful? Your head would be held up high, you would have a smile on your face, your eyes would be bright and shiny and ready to make contact, your body erect and so on.

Try completing the exercise below and take action on those areas needing more work. We are not asking you to mould yourself into something you are not. Your brand should be authentic to you. The goal here is to ensure that you are being consistent and true to you.

Look

30 mins

Values I want to project	Already convey	Need work on looking more

Sound

30 mins

Values I want to project	Already sound	Need work on sounding more

Behave

Values I want to project	Already behave	Need work on behavinh more

30 mins

Feel

Values I want to project	Already feel	Need work on feeling more

30 mins

Clarity

Another branding exercise is the Johari Window, featured in Spillane's *Branding Yourself*. This is useful for coming to terms with yourself and discovering inconsistencies in your personality, behaviour and perception. It allows you to recognise yourself more honestly and discover if you are sending out conflicting messages.

When you are communicating one on one with someone else, consider there are six 'people' present. You are simultaneously the person you think you are, the person you are giving the impression of being, and the real you. And the same applies to the person with whom you are communicating. In addition, there is a fourth element consisting of each person's blind spot. Ask a friend or your Blue Sky Team to help you identify any blind spots you may have about yourself. Use this exercise to identify any gaps and find out what may be holding you back.

Public Self	Blind Spots
What am I happy to share with people?	What things don't I see?
Private Self	Unknown Self
Dreams & aspirations – what I know about myself but only share with nearest and dearest. What do I want to be?	What you don't know about yourself – your potential

FOCUS ON SOLUTIONS

Now that you have examined who you are and what you're capable of being, you are able to create your own brand statement that identifies who you are, the essence of your achievements and what you have to offer. Once that's completed you should set some strategies on how you are going to get to where you want to be. Choose where to focus your energy and where you want to make changes. Be honest about what you really want rather than doing what you or others think you should be doing.

Ask yourself:
- What can I do to improve?
- What do I need to know?
- What can I learn from what has already happened?
- What will get me what I want?
- What actions can I take right now to move me in the right direction?

For the items you are already doing well, write down what you want to keep doing. Continuing to do things that you know you are good at is just as or even more important as improving other areas. Don't focus on your areas to improve to the detriment of your strengths. One line of thinking is to maximize your strengths and outsource your weaknesses. Or as mentioned earlier, turn your weakness into a unique selling point.

Self Marketing Tools

Your own website

Develop your online presence by creating your own website to post your CV and include related materials. Some people are creating online CVs. Your website is a place for you to more fully describe your mission, achievements and provide related proof. In this way your website can act as an online portfolio. Add a blog to it and a Twitter account and you are set to use the most recent tools for work search. Include a video to introduce yourself with your elevator pitch and/or demonstrate a skill you have. Tailor your use of this tool to meet the specific needs of your own work idea.

Wordpress.com can provide you with a professional looking theme and functional blogging platform for free which you can manage yourself and present in a way that looks like a website. Visit *www.wpbuildingblocks.com* for step by step information on building a website using WordPress. To start a website, you will need a domain name and website host. Richard Bolles recommends *http://bravenet.com* as a useful resource for work searchers wanting to start a website.

Proposals

Proposal writing is a skill you will need if you want to submit an offer or bid on projects. It is also a technique to use when you have a solution to offer to an employer who has no positions available. An effective proposal will include the following:

- **Executive summary** — A concise overview or snapshot summarizing the contents of the proposal. It is the key sales information of the proposal
- **Statement of need** — Identify the problem, provide support information like statistics and research findings, and introduce your service or project as the solution
- **Project description** — Provide more detail about the project including objectives, methods, staffing/administration, evaluation and sustainability. Include a timeline
- **Budget** — Include the projected costs of providing the service including professional time, project management time, travel time, supplies and engaging associates for the project
- **Organisation information** — Describe the competencies and experience you and your associates or employees bring to the project. Portray your capability to

provide the service or bring the project successfully to completion

- **Conclusion** — A few short paragraphs concluding the proposal and looking towards the future with the project/program/service in place

There is a free online tutorial on writing proposals available at *www.foundationcenter.org* under the 'get started' tab. Look under online guides and tutorials.

The professional portfolio

A portfolio can act as an archive or master CV for all your key information. Traditionally, artists, writers, photographers, models and designers have used portfolios of their work to market their talents in their constant search for freelance work. The benefits of a portfolio have now been recognised by other professionals. A targeted portfolio can be used to prepare examples to talk about during an interview; to literally show examples of the quality of work you are capable of performing and to substantiate the claims of the CV. It can also be used as a tool to support career and life transitions.

Compiling a professional portfolio is a rewarding exercise. It re-acquaints you with your own strengths and achievements and renews your confidence and self-esteem. This is especially helpful when going through a major career and life transition. I (Colleen) found by reviewing the accomplishments and activities preserved in my portfolio I was reminded of my passion and what I was capable of before I moved to a new country and had to learn a new language. It gave me the motivation to make one more networking effort and take another step in the direction of what I most wanted, instead of settling for what I feared might be my only option.

A portfolio contains artefacts as well as facts. In many ways it is an archive of your life's milestones and achievements. It can be made up of certificates, references, samples of work, thank you notes, employee or client evaluations, statistics or newspaper clippings. In his comprehensive book *Portfolio Power,* Martin Kimeldorf suggests you compile your collection using clear plastic wallets inside a ring binder. This allows content to be updated and rearranged as desired. He recommends items should be categorised into skills sections such as Learning, Communication and Persuasion Abilities, Managerial or Leadership Skills, and Information Gathering and listed in reverse chronological order. An alternative is to organise the portfolio around Work Experiences, Education and Training, Volunteer Activities and Leisure. He recommends displaying each item with a title and a caption using consistent type style and positioning throughout.

Before starting to organise the items in your box, first identify the purpose and focus for your portfolio including the specific skills you need to substantiate and illustrate. Kimeldorf suggests you start by collecting samples and artefacts into a box. If possible categorise them as you go, including detailed information answering the questions of 'what, why and when'.

There's no need to wait for a work search to begin on your portfolio — jobs are no longer for life and building and maintaining a professional portfolio is a way of managing your own HR file. It will help raise your awareness of all your skills and experience and keep all your information in an organised and accessible format. That way when opportunity knocks you will be ready to recognise it and respond more quickly.

Making a portfolio is a project the whole family can do, so get your kids involved in starting their own portfolios too. In addition to school activities, projects and accomplishments, include pictures of sports tournaments, vacation experiences and hobbies and make sure to write the story that goes with them: What skills were used and further developed? What key personal characteristics does it demonstrate? What does this experience represent to you? This tool will be an immense help when your child gets to the age where they are asked, 'who are you?', 'what do you want?' and 'what can you do?'

PORTFOLIO ACTION PLAN

1. Collect all the bits and pieces of your achievements from their different storage places.
2. Organise them in a way that makes sense to you.
3. Choose a way to store these items: digitally, website, paper, box, blog...
4. Note what is missing that you'd like to add or continue searching for, write stories with pictures to include if there isn't a readily available document representing this.
5. Read your portfolio and appreciate all you've done and who this says that you are.
6. Keep adding to it with every new experience and artefact.

25
mins

My portfolio is meant to:

_____

_____

My portfolio will be seen by:

_____

_____

It will be finished by:

_____

Date to gather items:

_____

Date to sort and group items:

_____

Date to organise items into your choice of format for review and presentation:

_____

Tools and tips for formal work search

A formal work search generally means preparing a CV (*curriculum vitae*) and cover letter as well as going through an interview process whereby the employer or contract-provider selects the successful candidate. It is possible that through networking you have already 'got the job' but you need to provide the required documentation to formalise it. Here we provide an overview of the tools needed for this process and tips to prepare them well.

TYPES OF CV

The CV is a concise, targeted, summary of your work and learning experiences. While it describes past experiences it is also a forward-looking document aimed at achieving your future goals. The CV will summarise your experience and highlight the most relevant points for the work you are wanting. The purpose of the CV is not to get the job but to obtain an interview. When submitting a proposal, the CV is often attached to detail the credentials and experience of the individual or team submitting the proposal.

To clarify terms, in North America it is referred to as a resumé while in Europe it is called a CV. To further clarify terms, an *academic* CV is a much longer document and includes details of all published papers, qualifications, research and presentations. Traditionally there have been three kinds of CV: the chronological, the functional and the combination. More recently some new forms of CV have been developed: the visual and the networking CV.

Chronological

The *chronological* CV lists your most recent experience first and progresses backwards through time. This is the most commonly used CV format and is preferred by employers as it is easy to see what skills were used when and where.

Functional

The *functional* CV emphasizes skills, abilities and achievements without direct reference to employer and timeframe. Employers are more suspicious of this format as it can be used to disguise gaps in work history. It is most effective for people who have worked for longer periods of time in similar positions or for people who want to market their skills in a new career direction.

Combination

The *combination* CV contains the best of the chronological and functional CVs. It provides the most flexibility to tailor your CV to your specific situation and goals. Generally in this type of CV, experience and accomplishments are listed under skill headings and a work history is also provided in a separate section. Creative headings such as 'highlights of qualifications' or 'summary of accomplishments' can be used to fit the targeted content.

Visual

A new type of CV is now available thanks to the advances and accessibility of technology. It is called a visual CV and incorporates more graphic elements like charts, maps, scales and pictures. Some employers may be more reticent to accept this type of CV, preferring to stick to what they know and not learn a new way of reading a CV. It may not be possible to scan this format so check to see if they use scanning software to sort through CVs. If done effectively, a visual CV should be easier to read and an employer will know within seconds if a candidate deserves more attention. Here are some websites which support the development of visual CVs: *http://re.vu; http://vizualize.me; http://kinzaa.com.*

Networking

The networking CV allows you to follow-up your elevator pitch and elaborate your skills further. It is not targeted at a specific company or job opening but at opportunities in your desired career direction or business sector. Using the vision of your ideal opportunity to guide you, write your networking CV as if you were using it to apply for that position. Incorporate elements of the above CV's formats.

Vehicles which also perform similar functions to a networking CV include your LinkedIn profile, your Facebook page and Pinterest collection. They are all ways to profile your skills, experience, interests and values.

GETTING IT RIGHT

The saying, 'You never get a second chance to make a first impression' is extremely relevant when it comes to your CV. Most CVs are read the first time within a few seconds with the intention to reduce the number of CVs to be read fully. The reader is looking for reasons to disregard your CV. Make sure your CV is well written, with the most relevant content easily found and containing absolutely no errors. Ask two or more people to read your CV for you before you send it.

Local requirements

Find out locally what is required in a CV. In some countries, it's standard to enclose a photograph. In others, such as the US, the employer is required to dispose of these CVs. Check with employment agencies, government agencies and local work search websites to learn about local customs.

Some countries and employers require original or certified copies of transcripts and references to be attached to your application. Prepare copies of these documents in advance so you can respond quickly to opportunities.

Targeting

Regardless of where you are, it is essential you customise each CV to highlight the skills required for the position in that company. You do not need to include every task that was part of your responsibilities in a particular position. A CV is a marketing document and summary aimed at getting you an interview for the work you want.

One option is to create a master CV with all your information so you do not need to remember it again every time you create a different version. Then all you need to do is tailor it to each position.

Page size

Be aware that page sizes in Europe are A4 while North America uses 'letter size'. Choose the appropriate paper size for where you are applying when writing your CV so it looks the way you expect when printed. If possible when sending your CV by post or courier, purchase stationery that has the same dimensions as the recipient's and mail or fax your resume and cover letter on this stationery.

Length

The average CV you will send will be two pages long. While for a work searcher with less than five years' professional experience a single page is sufficient, those with more experience should work hard to keep it to two pages. If you are struggling with the two-page maximum, try the following:

- Remove or condense your employment experiences that happened 15 years or more ago
- Reduce the size of the font to 11 points but no smaller
- Make the margins smaller
- Highlight or provide the most space for the information that is most relevant to the job you are seeking. Consider leaving the rest out

Scanning

Some agencies and employers may scan your CV electronically and for this reason you should use a simple font, such as Arial, Helvetica or Times New Roman, at about 12 points, using black ink on white paper. Fasten separate sheets with a paper clip rather than a staple and only print on one side of the paper to facilitate scanning and copying. Put your name on each page in case they get separated.

Emailing

When emailing your CV, ensure the CV received on the other end looks the way you intended. Word now allows you to save and send a document in Adobe (pdf) although this means it may not be saved in the employer's recruitment software system. Save your document in the version of Word most people are using at this moment, or call to find out which version will be compatible with the employer's software. Keep the formatting simple in order to ensure it comes out on the other end as you intended. Email your CV as an attachment called 'CV your name' and use the same approach for the cover letter. State the work title for which you are applying as the subject of the email. If you apply for more than one position in a given company, include the position name along with your name when you save your CV and cover letter. This will communicate that you have targeted your application.

The content of the email will be well written, concisely referring to the position title, the attached cover letter and CV, expressing enthusiasm and interest for the position and noting you will make contact to ensure it has been received and could be opened. It will also include your contact information.

Key words

Key words are used by larger companies to sort through resumes. The more key words you use which connect with the position you want, the higher up on the ratings your CV will come. Key words are used by search engines. As a result, if you post your CV content anywhere online you will want the most important and relevant key words to be there, so your CV will be found and read by your target market. You can learn more about the key words you will need to include in your CV by reading position descriptions, occupational profiles, and evaluating the effectiveness of your own search results using a selection of the words you think are most relevant. Reviewing the words in the results you find will also help you sharpen your list of key words.

THE BASIC ELEMENTS OF A CV

All CVs will generally contain these elements:

The objective

An objective can serve the purposes of providing an organising principle for the author and a guide for its readers. In this way the reader doesn't need to guess what kind of job you are applying for. A cover letter is often not read and can get separated from the CV. For this reason stating your objective in the cover letter alone is not an alternative. A good objective is stated briefly in a few words. In our opinion, if you are short on space, the objective can be left out as long as the CV is targeted and saved under the position name.

Highlights of qualifications

A 'professional profile' or 'summary of qualifications' or 'highlights of qualifications section' allows the reader to quickly find the most relevant points which demonstrate you are a candidate with a CV to read more closely and invite for the interview.

Your qualifications

As a general rule, you should list both your educational and professional qualifications in reverse chronological order, from most recent to least recent, regardless of the CV format you have chosen. Use bullets to make the content easy to read quickly and get you through the first speed-reading. Make sure your bulleted items begin with active and engaging verbs. Search online for 'action verbs CV' or 'resume'. These lists can help you find the right word to capture your experience on paper.

Educational achievements

Include the degree you earned and if directly applicable, specific courses. If your degree is recent, awarded in the last five years, and it bears directly on your objective, you may want to place the education section on page one, before professional experience. Otherwise it is equally acceptable to place it following your professional achievements.

Check out the standard terminology for your qualifications in the host country. Galen Tinder of REA notes that only PhD (doctorate), MBA (Masters of Business Administration) and TEFL (Teaching of English as a Foreign Language) are terms recognised worldwide. Find out what terms your potential employer will understand and make sure your qualifications will be clear to them. If needed, have your training and education evaluated locally so you can describe it in an understandable way for the employer.

Include any specific training you have undertaken within the last five years, such as informal computer courses, languages or personal development. Write them in the same format as other experience using the name of the training, training provider and dates.

Professional achievements

Also called 'work experience' or 'related experience'. You may want to consider grouping similar positions together in one section. Do not try to mask gaps of unemployment. It's no longer considered a black mark against you to have been out of the workforce, even for a lengthy period of time - especially if you give the reason in your cover letter. You can include volunteer positions here by listing it like work-experience with the word 'volunteer' in brackets after the position title. This allows your voluntary experience to be valued on a par with your paid experience and is especially useful when looking for opportunities related to your voluntary experience. State the position you held, the name of the company and its location. Always state the start and end date (month and year) for each position you've had. Then list your most relevant and important responsibilities and achievements. Answer the foremost question every reader of your CV will have in mind: 'What can this person do for me?' Make sure it's clear you are a person who has produced results in the past and will be able to do so for this employer as well. For past positions use action verbs in the past tense and for your present position use them in the present tense. Keep sentences as short as you can while also stating the concrete specifics of your achievements such as percentages, dates, profit margins, group size and so on. Include whether you worked in a team, the size of the team, noting if the members were multinational, and whether you were a team leader.

If you did much the same thing in another company, group the positions with one job title and then list the companies clearly indicating the dates you worked for each. A list of awards highlighting relevant and/or transferrable skills will help distinguish you and your qualifications from other applicants.

'When I first put my resume out, no one at all was interested. So I had to find someone who knew a little about hiring staff, as luck would have it I found a HR director at Qwest Communications and she sat and went through my resume with me, helping me re-word literally the whole thing. Even then it took a further 6 months for a company to hire me. If you are not fussy, commission jobs are ten a penny but in the current climate that does pay the bills.'

Lizzy, British in America, *www.expatwomen.com*

Volunteer experience and hobbies

If your volunteer experience does not connect directly to the position you are seeking, list it under its own heading using the same formatting as your professional experience. Include a short list of specific hobbies on your CV to provide a well-rounded impression of yourself. Stating you are taking guitar lessons demonstrates you are someone who is actively learning in their private life, and has self-discipline (as anyone who has tried to do this as an adult knows). Do not list reading and watching TV as hobbies. Do include what genre of book you read regularly, what magazine you subscribe to, what kind of travel you enjoy or you have done and whether you are a member of a club. Make sure if you do list these elements of your private life, they will not decrease your chances to be invited for the interview. In other words, be cautious or eliminate mentioning associations with, for example, a political or religious connection.

CV samples for portable careers are available at *www.careerinyoursuitcase.com.*

COVER LETTERS

A cover letter should always accompany your CV or proposal, using the same font and paper as the CV. They may also be called 'letters of interest' or 'motivation letters'. Your cover letter should be of the same quality as your CV and thus deserves equal attention and targeting effort. It may be read before or after the CV, so make no assumptions. Cover letters may also be used to assess your written communication skills. A succinct cover letter is a maximum of one page in length.

The cover letter will refer to the CV and encourage the reader to continue reading the CV. An effective cover letter will introduce your CV to the reader, establish the frame of mind the reader brings to the CV and provide your reasons for the application. It can add positive background and supplementary material that could not be incorporated into the CV. The cover letter should highlight and elaborate on the CVs most important elements in relationship to the particular position you are applying for.

The tone of the cover letter will indicate a motivated candidate and find the middle ground between formality and familiarity. Using a generic letter to cover all your CVs communicates you have no special interest in the particular position. Compare it to how you would feel when someone makes an invitation to you in a way that you know they don't really care one way or the other if you take them up on it. To prevent this from happening to you, while writing your cover letter imagine what it would be like to work for that company in that position. Can you see it for yourself? How does it feel? Now write the letter with that feeling and those images fuelling the process.

According to Galen Tinder of REA, an effective cover letter has three components:

The beginning

This is the first paragraph of your letter and sets the tone of the letter. Confirm to the reader exactly which position you're interested in and how the vacancy came to your attention. You can mention here in one sentence your motivation for applying.

The middle

Here you will summarise your qualifications (e.g. five years of direct or related experience) and elaborate on, or provide an example of, your best selling points. Focus mostly on what you have to offer the company and minimally on what the position will do for you.

- Summarise the critical skills, experience, and personality traits that make you an ideal candidate for the position. Galen recommends you:
- Be specific about what you bring to the table and concrete in your illustrations of what you can accomplish
- Talk about your achievements and how they benefited your previous employers
- Research the company to explain how your past qualifications can translate into benefits for this particular employer

The conclusion

Galen describes the last paragraph as 'clear and quietly confident'. Insights into the local culture will help you find the appropriate level of confidence. For example, my (Colleen's) usual approach of stating that I look forward to discussing my qualifications and experience in more detail with them may come across as aggressively confident in some cultures. Do keep the ball in your court though and state when you will call to follow up on the application and then make sure you do it. This will allow you to be proactive during that difficult period of waiting after you submit an application. Visit *www.careerinyoursuitcase.com* for a sample cover letter.

The interview

Once you are over the first hurdle of preparing your marketing documents, the next hurdle usually presents itself. We say usually, because through networking you may already have secured the job and later simply need to supply the documentation to make it official. The interview is a natural part of the process of discovering opportunities and determining if they are for you (and you for them).

It is a 'sales pitch' from both parties to convince each other of the merits of choosing that person and that company, as well as an opportunity for them to explore your knowledge, skills and personal characteristics, and hear concrete examples of how you have used each of these. They want to know what you can do for them and whether or not you will fit into their current team culture. In a field where there is a shortage of skilled workers, they will make more of a sales pitch of their company to you. In a field where you are one of many suitable candidates, you will need to differentiate yourself from the others in a way that makes you the chosen one.

In order to prepare successfully for an interview, you need to be able to understand the way potential employers think and what their selection criteria are. Galen Tinder of REA suggests you think of any additional skills not specified in the job description that will strengthen your chances. This will also demonstrate you have prepared well and set you apart from other candidates. As part of your preparations, get an idea of the potential salary to be offered by researching the internet.

Be honest and be yourself. Having prepared well, you will have a good sense of what you have to offer the company and how your skills match their needs. In this way you will find work opportunities to use your strengths to their greatest advantage without having to fit your square peg into a company's round hole. Understand the cultural norms where you are applying for work and the cultural backgrounds of the interview panel. Discussions regarding salary in western culture are generally reserved for the second interview or negotiation stage. What North Americans consider to be taboo in an interview may be perfectly acceptable where you currently are. Also, be aware of local practices regarding shaking hands, making eye contact, showing the soles of your feet, and body language.

INTERVIEW PREPARATION CHECKLIST

100 mins

☐ Research the company online using their website, LinkedIn, Facebook and searching the company name for online references

☐ Research the position using occupational profiles online (if you haven't already)

☐ Develop a visual image of how it would be to work in that position at that company and how it would feel for you. Keep this vision in mind and check its accuracy during the interview

☐ Prepare concrete examples of your experience and qualities relating to the position

☐ Prepare to explain how your portable career connects with the company profile and is of benefit to the position requirements

☐ Prepare to talk about previous experiences in a positive way, indicating what you have learned from them

☐ Research salary range to be able to state a ballpark figure you would be willing to accept

☐ Understand the interview process and the common questions asked during an interview (see the tutorial available at *www.quintcareers.com*)

☐ Understand the principles of establishing rapport (see *Chapter 5 — Networking*) and use them with everyone you meet at the company and during the interview

☐ Select your clothing in advance of the interview day and ensure it is ready.

☐ Visit the company in advance (or review their online pictures) to see what is generally worn and wear clothing one degree more formal or conservative than that

☐ Make sure your non-verbal communication is as well prepared as your verbal

☐ Prepare your list of references: ask them for permission to use their name, tell them why you chose them and which of your skills you would like them to elaborate on

☐ Conduct a practice interview with one of your Blue Sky Team members or supporters and record it using your mobile phone, digital camera or video camera. Review this, recognise what you did well and look for ways to strengthen your performance

INTERVIEW DO'S

• Be confident in your abilities and open to asking questions for clarification during the interview

• Sum up your responses with how they relate to the position

- Practice active listening skills: paraphrase the question to indicate you understood it and then give your answer while making eye contact with all panel members
- Find as many ways to agree with the interviewers as possible
- Enjoy meeting new people and expanding your network
- Follow-up with a thank you email
- Use the interview record form at the end of this chapter and online at *www.careerinyoursuitcase.com* to record your experience and insights following an interview

References

Interviewers will request your references if they are interested in following up on you as a candidate. In general, this may happen at the end of the interview or following their review of interviewed candidates. Some employers may choose to check references before the interview, so check to see when they would like references submitted if you are unsure.

Your reference list should include two to three names and contact information of individuals who the interviewer may contact for information about your performance in previous work situations. If you do not have professional references, choose the people who will best be able to speak to the skills needed for the position.

Prepare your references in advance by informing them of your work search, asking permission to use them as a reference and requesting they focus their comments on the specific skills and accomplishments most relevant to the position you are interviewing for. You may need to refresh their memory of the accomplishments you wish them to speak about. In this way you ensure your referee shares the information most relevant to the interviewer's needs. You are not telling them what to say, but supporting them to do their best as your referee. Make sure you let them know when they might be contacted and let them know whether or not you get the work.

'Backdoor references' are being conducted more frequently by recruiters using social networking to connect with former and current colleagues and gather additional information about you. Whether it's ethical or not, it is happening and helpful to know about.

Thank you and following up

A critical element of a well-executed work search is following up - the exercise of charming persistence. Frame this activity in your mind as you doing them the favour of making it easy to connect with you, rather than feeling like you are begging for their attention.

It is important to follow-up an interview with a thank you note. In today's instant world, an email is seen as even more effective than a hand written note. Jessica Liebman, managing editor of *Business Insider,* considers it an essential element in convincing the potential employer of your interest and enthusiasm for the position. According to Jessica, the three elements to include in the thank you are:

• The words 'thank you'.
• Confirming your interest in the position following the interview.
• A reminder of why you are the one for the job.

The e-mail note has the advantage of being received the same day as the interview, getting your name in the person's inbox to allow for searches, and opening the door for an easy reply and a potential conversation.

The same applies to a Tweet or text message. My (Colleen's) friend Linda Tweeted with an interviewer one week after being told she was the number two candidate for a position. She stressed what a positive interview it had been and invited him meet to explore the feasibility of her desire to work in this sector. She was inspired to do this after seeing a Tweet about another position with this same company and wondered if it was worthwhile for her to apply again. The immediately Tweeted response accepted her invitation to meet and scheduled it for the next day. She was offered the position immediately. Upon reflection she recognizes that because she was searching for a position that really fit her qualities and values she was able to exude an authentic confidence in the interview.

Also send a thank you after information interviews and when people in your network share information and tips with you.

INTERVIEW RECORD SHEET

What is your first impression of the employer?

_____

_____

_____

Which of your values match the company's values?

_____

_____

_____

What is the work culture in this company?

_____

_____

_____

How much will you need to adapt to fit in?

_____

_____

_____

Does this opportunity meet your requirements related to salary, commute, work times and location?

_____

_____

_____

What about this job and employer would make you happy working here?

_____

_____

_____

Rate this company from 1 – 10 (with 1 being 'prison sentence' and 10 being 'dream job'):

1   2   3   4   5   6   7   8   9   10

Chapter 6: Resources for Marketing Yourself

A Semple & M Haig, *The Internet Job Search Handbook,* How To Books

A Stead, ed. A *The Candidate Yearbook (Essays and statistics on job hunting in the UK,)* Career Counsel Ltd

A Vincent & J Valkenburg, *Career Management via LinkedIn,* Spectrum

CEPEC Recruitment Guide: A Directory of Recruitment Agencies and Search Consultants in the United Kingdom, CEPEC

Executive Grapevine: the International Directory of Executive Recruitment Consultants, Executive Grapevine

Government of Alberta, Human Services, Advanced Techniques for Work Search, *www.alis.alberta.ca/publications*

I Krechowiecka, *Net That Job,* The Times with Kogan-Page

J Adair King & B Sheldon, *The Smart Woman's Guide to Resumés and Job Hunting,* The Career Press

J Brownfoot & F Wilks, *Directory of Volunteering and Employment Opportunities Director,* of Social Change Publications

Key British Enterprises, (Lists the top 30,000 British companies) Dun and Bradstreet

M Kimeldorf, *Portfolio Power,* Petersons

M Spillane, *Branding Yourself,* Pan

M Yate & T Dourlain, *Online Job-Hunting – Great Answers to Tough Questions,* Kogan-Page

MA Thompson, *The Global CV and Resumé Guide,* Wiley and Sons

Personnel Managers' Yearbook AP, Information Services

R Nelson Bolles, *Job-Hunting on the Internet,* Ten Speed Press

R Nelson Bolles, *What Color is Your Parachute?,* Ten Speed Press

T Peters, *Brand You Knopf Doubleday,* Publishing Group

The Occupational Outlook Handbook, BLS Publications

The Voluntary Agencies Directory, National Council for Voluntary Organisations (NCVO)

V Reily Collins, *Getting into the Voluntary Sector,* Trotman

Volunteer Work, Central Bureau for Educational Visits and Exchanges

'When you work you are a flute through whose heart the whispering of the hours turns to music.'

Khalil Gibran

Chapter SEVEN

Working for Yourself

Starting Your Own Thing

Working for yourself is an excellent way to live out your portable career. If you know you're likely to be on the move again fairly shortly, and that no business you choose is worth the investment it would take to make it a big success in one location, then maybe you should think about starting a more modest concern. One that will preserve your sanity and your professional identity and also give you the flexibility you need. Think about starting small and growing the business organically, sharing costs, bartering skills and making your venture work for you. A venture that grows organically will often feel 'effortless' as you move from serendipity to serendipity.

> Many expatriate wives lose their identity and self-confidence when they go round the world. Many [women] lose the same when they have children. But for the trailing spouse they often have both of these to contend with. I have never suffered from this because I have always known that I could do something for myself, however small.
>
> **Pauline, British in Norway, *www.careerinyoursuitcase.com***

COLLABORATE

While it seems a bit of an oxymoron when starting your own thing, you will definitely want to find ways to collaborate. The owner of a small business, especially a home-based one or a consulting practice, can feel very isolated. There are no more coffee breaks or lunches in the company cafeteria with 'the gang'. The consultant can go from project to project, never developing close or lasting relationships. One antidote to this is to join a breakfast group or other support group for small business owners or consultants, a local networking group, or a forum or trade association. Check with the local Chamber of Commerce to learn about local entrepreneurial networking groups. These types of networks can empathise with and understand your problems and concerns in a way your clients and even your family can't. You may also be able to participate in forums and chat groups on the Internet. These might not provide the face-to-face contact you crave, but they have the advantage of being instantly accessible at almost any hour of the day. You could even start your own breakfast club or online forum. A mastermind group will allow you to ask each other for ideas and solutions. Joining a virtual network, such as Ecademy *(www.ecademy.com)* offers this kind of benefit and with hundreds of thousands of members all over the world and countless forums it is a boon to the sole trader. Their Blackstar membership offers the benefits of a mastermind group too.

Business owners and consultants also often work in isolation and complain about a lack of feedback. If you have created an informal support team, success team or as we call it Blue Sky Team you will always have a source of ideas, advice and feedback. If you move frequently, as I (Jo) do, then one of the hardest things about running your own business will be that you have to keep starting again in a new place, and you have to do so alone. It can be really tough finding the motivation to keep going and to make things happen when you are uprooted for the umpteenth time.

I (Colleen) have collaborated in developing and co-facilitating workshops with other freelancers many times over the course of my career. I find it's a natural way to develop my network and share resources for mutual benefit. It makes my work more enjoyable as well. During the last 25 years I (Jo) have also partnered with many others on a project-by-project basis. In Dubai, when I worked at the recruitment agency, running a computer training department, having an alliance with the agency was mutually beneficial. As their clients became my clients, mine became theirs. I have run workshops jointly with others. This has many benefits. Not only does it mean we share the work and the preparation time, but while we market to our network, the co-trainer markets to hers, and in this way we double our potential client base. Of course, it means we share the income too, but in our opinion the benefits outweigh the disadvantages. The partnership represented by the book you are now reading is another example of how we have used this model of 'effortless entrepreneurship' again.

Here are some ways to allow *effortless entrepreneurship* to happen for you:

Find associates

If you know people who do the same kind of work as you, consider making them 'associates'. Without the bureaucracy that comes with hiring staff, you can pass some of it over to a trusted third party. You can even profile them on your website. This will enable you to take on a greater volume of work without the risk of being overwhelmed by more than you can handle. Clients will be happy with the final product or service as long as you guarantee a uniform high quality.

In the past I (Jo) have worked with associates and used a finder's fee/commission arrangement. In this way, if my associate passes business to me, I pay her 15% of what I earn and vice versa.

I (Colleen) have used this approach in an informal way, collaborating with other likeminded professionals to provide workshops and services. I believe in the principle of abundance - the more we share the more there is for everyone. This belief allows me to turn the 'competition' into potential associates if there is a values and vision fit. Two advantages of forming associations like this are that your business will appear larger than it actually is, and you may be able to find ways to share marketing and publicity costs with others.

When I (Jo) returned to the UK in 1997 I wanted to find work as a bit of an expat expert, helping people solve their career problems. But, back home, I was no longer in the 'expat bubble' and felt isolated and unknown. So, I decided to form a group called Words That Work and invited fellow expat experts to pay me a very small fee, I think it was £50, to form a group of six of us and share a brochure, website and letterhead. I made no profit from this idea, but what I did receive was a place in a glossy brochure and the knowledge that when my associates handed out the brochure they would also be promoting me.

Join an established company as a freelancer

If you don't want to tackle the paperwork that goes with forming your own company, seek out an established organisation to which you can make a contribution, and determine its willingness to provide you with a work permit or visa. Sometimes you may have to pay them for this service, but the fee will often be less than you would pay to start up a business and obtain your own permits and premises, as is the prerequisite in some countries. Often a deal like this will also provide you with an office address and even a desk.

When I (Jo) was in the Middle East, I formed this sort of arrangement with a recruitment agency. I provided them with a computer training department and curriculum vitae writing service which they branded as their own. In return, I used their office and advertised under their name. I paid them a percentage of my earnings and the arrangement was profitable for both parties.

I (Colleen) have a similar arrangement in the Netherlands with an education management consultancy. I choose to operate from a position of abundance and the belief that there is enough for everyone. This has helped me find more 'pieces' of work that have added up to a complete work scenario for a portable and flexible career. See your competition as potential collaborators and a world of opportunities will open up to you.

'It is hard to work legally in Oman without a local sponsor. It is illegal to advertise or knowingly make money without one. When I was offered the chance to do some food hygiene training for a local company I knew I needed to be legally able to work. So, I approached the British Council, knowing that training is one of their objectives and asked them for their sponsorship as a consultant. We agreed that I would make myself available to any of their clients and they would organise my work visa. I did pay them an annual fee but it was worth it. Where there is a will there is a way.'

Sue V, British in Oman, *www.careerinyoursuitcase.com*

Teamwork

We all have strengths and weaknesses, so why not consider working in a team with a selection of other people? First, identify people whose area of expertise complements yours but with whom you share a common passion or purpose. I (Colleen) know I am great at having ideas, talking to people, teaching, networking and writing. But marketing, administration and filing are not in my list of favourite things to do. I believe it is better to focus on your strengths rather than expend energy trying to improve on the things you do well. If you put your best efforts into the things you do best and you work with someone with complementary skills you have a better chance of more success in less time. Even if each team member contributes only what he or she does best, together you can cover every aspect of the business from marketing to production.

The other advantage of having a team is you can spur each other on, you can have someone to share ideas with and you will not need to work alone. When Sue Valentine and I (Jo) decided to write the cookery book, *Dates*, I focused on writing, editing, desktop publishing and production while Sue focused on the photographs, the properties of dates and finding a sponsor and publisher. We shared writing the recipes between us. Separately, we would work on our specialist areas, and then we would set deadlines and meet up to discuss progress. As a result, we stuck to our original plan and the book took nine months to complete from start to finish. Today, writing a book alone, I know I allow myself to procrastinate terribly. If you have a partner or partners in your project you are accountable to someone which can make all the difference to your success.

'I met Irene at a professional conference in Paris. We liked each other instantly. Irene came to one of my cooking classes; I enjoyed one of her walks with Shopping Plus. We found that we both had something to offer each other. We also both had the same type of relaxed working style. We pooled our joined experiences and started "French for a Day".'

Sue Y, British and Irene, French, in Paris, *www.careerinyoursuitcase.com*

Barter skills

If you don't want to form a formal association with others and don't want to pay staff, but do need help with certain aspects of your business, consider bartering your skills. In the current economic climate, we think this form of entrepreneurial thinking is going to gain momentum.

Bartering can take all shapes and forms. A friend of mine (Colleen) designed my first website for me for a bottle of wine. Another friend of mine joined a bartering network and taught mosaicing skills in exchange for haircuts. The same can be done for many other skills and services. What skills do you have? What do people ask for your help with? Ask them if you can exchange it for learning from one of their areas of expertise.

What types of collaboration suit your personality, style and values?

'When I decided to write *Gardening in Oman and The Gulf* I had to learn to use a word processor. Expatriate life is full of talented women who are not working full time and a friend taught me how, for free. Another friend taught me how to take photographs. Sometimes we bartered skills, sometimes I paid nothing, sometimes I just paid less than the going rate.'

Anne, British, in Oman, *www.careerinyoursuitcase.com*

Forms of entrepreneurship

It's important to know all the forms this way of working can take. Each form has particular advantages and disadvantages for individuals with varying personalities, skills, and life and family situations.

Starting a business from scratch

This is perhaps the most adventurous of the options. Starting from your own idea (or a variation on others' ideas), you plan and execute your own entrepreneurial venture. In essence, you do everything yourself — generating the business idea, researching the marketplace, checking the competition, determining the form of ownership, formulating a business plan, obtaining funding and doing the finances.

Buying an existing business

This is often a good option for entrepreneurs who don't want to go through the hassles and procedures involved in starting a business from scratch. With this option, however, it's important to research and identify exactly what you're buying. You must carefully assess the financial health of the business (often with the help of an accountant). Interview the current owner thoroughly and talk to customers, employees (if any) and suppliers. You must also speak to the current owner about staying on to help you as you take over the operation. And of course, in return for the privilege of buying an existing business, you may have to invest more cash than if you were starting your own. You need to value the business accurately and to negotiate skilfully for a purchase price and terms fair to both you and the current owner.

Buying a franchise

There are thousands of franchise options which provide a business model and certain tangible assets along with a known name. Many internationally known food outlets, like McDonald's and Kentucky Fried Chicken, are franchises but there are many others out there which offer services ranging from carpet cleaning to colour consultancy. The costs of buying into an established franchise can sometimes be high, and franchisees are put through a rigorous screening process. The price also depends on how well known the brand is already and how much training and assistance you will receive along the way. Franchises can require long hours in order to make the anticipated earnings. With these levels of financial and personal commitment, make sure you select a franchiser committed to franchisee support and success.

Buying a franchise seems to have many advantages. After all, who wouldn't want to buy into an operation that has instant name recognition, protected territories, time-tested operational procedures and marketing methods and guaranteed profits, all at a reasonable price? The problem, of course, is finding a franchise like this in a very glutted market, full of hype and exaggeration. And even if you find the 'perfect' franchise, franchising itself may not suit your personality or satisfy the reasons why you wanted to start your own business in the first place, as it will often require a significant time investment in one location. There are people who specialise in start-ups and then sell them once they're off the ground.

> 'My mother always says that a vacation is just a change of work. I have always made a point of visiting all potteries and galleries wherever we have been on holiday. I also take lots of courses for up to two weeks at a time. They are really inspiring.'
>
> **Cheryl, American in Vietnam,** *www.careerinyoursuitcase.com*

What business form suits your values and potential business?

Do you have what it takes?

An entrepreneur is someone who likes to be in control, enjoys an element of risk, is flexible, loves to solve problems and is quick thinking. A successful entrepreneur finds ways of replicating his or her business and making money from that without necessarily doing all the work. In his book *The Emyth*, Michael Gerber explains how a successful entrepreneur needs to wear three hats — he needs to actually do the work, to *manage* the business and the administration that entails and to be *entrepreneurial*, creative and inventive. This can be a tall order for some people, while others thrive on being able to use all of their various skills this way.

Also, people with their own businesses will tell you that the self-discipline and self-confidence required being your own boss is not for everyone. The hours are long and the external rewards are few (at least initially) but there will be one undeniable, and immediate, benefit: if you have the right mix of skills and personal qualities, you'll finally have a boss you can respect!

Typical traits of successful entrepreneurs

Most successful entrepreneurs have experienced failure and according to Chamber of Commerce statistics, the majority of businesses fail in their first year. This is why many Chambers of Commerce offer coaching for first time entrepreneurs.

A successful entrepreneur has a specific set of traits more suitable for entrepreneurial endeavours. Here are nine of the most important:

1. **Competitiveness and drive**
   Entrepreneurs like to compete with others or themselves to achieve their goals.
2. **Action orientation**
   Entrepreneurs can take a good idea, develop the workable business plan needed to make it a reality and act on it. They will stick with it to make it a success.
3. **Risk tolerance**
   A successful entrepreneur will take risks that are informed. They thrive to a certain extent on risk but will not go beyond certain boundaries.
4. **Strong goal orientation**
   Goals are written down and followed through on. An entrepreneur loves the sense of completion and achievement that comes from meeting their goals.
5. **Ability to make decisions**
   Entrepreneurs step up and can make decisions without unnecessary delay, taking responsibility for their outcomes.
6. **Emotional resilience**
   Setbacks are seen as learning opportunities, not reflections on your worth as a person. Thomas Edison tried several hundred substances before he finally settled

on tungsten as the right element for a light bulb filament. If he'd considered himself a failure after the tenth attempt (or even the fiftieth) he never would have invented the electric light bulb. A typical salesman needs to go through nine rejections before he or she gets an acceptance. Failure and setbacks of one kind or another are a part of every entrepreneur's success story. As an entrepreneur, you will need to be able to withstand this kind of rejection.

7. **Some sales skills and experience**

We'd be no good at selling something we do not believe in, but when we are passionate about a product, our enthusiasm easily persuades others to buy. In addition to believing in the product or service, you need the commercial skills to negotiate and close deals.

8. **Preference for creativity over bureaucracy**

Most entrepreneurs enjoy and need to find creative new approaches, solutions and ways to deliver on their agreements. If you're the kind of person who is always consulting the company's procedure manual, beware.

9. **Optimism**

This is perhaps one of the key attributes of a successful businessperson. Optimists think failure is caused by something that can be changed or learned, while pessimists take personal blame for any failure, attributing it to a character defect they are helpless to alter. Given the number of setbacks a business is likely to face, the belief it can turn out otherwise is essential to achieving success

Self-employment questionnaire

Ask yourself, and answer honestly:

- ☐ Do you truly believe in the idea and business you are entering?
- ☐ Where did the idea come from?
- ☐ Have you seen the idea used elsewhere?
- ☐ Is this an idea for you, or would it be better for someone else?
- ☐ Can you clearly articulate your idea (in 50 words or less)?
- ☐ What will you do better than your competitors?
- ☐ Do you have a unique selling proposition (USP)?
- ☐ Do you really know the industry?
- ☐ Has this business passed its peak?
- ☐ Has your idea passed the time test? In other words, will you still love it tomorrow? Next month? Next year?

- ☐ Do you really have the skills to make it work?
- ☐ Do you have any experience in this business?
- ☐ Are you ready to commit yourself to the idea for the next five years or more?
- ☐ How well does this business fit in with the rest of your life?
- ☐ Are you plugged into the right networks to pursue your idea?
- ☐ Do you know the difference between a product and a business? (Having a good product is only one part of business ownership.)
- ☐ What are the potential rewards for you - monetary and otherwise?
- ☐ Can you afford to get into this business?
- ☐ How easily can you get out of this business if it were to fail?
- ☐ Do you have the traits of a successful entrepreneur? (competitive, action oriented, risk taker, goal oriented, decisive, emotionally resilient, sales skills, creative and optimistic)

Your To Do List

Okay. You think you have what it takes and you have decided to go ahead and further investigate the idea of working for yourself. These are the tools you will need to get you started on the right foot.

The business plan

One way to determine whether your entrepreneurial idea is practical and exciting for you is to prepare a business plan. Seeing the plan in black and white is often the 'litmus test'. Ask yourself (and also ask your Blue Sky Team or friends and colleagues, who can often be more objective), 'Now I have this business mapped out on paper, am I still excited about it? Would this plan appeal to potential backers? Would I be excited to be a customer of this business? Are there some things I haven't looked at carefully enough? How can I rectify that to the satisfaction of myself, potential backers and customers?'

'But,' you might protest, 'I just want to start a small home based business with no employees and almost no investment. I don't have to prove my credit worthiness to any backers. Why do I need a formal business plan?'

Most people who have started a business, however small and informal, stated later that they wished they had created a formal business plan. With a business plan you answer some very important questions to ensure it starts off on the right foot with no oversights:

- What is my business's mission?
- Who are my primary customers and what are my markets?
- How will I finance my business?
- How will I market and manage my business?
- What are the legal implications of and requirements for this business
- What are the risks and how can I minimise them?
- How can I keep my business on-track financially?

If you can answer these questions upfront, you'll run into fewer surprises and less trouble later on. And if you decide to expand your business vision, you'll have a basic plan to work with, which can be modified to fit the new realities and plans.

Often the Chamber of Commerce website for your area or an association of small and medium size businesses or a government service will offer support to help you create a solid business plan. These can range from individual coaching or group information sessions to a downloadable template.

Market research

Before you embark on any business it is vital you do some market research. You need to know who your competitors might be and how they operate. Further, you can choose whether to offer the same service exactly, the same service, only better in some way, or a slightly different service.

Take a look at the competition, or, if there is none, at similar services, and find out what makes them succeed, or fail. Is it because they have a prime location? That they offer out of hours service? That they have cool offices? That their overheads are low? They have great brochures? Are cheap? Or that the boss is a great networker?

You could use the Internet for your research of course, but, if you are starting a small business or have a fairly new idea you may find very little on the Internet. While this is changing rapidly, not everyone has a website or much of a presence online. Just because you cannot find another 'jewellery-making class' or 'publishing consultant' online in your area does not necessarily mean there is no competition.

Here are some ways other than the Internet to find your competitors:

- Check the member lists of networking groups, professional groups, business groups and Chambers of Commerce.
- Ask people who have been living in your location for a while, even your local expat advice service.
- Look in the classified advertisements section of local papers, magazines, newsletters and free sheets.

If you do find someone else is doing much the same thing you hope to do and, what's more, they live down the street, do not be disheartened. Meet this person. Maybe you will find that, actually, you are rather different, or your outlooks, experience or personalities complement each other. Maybe you could join forces or at least refer clients to each other? We do not believe you should be afraid of potential competitors.

We believe there is always room for more, and people do business with people they like and who are like them. People do business with people they know. Regardless of the proximity of your 'competition' you are bound to have different sets of friends and contacts.

Who is your target market?

'We had been running an After-School Tuition Centre in the UK for some years and due to a deep personal interest in living in Egypt decided to look at starting a similar project there, primarily aimed at expat families struggling with transitioning to a foreign country with their children. Before even beginning to set up the business however it was vital to analyse what had made the UK enterprise a success, and to evaluate whether the same key aspects would deliver the same results in an entirely different environment.

'It's really important not to assume that your product or service will succeed in a different country just because it did well in your home country. Market research is crucial and it might be necessary to change your business model. Setting up an after-school tuition centre in Egypt required introducing a completely different business strategy, and not taking this into consideration would have meant a much harder struggle.'

Diane, Canadian in England, *www.expatwomen.com*

What to charge

Whether you are providing a service, product or consultancy you need to employ the same basic rules if you're going to price it well.

Galen Tinder of REA advises you find out what other comparable services or products cost, and remember that going rates vary from country to country - and even from region to region. A public relations consultant, for example, may have to charge two thirds of her London rate to clients in the English countryside.

To find out about going rates or prices, you will ideally want to network with business and social contacts in your new area. You can speak to someone who provides similar services or someone you know who has used services similar to yours. Check also the prices on websites of businesses providing similar products and services.

Once you've established the average going rate, you'll want to position yourself within that range. If you're new in town and hungry for new business, you might be tempted to underbid on early projects. Stephanie Ward of Firefly Coaching advises you not discount your prices in her April 15, 2011 blog posting. She points out that discounting costs you a great deal of time and energy, increases your stress and can lower your confidence. It means you are not getting paid for what you are worth and it sets a standard for other clients. When one client knows another got a discount, they will want one too. You are the first person who has to believe you are worth the prices you are charging in order to project that to clients. Her advice is to focus on the value you deliver, set your prices and stick to them.

When producing a product rather than providing a service, you might like to provide extra benefits, or add-on products, in order to induce people to give your product a try. A buy-one-get-one-free offer often attracts new customers.

If you're charging a fee for your services then you need to think about your daily, hourly and project rates or retainer fee. Even with a service it is possible to offer packages, add-ons or buy-one-get-one free deals. When I (Jo) sign up a new publishing client I offer them what I call the *Toolkit of free eBooks,* documents and videos containing products for a value of over £200. If you are just starting out, not only do you want to attract new customers but you also need to practise what you do. It's at time like these a buy-one-get-one-free offer can be very useful.

Most of our business comes from referrals, and you won't get referrals if you don't get clients in the first place. Do whatever you can to tempt in those first few vital clients.

DAILY RATES

You need to establish in your head a minimum and a maximum daily rate. You'll propose a daily rate based on the marketplace in your new area, the size and budget of the client, visibility of the project and other factors. Of course, you may accept a beginning project at slightly below your minimum to help get you started, but try not to make this a habit. And if you're charging by the day, be sure to keep an accurate record of your time so you can document it for the client.

HOURLY RATES

An hourly rate can be computed as easily as dividing your daily rate by eight. You'll want to charge an hourly rate if you find you are putting in 12-hour days every time you visit the client to provide services. Hourly rates can be used in the initial stages of a project before it becomes a long-term assignment. Generally speaking, an hourly rate connotes less status, so you may want to avoid it for that reason. It also puts too much attention on time spent and not enough on results achieved.

PACKAGE FEES

If it is logical for you to charge by the hour (as it is for Jo), then consider offering a series of packages or programs. Clients can purchase a certain number of hours from you, usually paid in advance. Jo offers a better hourly rate to those purchasing ten hours than to those purchasing two, of course. Jo's Virtual Assistant also charges this way.

PROJECT BILLING

When you need to tailor a proposal to a client's budget, you can bill by the project. You then have the leeway to decide how much time you will spend on each aspect of the project. If the client doesn't demand itemised timekeeping, there's no need for her to know. The higher level the project, the less the client wants to monitor your time and the more appropriate project billing is.

RETAINERS

You know you've arrived when your client puts you on a retainer. A retainer guarantees you a certain level of billable hours, such as two or three days of work a month. The client is so dependent on your services she knows she needs to lock in a portion of your billable time on a regular basis. Any retainer arrangement should be clearly spelled out in writing and cover the exact fee, the time commitment and the type of work to be performed. In addition, you should establish a fee for the time that extends over and above the retainer.

> 'I really enjoy teaching people new things and there are always plenty of people on the expatriate circuit desperate to learn from an English speaker in a relaxed environment. I worked out of my home and had two computers so I could teach up to four people at a time. I taught beginners and intermediates about computers, operating systems, word processing, spreadsheets and graphics. I charged a rate that was satisfactory to my users. It took some while to pitch the price correctly I admit. Then the conversion rate kept fluctuating!'
>
> **Kitty, American in Norway, *www.careerinyoursuitcase.com***

Marketing your business

You may have the best, most brilliant idea in the world. There is a market for it. Everyone wants one, and it's cheap to make and cheaper to supply. But if you do not tell people about it you may as well not bother. Marketing is telling people what you have to offer, or communicating that you have the solution that your clients are looking for. When you believe in your product this generally comes naturally.

> 'Everyone has a Terrific Idea, but if you can't get out there and sell it, you might as well stay home and make cookies.'
>
> **Lisa, British in Italy, h*ttp://burntbythetuscansun.blogspot.com***
> **and *www.expatwomen.com***

If you are lucky enough to have your target market on your doorstep then you could do very well indeed - providing you get out there and tell people.

When Sue and I (Jo) published our cookbook, *Dates*, we were living in Muscat, in Oman in the Middle East. Dates were the local, indigenous fruit. They were everywhere: fresh in season and dried when not, on market stalls, in supermarkets and on the trees. They were plentiful and they were cheap. They were nutritious and delicious too. Dates were everywhere but few people knew how versatile they could be in your cookery. We had a target market on our doorstep. The first edition of the book was in Arabic and English, so our market extended from the English speaking expats there to the locals.

The market was easy to target back then too. With only two newspapers and one English radio station, we only needed to make three phone calls in order to ensure the local media interviewed us and ran our story.

Next, we had t-shirts printed with the words 'Make a Date with the Middle East' and wore them around the city. We asked the local shopping malls (there were only three) if we could stand in their lobbies, handing out bite-sized samples of our food, selling the book and packs of dates and jars of date syrup too. They agreed. We also stood in the school playgrounds, again wearing our tee-shirts, handing out samples and selling books. And we supplied the local bookshops of course.

Finally, we took a stall at the Christmas bazaars and had a big, sponsored launch event at the prestigious Al Bustan Palace Hotel.

With our market on our doorstep it is no surprise we sold thousands of copies in a short space of time.

Internationally, things were not so straightforward. This was before the Internet so, instead, we wrote articles for international magazines about dates or about our publishing experience and widened our net that way. Nothing, however, could beat the effect of having that market on our doorstep.

Ten years after its first publication, a second version of *Dates* was published by Zodiac Publishing and is available worldwide, including in Harrods in London, where there is a special section devoted to dates.

How well do you know your market? And how easily can you target it?

Every business needs customers and every business needs a marketing plan. It can be simple or complex, largely written or largely intuitive — but you do need one to succeed, even if it's all in your head. Bill Gates didn't start out with an elaborate marketing plan, but he probably has exceptional brainpower with an ability to store data. And today, even he has a mammoth marketing department.

Here are some ways you can market your business without (yet) developing that mammoth marketing department.

> 'Never miss a marketing opportunity and use all available avenues. Don't lock yourself inside a box. Use both printed and electronic media. Join groups and organisations that are like-minded, compatible and complementary to your business. Know your competition. Take advantage of any and all networking opportunities. Remember to provide some services gratis and consider volunteering for charitable organisations as well. People remember those who take the extra initiatives.'
>
> **Carol, American, http://delhi4cats.wordpress.com and**
> *www.expatwomen.com*

ATTEND BUSINESS AND PROFESSIONAL MEETINGS

If you are a brochure designer, you will not just want to attend meetings of your own trade association. You'll mostly meet competitors there who, while helpful and potential collaborators, are not potential customers. However if you attend advertising or direct marketing association conventions, you'll be a lot more likely to meet potential customers. You might also want to give a talk at one of these conventions, such as 'How to design a truly effective direct mail brochure' or 'Using Mail Chimp to Market'. If you don't have enough experience or credentials to speak at a large national meeting, begin your speaking for smaller community and business groups such as Rotary or Lions. They may be small business people like yourself, so may see you as a colleague. They may also refer you to people they know in larger businesses.

ASK FOR REFERRALS

As soon as you have your first successful engagement or product delivery, ask your customer if they will refer and recommend you to others. Ask if you can use their testimonials in your marketing literature and on your website.

WRITE A BLOG, ARTICLES OR COLUMNS

Write your own blog or contribute articles or a regular column for a publication your potential customers read regularly. An example might be a regional newspaper or a professional journal or newsletter. The articles should show your knowledge of your field and your business savvy. Join related groups on LinkedIn and participate actively. Many small businesses get their first clients in this manner. Don't forget you can write for websites and free publications too. A blog can be created free of charge at hosts like WordPress or Blogspot.

> When *Live and Work Abroad: A Guide for Modern Nomads* came out, people started writing to me with offers of work. The best promotional tool I ever found was that book – and, like most advertising, its creation cost me more money than the publisher was paying for it.'
>
> **Huw Francis, Author of *Live and Work Abroad: A Guide for Modern Nomads***

ISSUE A PRESS RELEASE

Send a press release announcing the opening of your business to the local paper. A press release is free advertising and lets potential clients know of your existence and the variety of services you offer. Find any excuse to send out a press release to the publications, radio or TV stations your target market are known to use. If you can find a link between your product, service or recent success and say, Christmas, Valentine's Day, summer holidays, the cold and flu season or whatever do so. An example of a press release can be found on *www.careerinyoursuitcase.com*

ADVERTISE

You don't need to spend thousands on advertising when you haven't made a penny yet. Put a display advertisement in your local paper. Get your business listed in the Yellow Pages, their website *www.yell.com* or your local equivalent. You can also buy a display advertisement in Yellow Pages type publications as your business grows or as an initial investment in its growth. If your target market is local expat women, then you may be better off advertising in the local school or women's club magazines. Go where you feel you have the best chance of finding potential clients. These days you can also advertise on the Internet using Google's AdWords, Facebook adverts or LinkedIn's targeted advertising features. All can be tailored to your market and your budget.

A word of advice: advertisements cost money, particularly if they are large and glossy. Classified ads are much cheaper. Online classifieds may be cheaper still. If you can get to write an article or be interviewed, chances are you may get a whole page devoted to you free of charge. If you want to find out how to write these articles you might like to consider Jo's workbook *Definite Articles.*

MARKETING SEQUENCE

Develop a series of messages that are automatically sent to a client over a period of time. When a client, contact or website visitor signs up for one thing it triggers a marketing sequence developed for that client type. This is a way to build up your connection and relationship with a particular client as well as a way to increase the possibility that the client will buy additional products or services from you without a great deal of effort on your part. Google 'marketing sequence' or visit *www.expertsacademy.com* for more information about this technique.

NETWORK

Informal networking can be one of the biggest sources of business development. Word of mouth is the best marketing tool available. Don't keep your new business venture a secret. As you meet people in your new community (at professional meetings, a synagogue or church, social gatherings) introduce yourself and your new business using your Elevator Pitch. The person you're speaking to may not have the need for your services, but could have a colleague or a relative who does. *Chapter 5 — Networking* is devoted to this subject and includes a section on your Elevator Pitch.

Ask clients to provide a testimonial for your website or brochure and to tell a friend they think could also benefit from your services.

GIVE GIFTS

Offer something for free. Create a free booklet or article, you can offer to people every chance you get. It will help create the type of abundance talked about in *Chapter 5 — Networking*. I (Colleen) recently received a bottle of wine from the local garage mechanic because it was December 23 and in an unrelated event the bill for my dinner out was tucked into a gift CD of two music singles of the restaurant owner's music. Find your own unique way to give a gift. Many entrepreneurs offer this free gift through their website if the person signs up to the mailing list. I (Jo) give away my free report on how to write life story to anyone who signs up to my blog or newsletter, *The Inspirer.*

WORK FOR FREE

What? Work for free? You have put in all this hard work and now we're suggesting you do it for nothing? Well, yes. Something like that.

Just as a new journalist finds it hard to find paid work until he or she has been published already — but finds the only way to build a portfolio of clippings is to write those first few articles for publications that do not pay — you too may find you need to follow similar principles.

The best way to persuade strangers to buy your services or products is to show them testimonials from past, satisfied customers. But, until you have some customers how can you get hold of those testimonials?

Offer to work for the first few clients either free of charge, or at a substantial discount on the understanding that they will provide you with a testimonial. Easy.

After moving to the Netherlands and learning the language, I (Colleen) was invited to contribute (voluntarily) to a program for people looking for work as often as I wanted. This was an 'informal internship' which lasted four months before I was asked to fill in (and be paid) for one of the program's coaches while they were on holiday. Shortly after that I was offered a contract to develop and deliver training in another program on a regular basis. The experience I gained allowed me to become more aware of the differences between the Canadian and Dutch labour markets and government support systems as well as practice my Dutch. It prepared me to work in my field in this country. I think it's unrealistic to assume you can seamlessly apply your experience in another country without first learning about that country and how to apply your experience there within its culture.

I (Jo) have also employed this method many times. When I am trying out a new course, I will usually offer it at half price to students the first time. I explain they get a special price but I would like their honest feedback on the course and a testimonial in exchange. Sometimes I give students free places on my courses even though the courses themselves are established and successful. I do this for several reasons. One is that I like to mentor new writers and allowing those who cannot afford to pay to attend my classes free of charge is one way I can help them that fits with my mission. Often I ask them to provide or help serve the refreshments in exchange. Sometimes I ask them to help me in my other work, doing some proof reading or research for example.

A benefit of giving away one free place to each workshop is my classes are always full, the interaction among students is better and, after the course, I have an extra testimonial and one more person who will refer me to other clients, who, hopefully, will be able to pay.

'In the beginning it was very difficult to find paid work when I first arrived to Saudi Arabia. I am fortunate to have had diverse experiences and skills, which are in demand so receiving calls and being asked for interviews was not a problem. However it is fairly typical in Saudi Arabia to request a prospective employee to first work on a trial basis to better allow the employer to gauge the skills, expertise and "fit" of the candidate into the organisation. This seems to be especially true when the candidate is a woman and looking for work, which is outside the traditional occupations woman generally hold in the Kingdom such as teachers, women's banks or at a hospital. Initially I "went with the flow" and performed services such as marketing analysis, risk assessments and custom curriculum design that I would have typically charged several thousands of dollars for my work. After two specific instances where, after performing work I was told I would be contacted if needed for future opportunities, I began to realise that I did not have to "go with the flow" and learned the hard way to never feel I needed to undersell myself or my qualifications.'

Carol, American, *http://delhi4cats.wordpress.com* and
www.expatwomen.com

> 'I believe strongly that you should do things for free. I also treat some people for free if I know they can't afford it. An open hand both gives and receives therapy.'
>
> **Angelika, German in Norway, *www.careerinyoursuitcase.com***

Marketing materials

Your well-designed brochure and business card can be produced inexpensively (perhaps even on your own computer if you have some talent in this area as well as the right software). They communicate a professional image even if at present you are sharing your home office with your son's gerbil. Business cards can be designed and printed for free at *www.vistaprint.com* in many worldwide locations providing you leave the back free for the Vistaprint logo. Vistaprint can also help with postcards, stationery, brochures and banners.

You will want a logo and business card that fits the character of your business and connects with the look and feel of your website. If you provide accounting services, your materials will have a more staid image than if you produce brochures and so on. Don't despair if you're not highly artistic. There are a number of easy software programs that can help you create these materials and special paper can be purchased at a stationery supplier. If you possess absolutely no artistic talent, take your design ideas and copy to your local printing and photocopying shop, where they should be able to help you design the brochure. I (Jo) usually create a tri-fold brochure (that's a sheet of A4 folded into three) in Word, and then pay a freelance designer to make it look professional. My latest brochures were produced by Vistaprint too, while I had bookmarks made at a local copy shop.

Marketing letters

You may also want to compose a marketing letter to be mailed with your brochure. In order to really attract attention you could consider finding out more about NLP (neuro-linguistic programming) techniques that draw the reader in. Ian Halsall's book, *NLP 4U* is particularly good for this. And Gary Courtenay's *How to Write Sales Letters with Clout* is also packed with good tips. Some of these tips can be applied to the writing of cover letters as well.

The letter should consist of:

Introduction — who you are and what you are offering in your new community
Attention grabber — in dramatic fashion, state the problem your services can solve for the potential client and address the consequences of not solving this problem
Benefits — describe how your unique expertise can benefit the client and help her solve her problems
Action close — tell the potential client you will be calling in a few days to follow up. Then do it

Follow up. Even if the client has no immediate need for your services, she may refer you to a colleague in another department or company. Make a personal connection rather than trying to be all businessy and slick. It rarely hurts to mention you are new to the area and especially eager for a chance to perform your services in this new environment.

Take a look at the home page of many websites and you will see they too read a bit like a sales letter and draw you in, ending in a call to action, usually, signing up for something. Look at Jo's *www.writelifestory.com* and Alexandria Brown's *www.ezinequeen.com* for more inspiration and examples. Consider using a video to convey your message. Your website is your shop window - you want people to stop by and browse, to make a connection with you and to return.

Internet marketing

Selling your product or services via the Internet can be very effective. Of course, you will need to have a website or a section on someone else's website. But it is no good putting up a website or webpage and leaving things to chance. You need to ensure that the search engines can find you, that your site is placed high on the ratings, preferably on the first page and your site is in some way interactive. The static formal website is a thing of the past. Here are some tips to create your online business presence.

CREATE A WEBSITE

Today, one of the first things you should do when you are setting up your business is to start a website. After all, what do you do when you want to find out who, say, teaches German in your city, or where you can buy size 9 shoes? You look on the Internet. You too need an Internet presence. At the very least you should have one single page of information and your contact details. But do consider the advantages of having a newsletter sign up form, a blog, lots of articles, links, a shop, your testimonials and free gifts.

Get a domain name

First you need to buy a domain name that will be easy for people to remember. You could play safe and buy your name. I (Jo) own *www.joparfitt.com* in addition to my other websites *www.summertimepublishing.com*, *www.expatbookshop. com* and *www.writelifestory.com*. You can search to see which sites are available at *www.yahoo.com* and from many other sites including *www.godaddy.com*, which I use. Key in the name you would like and see if it is available. If it is, then great, buy it and ask a webmaster to help you to move forward with its creation and hosting. Often the domain name will be very inexpensive. Sometimes, someone else has already had your idea and bought the domain you want but rather than using it themselves they offer it for sale at a higher price. Now it is time to be clever and inventive and devise another domain name you like. Maybe, if .com is not available you could still buy .biz or .co.uk, but generally it is best to buy a .com as this is the suffix most people will guess first.

Advertisers on your website

Unless you have a very popular website that sees heavy traffic, you are unlikely to be able to sell expensive advertising on your site. However there is much scope for setting up reciprocal links with important sites, and getting publicity for your business on other people's sites. Offering free content on appropriate websites is a good way to get yourself some publicity and a hyperlink that takes people directly to your own site.

If you find it hard to encourage people to advertise on your site, think about setting up affiliations with other sites and receive commission on sales resulting from all business that reached the affiliate's site from yours. *www.amazon.com* offers such a program.

Search engine optimization

Search engine optimisation services will help you to appear first on the list after a search by Google, for example. Paul Herbert of Where On Earth *(www.whereonearthgroup.com)* helps people with search engine optimisation (SEO) and says websites act like either 'corks' or 'stones'. The more links you have to sites that have many links of their own, the more like a 'cork' you will be and the further up the ratings you will appear. Additionally, the more pages you have containing the more keywords (the ones search engines look for), the more 'corklike' you will be. There is plenty of information on this available so study it carefully. Tim Ferriss' book, *The Four Hour Workweek,* is particularly helpful here, as he explains how to earn lots of money working just four hours a week running an Internet-based business that sells a product. Other Internet gurus I (Jo) have had dealings with are Graham Jones of Infoselling *(www.infoselling.com)* and Tom Antion (*www.antion.com*). Graham states on his home page that he learned everything from Tom, by the way. Try the new book, *Laptop Entrepreneur,* by Nick Snelling and Graham Hunt, created specifically for people overseas.

Content management

Depending on what you want your website to achieve you need not spend too much money on your site. Regularly updated content is the key to maintaining and increasing the number of visitors to your site. Learning how to do update your website content yourself is made simple by today's platforms, many of which are Open Source (free). If you decide to run a blog (which is available from many places including WordPress *www.wordpress.com* and Blogger *www.blogger.com* amongst others) and keep it active this will ensure you have new content on a regular basis. Incorporate your blog into your website and LinkedIn profile for the best results. Tweet about your blog posts to get further mileage from them.

Maybe you want your website to be a brochure online. And indeed, no self-respecting business should omit the value of having a website of some kind, however small. But if you want to sell goods and need a shopping cart and payment facility, search options, hundreds of pages of content and a sophisticated site it can cost considerably more.

Interactive tools

Your website is a living part of your business. It is very versatile and much can be sold or promoted through it. Artists can sell their creative work, publicise their exhibitions or advertise seminars. You can buy just about anything on the Internet these days. You can also find freelance staff to work for you. You can advertise your services, source clients, information or staff. The channels for selling are multiplying almost as fast as the Internet itself.

Consider your website as a tool to communicate on a regular basis with your target market and potential clients. By incorporating all the social media elements you will be able to keep it current without devoting all your work time to it. Put a survey on your website to engage your visitor's and learn more about their perspectives.

Blogging

As mentioned previously, many websites have a blog as an integral feature. Consider how blogging could benefit your business and create your own unique approach to blogging that suits you, your business and your target audience. Do not parrot what others are doing. Give it some thought to make it an effective tool for yourself. In a nutshell, a blog must be focused on one main theme, entries should be short (400 words is fine). Ensure you use lots of key words and tags. Include an eye-catching image or video clip too, without infringing on copyright. Try to blog three times a week and to build a following through the comments you receive. You will generate a group of followers who will automatically receive your blogs every time you post an update.

Tweeting

Once you have posted a blog, it is a good idea to Tweet about it. This communicates in a succinct nugget of 140 characters, information that can draw the reader of your Tweet to your blog and website, thus increasing traffic to your website. Again, know who your Tweeting target group is and Tweet only information relevant to them. Consistent messaging is key to developing your online brand as you will read in the next section.

Ideally, every Tweet you send should include a link to a website. If you are short on ideas then reTweet other people's Tweets. This has the knock-on benefit of helping you to build relationships with the people you reTweet. I (Jo) find Twitter to be great for networking. I link it to my Facebook and LinkedIn accounts so whatever I Tweet is automatically posted in multiple locations.

Video clips

Posting video on your website is very simple. You record your video on a host like YouTube or Vimeo and copy and paste the URL into your website updating page. Coach Stephanie Ward posts short two minute interviews with key authors and experts in the field of marketing as well as her own tips on very relevant topics. It allows you to feel as if you know her, profiles her knowledge and expertise, and increases the likelihood you will contact her when you need the services she offers.

'You can significantly increase the odds of success this year, if you know who you are, what you want, where you are going, how you will get there, and what you will do once you arrive.'

Nigel Risner, *www.nigelrisner.com*

'Having a business plan is essential regardless of the specific nature of the business. It allows one to identify goals and objectives, form a mission and vision statement as well as be used as a reality check to gauge progress.'

Carol, American in Saudi Arabia, *http://delhi4cats.wordpress.com* and *www.expatwomen.com*

'I think a business plan is often the kiss of death. It's better to have an articulated vision, which outlines what you need to do and go from there. It's a lot more flexible. And, do we really have all that time to evaluate our potential customers and marketing programs? If you're looking for outside financing, well then, go ahead and make the plan.'

Lisa, British in Italy, *http://burntbythetuscansun.blogspot.com* and *www.expatwomen.com*

Some bureaucracy

Because this is a general introduction to starting your own business, and not a detailed 'how-to' manual, we'd like to call attention to some other issues that should not be ignored by any prospective self-employed person but which can't be treated in detail here.

LEGAL ISSUES

Your business idea and plan may be simple enough that you don't need the services of a lawyer immediately. However you should be aware of the legal needs of a business such as establishing a legal form and securing any relevant licences and permits. You should also recognise when you are out of your league or when your business has grown to the point you do need legal help.

EMPLOYEES

Perhaps you're a sole proprietor who wants to keep it simple. You may have no plans whatsoever to have any employees, let alone a huge operation. That's exactly how Ben and Jerry started out. You still need to know about employee issues in case your business takes off in a way you never imagined. And if you plan to take on employees, you must consider this in your business plan, even before you establish your business. You will want to attract and retain employees who have the right skills and motivation and who fit your personality and working style. You have the opportunity to design a company culture and reward structure that truly motivates and engages your employees.

You may, however, decide to work with freelancers or associates instead of employing people on a full or part-time basis. If you employ freelancers you will pay them an agreed hourly rate or per task. Many small business owners employ a virtual assistant (VA) to do much of their administrative work. When you work with associates you may agree on a commission rate or other method of reward. Commission rates tend to range from 15 percent to 60 percent. Perhaps you could work with someone who will do all your marketing and production and decide to share the workload for a 50/50 split. There is no one size fits all approach to this, so our advice is to talk to other people in a similar business and learn from what they do. Finally, you could pass work onto third parties in exchange for what is called a finder's fee. This could be a one-off fee or a percentage of the first invoice, perhaps.

TAXES

You will want to enlist the services of an accountant who has experience with the tax needs of a small business and one who can cope with the fact you are not local and may have foreign business in other currencies. And you'll also want to meet with him or her as you set up the business, not at the end of the tax year when it's too late to develop the proper record keeping system and tax saving measures that you should have been applying from day one. You don't want to undermine your great idea and start by not having adequately accounted and paid for the appropriate taxes.

VAT

In some countries your service may be liable to value added tax, or some other equivalent. VAT is a percentage that must be added to your invoices and it differs from country to country. Not only must you add this to your invoices, but you can claim a tax rebate for VAT from goods purchased for your business too. VAT rules vary from country to country and in some it is optional until your business has a turnover of more than a certain amount per annum. Make sure you know the rules that apply where you are operating and strictly follow them. You don't want a sloppy approach here to haunt you once you are wildly successful.

Other considerations

TIME MANAGEMENT

Time management can be a real problem for the less organised. If you are working for yourself, your time will be your own and, for this very reason, you will have to structure it. In many jobs, we structure our time based on the job description, or on the organisation's priorities, which have been handed to us by our boss or those above him. When you have your own business, you need to structure your time based on your own priorities. This can become even more complicated if you're trying to take advantage of the fact you are in control of how you spend your time and apportion less time on work than your business requires. Yes, it's great you have the flexibility to attend a school play or take long lunches with friends. But you need to consider setting limits and boundaries too. In some ways, the needs of your clients will also help you set priorities, limits and boundaries.

'Anyone who is serious about building a sustainable and profitable business needs to be sure they are spending their time and energy on the right things. Are you beginning to see that a long to-do list that isn't prioritised with actions that aren't connected to actual dates for completion isn't efficient?

'It can be scary to integrate your to-do list into your calendar and I promise, it is worth it. What do you have to lose? Try it and if it doesn't work you can always go back to the never-ending list of things that never get done. Stop living in denial about what you can realistically get done and choose to plan and execute profitable actions that will grow your business.'

Stephanie Ward, *www.fireflycoaching.com*

Priorities and balance

Few things sap motivation more than an impossible workload. Life throws the unexpected at us too, and we need to ensure we have enough slack in our time schedule to be able to cope with emergencies, urgent jobs or ill children. If you aim to write a manageable number of tasks into your weekly and monthly lists then you can keep your motivation and optimism alive. In addition, we find that while some plans sound fine, it is only when we see them on paper we realise we have bitten off more than we can chew. Hence the value in having all these lists and charts printed out.

Make sure too, that you plan time off in advance, a short lunch break, opportunities for fresh air and to recharge your batteries. Be aware you may need a mixture of solitary and less solitary activities, so try to create a balance. When I (Jo) worked from home and lived alone in my mid twenties, I would make a point of taking a good walk each lunchtime and plan social activities for the evening. Now I live with my family, yet also work from home much of the time, I know myself well enough to realise I can only handle going out two or three evenings a week, and business trips abroad can only happen once a month. Equally, I realise I work best alone, in silence and I dislike interruptions. However, as an extrovert I need the company of other people regularly in order to feel energised and connected. Because of this I try to plan my weeks so I have time for being alone as well as time to be with other people. I have found that while writing provides the solitude I crave, teaching and consultancy provide the lively atmosphere I welcome too. Read more about work-life balance in *Chapter 8 — For the Journey.*

Accessibility

Email, mobile phones and other labour saving devices only serve to make us busier than ever. It's increasingly difficult to switch off. It is not uncommon for people to receive more than 200 emails a day. Luckily spam filters are very effective these days, but you will need to discipline yourself to set different priorities for what email you read when. Maybe you could try to answer emails only once or twice a day, or perhaps to not allow yourself to log on until you have done at least three hours of work? Switch off your mobile phone at weekends or in the evenings. If you're one of those people who always attempts to respond to every message you receive then you'll find your inbox rarely reduces in size as your recipients, in turn, reply to you — even if it's a simple 'thank you'! Give yourself permission to let someone else have the last word.

> 'It's a fact that the key to successful time management is discipline.'
>
> **Carol, American in Saudi Arabia, *http://delhi4cats.wordpress.com*
> and *www.expatwomen.com***

Goals and structure

When transitioning to a new location and looking for opportunities, it's important to use your time management skills. You are faced with days and weeks that seem wide open and you can fill any way you choose. This is the gift you long for when your agenda is full and it is also a potential burden as you seek to fill those days now without your usual activities. I (Colleen) watched a program once where individuals described the experience of going on an extended retreat where their time was completely their own. All of them went through a period of disillusionment, even depression, and then they re-emerged with their own daily structure. They needed to give their day some structure to avoid the energy drain of having to make choices for every moment of the day.

Here are some tips:

1. Structure your day and create your own balanced routine that reflects your desired lifestyle, needs and energy levels.
2. Align your daily structure with your personal and professional goals.
3. Recognise a transition takes energy and you may not get as much done as you are used to: set realistic goals as to how much you can accomplish and include breaks, treats and rewards for yourself.
4. Eat meals on time and at the table (not in front of the TV), or take healthy food along.
5. Get enough sleep and exercise.
6. Schedule time with others as well as time alone.

Here are some tools to help you organise your time:

Organisers

In your diary, online agenda or other scheduler, you'll want to map out your days and weeks very carefully, with adequate time allowed to transition from the business to the personal and to get from appointment to appointment. Remember: You cannot fill every blank space with an activity.

A good planner can cover several essential functions. Between two covers it can house monthly, weekly and daily schedules, daily To Do lists, records of each day's significant events, an address book and more.

I (Colleen) use the colour categories in Outlook to be able to easily identify different projects as well as personal activities. It keeps my to-do list in front of me and reminds me of things I need to do on a one-off or regular basis. It helps me see if there is a good work-life balance and it helps me to prioritize. I love that I can easily shift items around so my agenda becomes the diary of what I actually did and how long it took.

Notes

When you go to meetings, do you take along a lined note pad or your tablet? Do you have another pad or book by the telephone, and another where you jot down leads or ideas? If you're anything like us, you will either rarely get around to sorting out all these pieces of paper, or you will forget where you've put important notes. If, instead, you take to using a large format lined hard backed book, and use this same book for all those notes, ideas and messages, you will find it much easier to trace your movements, find a telephone number or remember what exactly it was you promised to do at a meeting with a potential client.

Lists

They say you have more chance of meeting your goals if you write them down so I (Jo) use a number of other lists too. First I write my tasks for the coming year or more onto the Long Term Master Plan sheet, then I transfer a few of each onto the Monthly Task sheet. At the start of each month I divide the monthly tasks between the available weeks. You can find samples of my charts on www.careerinyoursuitcase. com. I (Colleen) am visual and find when I can see things, I remember them and they get done.

Regardless of the tools you prefer, it is important for entrepreneurs to plan, take notes, keep records, and stay organised.

Career in your suitcase weekly planner

On the following page is a weekly planner. Schedule your time so you have the right balance for yourself between solitary activities and time with others, exercise, productive time, time to invest in learning and personal growth. Use a specific colour for each kind of activity so you can easily see how your time is balanced between activities. Schedule the appropriate activities for your natural rhythm: when do you have more energy for certain activities and when do you have less? Remember when you are 'working from home' that you can work in a much more concentrated way than if you were in an office. Don't expect yourself to work eight hours at such a concentrated pace. Pay attention to these factors when developing your daily and weekly structure.

Here is an example of how it could be filled in. Obviously you will need to take your own realities, fixed activities (e.g. school drop off and pick up times) and priorities into account.

Time	Monday	Tuesday	Wednesday	Thursday	Friday	Saturday	Sunday	
6 a.m.								
7	Get up & ready; breakfast; kids to school if applicable	Get up & ready; breakfast; kids to school if applicable	Get up & ready; breakfast; kids to school if applicable	Get up & ready; breakfast; kids to school if applicable	Get up & ready; breakfast; kids to school if applicable			
8	Exercise	Read the news, emails	Exercise	Read the news, emails	Exercise			
9	Shower and prep for the day	Brainstorm opportunities coming out in the news	Shower and prep for the day	Brainstorm opportunities coming out in the news	Shower and prep for the day	Brunch	Brunch	
10	Plan meals, make grocery list	Goal related activities	Read the news, emails	Goal related activities	Read the news, emails			
11	Buy groceries		Brainstorm opportunities coming out in the news		Brainstorm opportunities coming out in the news			
12	Blue Sky Team Lunch and weekly meeting	Lunch	Lunch	Lunch	Lunch			
13	Review goals as a group	Take a walk		Take a walk		Hobby		
14	Read the news, emails Brainstorm opportunities coming out in the news	Reading for personal growth; research opportunities	Coffee date	Reading for personal growth; research opportunities	Coffee date			
15	Devise action plan for week	Reading for personal growth; research opportunities		Reading for personal growth; research opportunities				
16	Goal related activities	Household tasks		Household tasks				
17								

If seeing a schedule like this gives you a case of claustrophobia, remember it's meant to be a guideline and you can always shift things around according to how life unfolds and according to the opportunities that serendipitously come along and according to your energy levels on a given day or time of day. What it does is give you a sense of your ideal day and week and assign appropriate time to your priorities. Give it a try on the next page. Copies of this form can be downloaded from *www.careerinyoursuitcase.com.*

'You do need to be a very motivated, dedicated and determined person otherwise you would never get anything done. I planned my day the night before — listing what I wanted to achieve and then would make sure I would get those items completed (my plan also included the household chores and so the daily plan was very realistic and included things that were important to my 'wellbeing' and work life balance such as friends and exercise.'

Victoria, New Zealander in India, *www.expatwomen.com*

Time	Monday	Tuesday	Wednesday	Thursday	Friday	Saturday	Sunday
6 a.m.							
7							
8							
9							
10							
11							
12							
13							
14							
15							
16							
17							

WORK LOCATION

It is not a given anymore that if you don't work for someone else that you must work from home or set up your own independent location. Flexible work spaces are increasingly available that allow entrepreneurs to work from an office location with other entrepreneurs and book only the amount of office hours they need or want. This allows for connections to be made, collaboration to happen, exchange of ideas and provides an antidote to the sometimes lonely pursuit of working for yourself. Visit *www.loosecubes.com* for one business model and if you have a work location with extra space, consider opening offering to a loosecubes member. Google flexible workspace or entrepreneur workspace and follow your leads.

Working From Home

With a home-based business, you have the perfect opportunity to set up the exact environment with the right business tools at your disposal. With today's technology, a highly technical home office operation can be set up at relatively low cost. These things are all possible, but they don't fall into place automatically. As you read earlier in this chapter, to start any successful business, you need to plan. And for the home-based business you need to think particularly about how you will structure and balance the priorities of home and family without each one intruding on the other or suffering in some way.

One advantage of commuting to an office is there's a natural separation between the 'working' you and the 'at home' you, with some transition time in the car or train to change roles. In the home-based business, you have to work harder to delineate and differentiate these roles — but it can be done and the work/life balance can be significantly enhanced. So it's important to create a working environment for yourself that will make you feel professional and will help you switch roles easily.

You can start thinking about what you want in your home office before you even arrive at a new location. What follows are a few helpful hints.

Home office checklist:

- ☐ Identify the space requirements for your home office
- ☐ What equipment do you need:
  - ○ Computer
  - ○ Printer
  - ○ Software
  - ○ Separate telephone number
  - ○ Ergonomic office furniture
  - ○ Internet connection
  - ○ Wireless router or network
- ☐ Technical support
- ☐ Virtual assistant support
- ☐ Financial administration support

Family matters

Because your family is in such close proximity to your business, you will have to manage them as well. You need to let them know when you are at work and when you are free to attend to family matters. Not to do so can interrupt your concentration on your business and result in dissatisfaction and grumbling among family members. Don't make them feel that they never know when they can ask you for a simple favour. Have a chat with your partner or significant other before you start your business. Discuss how your respective roles will change once your business gets rolling. How will household responsibilities be adjusted? How will child care arrangements change? Will you need your partner to be available during evening hours for some childcare if your business schedule demands some evening time? This is not as simple an arrangement as a family with one wage earner and a stay-at-home partner, nor is it even as simple as the typical two-career couple (and no one ever said *that* was really simple). This is a brand new working arrangement and it can bring your marital relationship much happiness or dissension depending on how you communicate to structure it.

You also need to take time out from the business. Remember, one of the advantages of the home-based business is the time flexibility it offers. But if you let the business run *you*, you'll soon find it affecting your partner relationship and your own sense of wellbeing. No one is going to give you a specified holiday period. You have to allot this to yourself and plan it to coincide with your partner's holiday schedule. And like a standard two career couple, you have to make time in the week to spend quality time together and coordinate with each other to ensure all the home and family responsibilities are covered.

Kids are another matter. They may be the most important reason why you elected to work from home. But you cannot expect work and life to fall into balance because you are home. However, you will be more in control and be in closer proximity to family in times of need or crisis.

I (Colleen) have chosen to limit the hours I work from home to the amount of day-care I was willing to have my son in during his pre-school years. I didn't see myself juggling child care and working during the same times and didn't want my son to feel he wasn't as important as my work. However, one advantage of juggling both together, if you have a nanny or your children are able to play independently while you work from home, is your children can see what you do all day. They get to know the whole person you are, the working self and the family self. And children can even give you ideas or contribute effort to your business. It helps to be realistic about the effect a home based business will have on children of different ages and the effect the children will have on the business.

The home-based business can be a true blessing to the parent responsible for a baby, toddler or pre-schooler. These are the years when a child is most dependent, and the most emotionally difficult for parents who must work. During this stage, though, you must be flexible to the needs of the child. For younger children, crying and feeding usually can't wait long for a response. You may not need all day childcare, but you might want some help during peak activity periods (your business' or your child's). The child in the middle years (five or six to twelve) is in school most of the day. Your flexible at-home schedule can make for a more relaxed morning routine. You don't have to rush around like a crazy person, trying to get yourself ready for work and your children ready for school by 7:30 am. And if they miss the bus, you can take them to school without being late for work yourself.

A child of this age needs to be taught the boundaries of the business. You may be at home, but you're also at work. The child needs to know when one begins and the other ends. Let him know your office schedule - and that when you are in your office, you can only be interrupted for emergencies. Set some ground rules. Maybe you could suggest they may interrupt you only in the case of 'blood or fire' as one stay at home novelist mother would stipulate when her children were small.

The high school child can understand these boundaries better and is more self-sufficient. One was even heard to comment: 'I like it when Mum is holed up in her home office. It keeps her out of my hair.' On the other hand, you can enlist the child of this age to help with the business. The caveat here is the help should be mostly voluntary (a little prodding is allowed for all parents) and it should represent a true contribution to the business that matches the child's skills and age level. A seven year-old can stamp envelopes, an 11 year-old can sort index cards alphabetically and a 16-year-old can probably give you some pointers on setting up your computer system and using the software.

'I have had a home office twice, first after my first pregnancy leave and now.

'After having my first child, I had negotiated with my employer that I would work 1 day 1/2 from home. I managed to convince them by acting very professional and putting together a "case": a Word document of 50 pages with the benefits of working from home and many success stories. BUT reality seemed a bit more difficult. It worked pretty well till my baby was 6 months old but became impossible afterwards. My baby wanted of course to be with me and was making very sweet noises that sounded quite inappropriate during my conference calls. Also, I had many interruptions to feed her, change her nappy. At the end, I was feeling like I had to work 10 hours to accomplish work requiring 5 hours. In the end the benefit of being with my child was becoming a huge stress. I think that a home office does not really work with small children at home unless you have a nanny to help you.

'I also work now exclusively from home. My two kids go to school so the house is very quiet. Now the problem is the opposite: it is too quiet and I sometimes feel rather isolated. I managed to sort this problem by working a bit at the nearby Starbucks. Working from home is a big plus: I work when I want to work. Perfect for a mum with small kids.

'I tend to work a lot at night, which could be a problem but I am working for my own business so I am happy to do that!'

Jasmine, French in China, *www.inspiredbeijing.com* and
www.expatwomen.com

'We run our business from home and from an office located a few miles away, but we need to be in constant communication with several other countries as well so having Internet connections is vital. We are in the process of starting an Internet-based business as well, and the beauty of this is that it can literally be run from a beach in the Bahamas or your front room. I can't imagine being without a computer within a few yards of me at all times. It's great to be able to have a meal bubbling on the stove while I work in the office and yet can keep an eye on what's going on in the kitchen.'

Diane, Canadian in England, *www.expatwomen.com*

'I appreciated the convenience (and the commute) of having the office in the home but at the same time, because it was within the corporate residence, the company corporate headquarters always expected me to be readily available in spite of the 11 hour time difference.'

Carol, American in Saudi Arabia, *http://delhi4cats.wordpress.com*

'I have a designated work-space, which is off-limits of the rest of the family, so to convey the sense of "I-am-at-work" to the others. But the reality is that working from home, no matter how virtually connected you are still in many ways lacks the human enriching experience of the "coffee-machine gathering", where you learn and stay on top of everything by being exposed to other people's problems, views and interests.

'The hardest part is to combine social availability with work schedule. In my network few people work and they have got the time and the desire to pop-in, therefore finding the right balance is essential to avoid being removed from the social scene for lack of response and yet prevent to be overwhelmed by it. After all who would not trade a menial web-research for a nice chat with a friend while strolling along the Seine?

'Also, recognise the importance of the work-mode: think of it as funny, but when I have important meeting online, I dress up as if I were to show up in a conference room. It helps me focus and gear up for the conversation to come.'

Patrizia, Italian in France, *www.paguro.net*

'Use your office space only for your work. Don't take your laptop to the other parts of your home. Separate your work from your personal life.'

Ursula, South African in America, *www.marketingmentorexpert.com* and *www.expatwomen.com*

'I love the 15 second commute from my bedroom to my "office", in the morning, as well as the casual dress code. Pajamas or jeans are acceptable forms of attire many days of the week.

'Currently I have clients in 14 countries. Because of this, I work with 80% of them on the phone or through video chat (I am set up with VoIP and a wireless Internet connection). This means I can work wherever I can take my laptop – even out on my terrace when the weather is nice. Technically, I am completely portable, so my office is more of a virtual office than a home office.'

Megan, American in Italy, *www.careerbychoice.com*

'For about a year I worked from home helping Brits obtain financing for homes in the States. The down side was that I felt isolated and not part of a team. Something I particularly like. I would also find myself doing housework in between working.'

Lizzy, British in America, *www.expatwomen.com*

Chapter 7: Resources for Working for Yourself

A Robbins, *Unlimited Power,* Free Press

C Barrow , G Golzen & H Kogan, *The Daily Telegraph Guide to Taking Up a Franchise,* Kogan-Page

D Chopra, Synchrodestiny: *Harnessing the infinite power of coincidence to create miracles,* Rider Books

DP Moore & EH Buttner, *Women Entrepreneurs: moving beyond the glass ceiling,* Sage Publications

DP Moore, *Careerpreneurs: lessons from leading women entrepreneurs on building a career without boundaries,* Davies-Black Publishing

G Courtenay, *How to Write Sales Letters with Clout,*

Government of Alberta, Human Services, Self-Employment: Is It For Me?, *www.alis.alberta.ca/publications*

I Halsall, *NLP 4U,* Lloyd West Publishing

J Parfitt & J Tillyard, *Grow Your Own Networks,* Summertime Publishing

J Parfitt, *Definite Articles,* Summertime Publishing

J Parfitt, *Expat Entrepreneur,* Lean Marketing Press

J Scala, *25 Natural Ways to Manage Stress and Avoid Burnout,* McGraw-Hill Trade

K Matheny & C McCarthy, *Write Your Own Prescription for Stress,* New Harbinger Publications

LR Kohls, *Survival Kit for Overseas Living*, Nicholas Brealey with Intercultural Press

M Chapman, *Emotional Intelligence Pocketbook*

M Gerber, *The Emyth,* Harper Business

M Seligman, *Flourish Nicholas*, Brealey Publishing

M Seligman, *Learned Optimism,* Knopf Doubleday Publishing Group

N Snelling and G Hunt, *Laptop Entrepreneur,* Summertime Publishing

P Kurtz, *The Global Speaker,* Amacom

S Covey, *The Seven Habits of Highly Effective People,* Free Press

T Ferriss, *The Four Hour Workweek,* Crown Publishing Group

TL Friedman, *The World is Flat,* Penguin Books

V Peale, *The Power of Positive Thinking,* Simon & Schuster

'Life is change. Growth is optional. Choose wisely.'

Karen Kaiser Clark

Chapter EIGHT

For the Journey

Change

Change is a constant element of life. To think otherwise is to invite disillusionment. Kids grow and change constantly. In adults the process slows down, but it continues. The stability the workforce had a few years ago is no longer the reality for most. Finding work-life balance is often elusive when responding to and initiating change. And stress accompanies change.

Two kinds of change

There are two kinds of change: voluntary and involuntary. Voluntary change is something you have actively chosen, such as accepting a promotion, starting your own business or relocating to another country. Involuntary change is caused by events beyond your control. Being laid off or experiencing the death of a loved one are examples of change that happens to you. They are not mutually exclusive and how you perceive an event influences whether or not you categorize it as voluntary or involuntary.

When I (Colleen) moved to the Netherlands I did so of my own free will. Some of the consequences of this move I didn't actively, knowingly, choose. For example, retaking my driving theory and practical exams in order to have a driver's license was not an active choice on my part. I perceived them to be involuntary changes resulting from the change I voluntarily made. However, I could still take action to deal with them effectively.

Relocation and change

Relocation creates change on at least three levels according to Galen Tinder of REA:

Physical relocation: Logistical details of selling or renting a house, securing housing in the new location, packing and transporting family goods and the endless but necessary tasks of 'settling in'

Family relocation: The entire family needs to adjust to everything being different in the new location. Nearly every aspect of common family life changes -

314

daily routines, schools, service providers, and friendships. Children will need various kinds of extra attention according to their age and the move itself

Social and emotional relocation: It is a time of saying goodbye to friends and to familiar and beloved places — a time, in other words, of loss

People who have moved within and across borders agree foreign relocations make the heaviest demands on a person's emotional resources due in large part to the language and cultural changes experienced.

'In a country like Egypt you need to have unlimited reserves of patience, as things simply don't happen overnight or in the way you expect. Whatever your time-line is, it'll be best to double it! It's also crucial to have someone who has the ability to speak the language, preferably a local, as misunderstandings are inevitable if you do business in English only.'

Diane, Canadian in England, *www.expatwomen.com*

'It is a not to be missed opportunity. Come with an open mind and not your predisposed concepts of the world. This way you will leave with a box of ideas. It is a time for you to discover your ability to add value to your environment and those around you.'

Ogbah Sokoh, Nigeria

Change and transition

William Bridges, an organisational psychologist who has studied and written on how people react to change, differentiates between change and transition. Change consists of external events, while transition is the set of internal processes we go through in adjusting to change.

THE TRANSITION PROCESS

Bridges observes that most people react to change by making an inner transition of three distinct stages — *Endings, a Neutral Zone* and *New Beginnings.* In other words, a transition starts with an ending and ends with a new beginning. People achieve successful transitions when they adjust to change through the healthy navigation of each of these three transition stages. When we fail to accomplish the essential tasks of each stage, we can get stuck in an incomplete and unsatisfying transition characterised by prolonged stress and maladjustment.

Broadly speaking, *Endings* consist of saying goodbye and leaving. *The Neutral Zone* is a way station between departing from one place and arriving at another. This is where we pause to gather our energy and inner resources for stage three. *New Beginnings* signal the stage of investing energy in our new world.

Here are several of the most common 'sticking' points in this three stage process as described by Galen Tinder of REA.

Endings

For most people, the endings stage of relocation begins when the final decision has been made. At this point, whether we realise it or not, we begin to disengage psychologically from the place we're leaving. This disengagement begins subtly, becoming more conscious and intentional as we grow closer to the move.

When we prepare to move we're confronted with a combination of logistical and emotional challenges. We tackle a seemingly endless list of tasks that come with uprooting ourselves from one place and settling into a new 'world' in which we are a stranger. At the same time, we typically feel a sense of loss about everything we are leaving behind, not only the concrete places but also a way of life.

These feelings are natural and normal. They're part of ending our relationship with the tangibles of a given place. We may fear that if we give such feelings the recognition they deserve, they will exhaust us and leave us no energy for the future. True, strong emotions like sadness and fear can tire us out over the short term. But this stage clears the way for healing, a newfound energy and a creative engagement in our new location. Over the longer haul, it is the feelings we don't acknowledge that wear us down.

The truth is, life involves discomfort and it includes painful feelings, especially at points of ending. A healthy reaction is to feel fully and move through them, not around them, talking about them with people who understand us. This will help prevent us from getting emotionally stuck in the old location while our bodies and our lives have moved to the new one.

> 'I felt unfulfilled… while working I felt that I made a difference, I contributed to the success of companies, and all of a sudden I had this empty feeling. I missed my colleagues, peers and my clients. I felt I didn't belong.'
>
> **Ursula, South African in America, *www.marketingmentorexpert.com* and *www.expatwomen.com***

What can help us say goodbye? Every year thousands of domestically and internationally relocating families have discovered that parting rituals don't have to be fancy to be helpful. A last visit to a favourite pizza parlour, a romp at the local playground, visits to important sites like schools, and special goodbye times with friends are examples of simple, but effective, leave-taking rituals. Some children host a goodbye party for their friends a week or two before the move. What is important is that the ending is acknowledged and marked in a meaningful way.

The neutral zone

This period occupies the middle stage of transition; it begins with the departure from the old home and extends into the initial period of resettlement. Its duration varies anywhere from one to several months.

The *Neutral Zone* is often marked by a sense of dislocation and anxiety. Change means heading into unfamiliar territory, and during this passage it's common to confront a feeling of emptiness. People often feel in limbo; they miss their familiar surroundings but haven't yet planted firm roots in the new area. During this period family members are especially vulnerable to disappointment as they find their new location doesn't offer the same features, attractions and apparent advantages they had appreciated 'back home'.

Despite its unsettling aspects, the *Neutral Zone* provides time for rejuvenation, self-examination and redirected focus. In the *Neutral Zone* people discover new talents and passions, and a capacity for closer, more rewarding relationships. It is in this neutral zone that completing the exercises suggested in *Chapter 2 — Find Your Passion* can be most helpful. Take the gift of time at this stage to do the inner work of reflecting on who you are and begin the external process of exploring your options. Create a temporary elevator pitch for this time so when answering the question 'And what do you do?' you don't feel the emptiness of the ending or the pressure to find a new beginning before its time.

We may need to make time for the *Neutral Zone*, settling into the new location at a reasonable pace without feeling as though we must master the entirety of our new environment in the first week. We give ourselves a gift by not pressing hard towards premature new beginnings. No, our goal is not to dawdle. It's to break away from our incessant doing and to create space in our minds and our lives for self-discovery and creativity; to create space for a new beginning.

New beginnings

Veteran movers learn the unpacking of their belongings scarcely concludes their relocation. Experience teaches them it takes six to nine months to functionally acclimatise to their new world. In her book *Beyond the Sky and the Earth*, Jamie Zeppa described it as the difference between arrival and entry. Entry is the new beginning, when you suddenly realise you did something easily without thinking. Something which was a real challenge for you when you first arrived. I (Colleen) remember how nice it was to drive somewhere again and not have to carefully read every sign along the way. Prior to moving, I had taken for granted being able to recognise place names on signs by the shape of the words and not having to read every letter. Trying to fully read road signs in Dutch had left me feeling over stimulated on road trips.

So it can be difficult to pinpoint where the Neutral Zone merges into New Beginnings. But at some point people look back and realise they've made the shift. It will happen for you too. '[Not having work made me feel] devastated and insecure. I have worked all my life by choice and I did not know how to easily adapt to finding myself at home and without a job when I first arrived in the Kingdom. After allowing a "reasonable period" for self-pity I then gave myself a harsh pep talk and put together my action plan in marketing myself, my qualifications and making contacts.'

Carol, American, *http://delhi4cats.wordpress.com* and
www.expatwomen.com

People who work through their fear of change and resistance to it will have more success making desired personal changes. People who bring this capacity for self-change to meet the challenges of external change are rewarded with a rich and dynamic life.

People who manage change well are those who can make and accept changes in themselves. When a major change appears on the horizon, they're not immune from normal feelings like fear, sadness and anger. But by facing and expressing these feelings, they move towards the future with hope and a sense of adventure.

Think of a transition you have gone through in the past five years that you would say is 'behind you'. Answer the following questions about this transition.

1. How did you feel when things ended?

20 mins

_____

_____

_____

_____

2. How did you feel in between, before the new beginning was in sight and identified?

_____

_____

_____

_____

3. How did you feel when you had found the new beginning?

_____

_____

_____

_____

4. What insights from that transition could you apply to help you be successful in your current transition?

_____

_____

_____

_____

'Not having any work in the first eight months after moving to Beijing with my family was extremely hard for me. Not only had I lost my professional identity but also a sense of where I was going. I started losing my self-confidence and would only speak to women at the evening social gatherings my husband and I were attending. I suddenly thought that if I was not working, I had nothing very interesting to share with the gentlemen. Obviously I was wrong.'

'It was actually after one of those evenings that I realised how bad I was feeling about myself. I then took the decision to start my own business and by then save myself from depression.'

Jasmine, French in China, *www.inspiredbeijing.com* and
www.expatwomen.com

'Expatriates often sense their differences from the local community, but a couple consisting of a working woman and an accompanying male partner is likely to be different not only from the local community, but from the rest of the expatriate community too. This complete sense of difference can be an isolating experience and can become problematic, especially for the male accompanying partner who doesn't even have his job to base their joint identity on. Problems are most likely to arise when the male accompanying partner feels undervalued by his partner and friends, or when he suffers from a loss of self-esteem and subsequent depression due to his change in situation.'

Huw Francis, *Author of Live and Work Abroad: A Guide for Modern*
Nomads

The Challenge Of Change

To paraphrase the international bestselling psychiatrist, M Scott Peck, author of *The Road Less Travelled,* change is difficult. Add to that statement the reality that life is change. It is growing from one stage to another, learning and accepting the changes that accompany each stage. Whether it is changing ourselves or adjusting to changes in external circumstances, our relationship with change engages our vital energies. Change is something our bodies are designed to minimize; they like a 'steady state'. This is what Susan Jeffers in her book *Feel the Fear and Do it Anyway,* tells us. So when you are initiating change in your life, it's quite possible you will work against yourself in some ways. This is normal and to be expected.

Using the tools listed below can help increase your awareness of how you are resisting change, help you make a plan to address the resistance and get the most out of the changes you are going through.

Blogging, journaling and your lifestory

Writing can help you process and put into perspective what is happening in your life. Take the time and value your experience and your story enough to put it down on paper. It is a tool for you to use to help you gain insights, become more conscious of the choices you are making, how they reflect your values and the effect they are having on how your life is unfolding. Review the writing techniques described in *Chapter 2 — Find Your Passion,* on writing Lifestory and Shining Moments.

Portfolio

On days when you feel you are not doing well, looking back at your achievements will remind you how great you can be. As described in *Chapter 6 - Marketing Your Skills,* a portfolio can be a key tool for you during these times.

Creating a portable career, work search, starting to run your own business and adapting to changes all take hard work. Of course you will have down times, and times when you feel like giving up and retreating from the world. Self-motivation is one of the key attributes required by anyone who repeatedly has to reinvent themselves, or pick up a temporarily shelved career. Margaret Chapman, author of *The Emotional Intelligence Pocketbook,* recommends four essential actions you can take to stay self-motivated. She suggests we employ positive self-talk, think about our inspirational mentors or role models, create an environment which lifts our spirits and build our own support network or hire a coach.

Successful changers have often developed these skills in order to deal with change — changes they initiate as well as changes outside their control. They are attitudes or ways of thinking which can be learned and help you respond well to change. See the techniques for coping with stress later in this chapter for more approaches for handling stress and change.

RESILIENCE

Studies are showing one of the keys to successfully dealing with change and transition, as well as life's other challenges, is something called resilience. We have mentioned it several times throughout this book as a key skill for your career development. What do you do when Plan A doesn't come together? When your computer dies with your masterpiece business plan or CV unsaved?

Duncan Westwood, director of Expat Care for International Health Management in Toronto, believes that you can look to your past for inspiration. If you look back to other times when you have failed but managed to pull through, you should be able to identify the actions you took and the traits you demonstrated that pulled you through.

I (Jo) attended a workshop by Duncan at the 2011 Families in Global Transition conference on the subject of resilience and did the exercises he gave us. As a result, I discovered that my own resilience tactic was to allow myself not to be perfect. As a writer and editor, I know that it is really bad to put out work that contains errors. However, I know that to achieve perfection is almost impossible.

I published my novel, *Sunshine Soup*, in 2011, after having paid three separate proof readers to check it for me. I discovered mistakes in it and received lots of, ahem 'helpful' feedback. So, I pulled the book, corrected the mistakes and republished. In order to be 100 percent sure of accuracy I asked more than 10 people to proof read it. They each came back with approximately 20 errors – only those errors were not the same 20. There were actually over 100 errors. Such a 'failure' could be considered a good reason to quit my profession, but after much scrutiny I realised that I can accept being 98% accurate with my own work. I am only human after all, and I had tried my best to ensure the book would be error free.

This ability to pick yourself up and start again is the stuff of resilience. It is what some people call 'bouncebackability'.

I have accepted that it is okay to get things wrong and that I am humble enough to take the criticism but am always prepared to fix those mistakes and carry on.

Each time I have moved countries, I have found that I feel impotent and disorientated in the new location. I have failed time and again and certainly been less than perfect. After admitting defeat, asking for help and accepting that it is okay not to be bionic, I have been able to stand tall and keep on going. This is the stuff of resilience.

What you believe about the world, as you explored in *Chapter 4 — Creating Your Career* will influence your thoughts and reactions to adverse situations when they occur. The ability to make a shift in thinking, to actively choose a way of seeing the event from a potential benefit perspective, one which helps you find constructive actions for yourself, will ultimately influence the results that event will create. Flexibility and adaptability are two fundamental elements of resilience.

CULTURAL INTELLIGENCE

Cultural intelligence or CQ also plays a role in your ability to adjust to a new culture. A 2010 study by Regula Sindemann, as described in the February 2012 Expat Women blog, provides some insights. CQ is defined as one's ability to function effectively in culturally diverse situations. This study found a significant correlation between CQ and the expressed satisfaction level of expat spouses and partners. CQ motivation, strategy and action all play an important role, in many cases more important than CQ knowledge alone. Learned capabilities are emphasized in CQ more than personality traits. It is encouraging to know CQ can be influenced by experience and training and can therefore be learned. Your CQ will have an influence on how effectively you will cope in your new location and it will free up the energy and clarity you need to create your portable career.

'Living in different cultures as a child and as an adult was an unbelievably enriching experience and has brought me opportunities I could never have imagined. Perhaps the most important of all an open mind and a conviction that there is always someone around who can help, if you only start talking and asking for what it is that you need.'

Jutta, Dutch in Singapore, on LinkedIn Group: Expat Web

LEARNING THE LANGUAGE

One thing you can do to set you ahead of the game is to learn the local language. Culture and language are inseparable. The key to understanding most cultures lies in the languages spoken there. The standard greeting in most Asian countries is 'have you eaten rice yet?' What does this tell you about the importance of food in these cultures? Yet, strangely, many expatriates will decide learning the local language is unnecessary, too much work, impossible, or all three and not attempt it. Showing a curiosity for the local people and their culture through learning the language demonstrates respect for them and where you are now living.

Mary Farmer has lived and worked in six different countries and speaks the languages of all of them. 'I do not consider myself gifted linguistically,' she says, 'but I am both motivated and stubborn. And as a media addict, I could not conceive of living happily in a place where I couldn't even read the local newspaper. I'm also convinced that forcing everyone in your vicinity to speak your language raises an insurmountable barrier between you and your new neighbours, colleagues and so on, and that you will never truly feel at home. And a final motivator: cultural experts have proven that being surrounded by an unfamiliar language for a long period of time almost always leads to alienation, paranoia and culture shock. Yes, perhaps you are the topic of conversation in the market when everyone suddenly bursts into riotous laughter - but wouldn't you rather know for certain? And wouldn't you rather be able to laugh along with them?'

Choose a course of language study which suits your learning style and don't be dissuaded by the inevitable naysayers around you. Imagine how you would feel if you had been living in a foreign country for five years and were still unable to speak the language, only to see Jane-Just-Come (that's you) blithely master the tongue in months?

'I spoke the language, but, if you don't want to end up as a secretary for some export office, it's best to learn the language. Take an intensive course. This is your greatest tool in getting the job you want. Not knowing the language means you will always have a problem inserting yourself in a local company.'

Lisa, British in Italy, *http://burntbythetuscansun.blogspot.com*
and *www.expatwomen.com*

'When I moved to Beijing with my husband and my two kids, I thought that finding a job in China – land of opportunities – should be no problem. After all, I had 7 years work experience as a UK chartered accountant and had worked in Paris, London and Zurich in prestigious companies. But I soon realised after our move that Beijing was already flooded with local, BILINGUAL number crunchers. When I was telling recruitment companies that I could speak French, German and English but not Mandarin, they used to tell me "Poor you, we are really sorry, but you have really NO chance. Learn Mandarin for 1 year and then come back to us".'

Jasmine, French in China, *www.inspiredbeijing.com* and
www.expatwomen.com

'Naturally without having fluency in the Arabic language results in communication gaps and loss of revenue. In my capacity as a founding partner of Global Watchers Arabia the focus at present is predominantly on the expat community within Saudi Arabia and clients from the rest of the English-speaking world […] any business with a Saudi company requires discussions and written communication in Arabic, especially in regards to legal documents and contracts. Therefore to pursue and interact with Saudi clients results in GWA having to engage fee-for-task consultants who are native Arabic speakers to represent GWA with non-English speaking clients.

Carol, American, *http://delhi4cats.wordpress.com* and
www.expatwomen.com

'I was not as expressive in English as in Afrikaans. I couldn't make fast progress in my career, because I couldn't express myself well. Business language in South Africa is different than in the United States.'

Ursula, South African in America, www.marketingmentorexpert.com
and *www.expatwomen.com*

OPTIMISM

Optimism is a key quality needed for successful entrepreneurs. Psychologist Martin Seligman has studied optimism and found it to be a learnable trait. His book, *Learned*

Optimism, and most recent publication, *Flourish*, will teach you his scientifically validated approaches. His website *ww.authentichappiness.com* has free questionnaires you can use to measure your optimism, as well as your signature strengths, hopefulness, work-life and happiness. Also available are links to video recordings of his talks.

Optimistic thinking can make the difference between success and failure in any new venture, especially one with so many obstacles and problems as the launch of a new business.

Positive thinking is not the same as optimism and neither is happiness, but somehow they are all connected. If you want to put more positivity into your life and work think back to your last year of education. Think about the things you enjoyed doing then, but you no longer do now. Try to put at least one of those things back into your life. Try to give yourself ten minutes of 'me time' each day. And when you go to bed at night, think of three things you are grateful for.

POSITIVE SELF-TALK

Most people repeat negative statements to themselves such as 'I hate myself', 'I am stupid' or 'I can't do...' They spend so much of their time focusing on the negative they see faults in everyone as well as themselves. This creates a process called 'self-fulfilling prophecy' and they set themselves up for failure as they get caught in a vicious circle.

Your subconscious doesn't know the difference between a real and an imagined experience. If you keep telling yourself you are going to fail then you will — because the next time you attempt the same thing you will find yourself remembering the previous failure. As soon as you expect to fail, you do. One way out of this self-destructive loop is to condition your mind with positive thoughts, self-talk and affirmations.

An affirmation is a statement you read and repeat throughout your day. If you like you can write yourself notes and post them all over the house, so they are never far from your thoughts.

The requirements for effective and powerful affirmations are that they must:

- Start with the pronoun 'I'
- Be stated positively

- Be in the present tense
- Relate to your goals
- Be visual

For example: 'I, (insert your name) am confident and a competent public speaker'.

For extra emphasis you can try repeating the same basic affirmation but in the second and the third person.

For example: 'You (your name) are confident and a competent public speaker. She (your name) is confident and a competent public speaker.'

The reason for this is that our current views of ourselves tend to be formed by a mixture of what others say about us, what we say to ourselves and what others tell us.

Read your affirmations at least once a day. Alternatively record them and listen to them in the car, before going to bed or first thing in the morning. Stand in front of the bathroom mirror, look yourself directly in the eye and say your affirmations to yourself, ending with 'I love you'. When you are reading or listening to your affirmations, make sure you visualise them in vivid detail. The more clearly and deeply you can visualise, the more you will program the mind to believe it and make it true. If you think you can, you can. Always think and tell yourself you can. A lot of people see themselves in the past or in the present when they read their affirmations and visualise. Try to visualise yourself the way you want to be and make sure you are looking into the future. Don't dwell on the past, unless it is positive and helps build the way you want to be.

If someone instructs you not to think of monkeys, it is impossible not to picture one. Your unconscious mind doesn't recognise negatives. If you ask it not to worry or make a mistake, you are setting yourself up to do just that. Successful people, in particular sports people, know they are more likely to achieve positive results if they focus on positive outcomes. Our thoughts strongly influence our performance. Concentrate on what you really want, and your mind will propel you forward to achieving it. The how will become apparent as you go so you don't need to have it all figured out in advance.

Like negative self-talk, optimism will also create self-fulfilling prophecies. Studies have shown that people with a positive sense of self will work harder and longer, and in turn their perseverance will allow them to do better.

'Have the courage to take a risk. Practise believing the *impossible* until it becomes *possible* and then *actual*. Remember achievers achieve the unachievable,' writes Norman Vincent Peale, author of *The Power of Positive Thinking*.

Work-Life Balance

Work-life balance does not mean having it all. And even when we do manage to 'have it all' we're usually too tired to enjoy it.! A working woman can indeed have a nanny, and a cleaner, and live off ready meals — but business dinners mean missing out on bedtime stories. And then there's the guilt. In her book *Foetal Attraction*, Australian novelist Kathy Lette suggests that when we give birth, a 'guilt gland' appears from nowhere.

For women, the issue of work-life balance rears its head daily, as we race from packing lunchboxes, to school runs, cram in some work, scrabble together supper, then start ferrying children to Brownies, swimming lessons or karate. Action is everything. And it is not until the house is silent that we can flop in front of the television and sigh.

Even if women abroad are not working, balance is no more achievable. And, in many ways, the rollercoaster life of the 'multimover' is even tougher. In order to stay sane, we need to maintain social contact, and fill our time with work, volunteering or learning. Add to the usual list of daily tasks, the need to prepare for and recover from regular moves, and each day can feel like a crisis. Whether we work in the traditional sense, or provide support services to our employed partner and family, what we do outside of 'me-time' must still be regarded, and valued, as work. Keeping soul and home together is a lot like spinning plates. Try to stop *juggling* and start *balancing*.

REAL LIFE SOLUTIONS

I'm the first to admit it is easier to talk about taking time off than asking for permission to go, particularly if the person who gives the permission is you. Years of conditioning have made women, particularly mothers, willing to accept a martyr's role. Read some real-life examples in the text-box below:

'Without setting work hours and a designated workspace it can be more difficult to "leave the office" and "call it a day". Being strict about setting those limits and spaces is important for balancing work and life. In my opinion it is essential to create structure and schedule for your days. Although it is in my nature to plan and schedule (I am a coach after all) for those to whom this does not come

easy, too much unstructured time can lead to procrastination, inefficiency and hence longer working hours. And for extroverts who are energised by working with others, creating opportunities to connect with people if you are at home most of the day by yourself is also important to do. In the end, no matter what your strategy, it really comes down to identifying your priorities, allotting time for them by creating a reasonable schedule, and then keeping to your schedule. You can adjust your schedule as you go along and discover what works in practice. The real challenge is keeping to the schedule. I have found that different people have different blocks — and different strategies for getting around those blocks – to sticking to a plan of action. For me, the benefits of having balance – such as health, peace, opportunity to spend time with friends and my husband – are things that keep me in check. Since I work with expats, I often work with them to identify what drew them to their new home country and find ways to get them to use that interest to engage with their home/community. I find that helps many people find more work/life balance.'

Megan, American in Italy, *www.careerbychoice.com*

'One thing we have begun to insist on is regular holidays. It's so easy to go through a whole year without stopping. Now we book breaks ahead and make sure we work to deadlines to ensure we can get away. The other thing I find important is to have a hobby or interest that is completely different from work. For me it is cooking and reading, as well as walking in the countryside when I can. That offsets the brain-strain a bit.'

Diane, Canadian in England, *www.expatwomen.com*

'If you are considering working from home I suggest you take on board commitment outside of the house that forces you to interact with people. In my case I volunteer for a women's network and organise breakfast events for entrepreneurs, where I work with another lady and seek speakers, decide topics advertise the venue etc. There is a double gain there, I get to meet other entrepreneur and to be exposed to topics I have a keen interest in.'

Patrizia, Italian in France, *www.paguro.net*

STRESS BUSTING

It can be hard to remain calm and stay positive when it's slow going, or when external events get in the way. When things appear not to be going our way it is easy to feel stressed, negative or demotivated. Stress is a normal part of life and something we need. There is 'good' stress and 'bad' stress. All stress releases a mix of hormones and chemicals in your body which can cause physical and psychological damage if they are not brought back into balance.

Gail MacIndoe says the first step to addressing stress is to determine what triggers it for you. Start to notice where the ongoing stress is — is it at the office or at home, with particular people, before certain events, doing a particular task, or when something specific is said to you? Getting problems down on paper sometimes helps to give you a more objective perspective and stops the negative thoughts going round and round in your head.

Once you've identified the source of your stress, you can make a plan to neutralise it. For example, if a client is repeatedly finding fault with your work, do not allow yourself to get repeatedly stressed about it. Why not ask him what you could do to improve your service? If it is a case of him picking on you, try humouring him or ignoring it.

Having identified your stressors, spend some time building coping resources and avoidance strategies. Mary Pritchard, as quoted online in the *Huffington Post* talks about problem-focused coping, avoidant coping, proactive coping and emotion-focused coping. Broadening your toolkit of coping resources will better prepare you to respond to, and prepare for, the various sources of stress for you. This will serve to increase your self-esteem and energise you. Take a look at the following coping strategies and consider which ones may help you.

Coping resource list

When our attention is dominated by a stressful situation we often forget or don't realise we have coping resources. Matheny and McCarthy, authors of *Write Your Own Prescription for Stress (2000),* suggest making a list of possible coping strategies you have used in the past or intend to use in the future. The exercise you just did on transition should have reminded you of some of the coping resources you have used in the past. Then you just have to remember to put them into practice. You possess many skills and resources. Recall past successes and visualise yourself coping. Build your confidence by spending time making an inventory of your resources and thinking about past successes.

Stress diary

James Scala, author of *25 Natural Ways to Manage Stress and Avoid Burnout*, recommends keeping a stress diary. In this way you can identify your stressors, think up solutions and then look back to see how far you have come in eliminating it.

Start by summarising the stressor in general terms using one or two sentences. Then write beneath this how your stress manifests itself. Perhaps you have headaches, stomach aches, feel depressed, tired or angry? Or perhaps you procrastinate? Write down how the stressor is making life difficult for you. Next you need to write down the actual problem, or cause of your stress. Finally, you need to write down a possible solution.

An example could be:

Stressor: Having to make cold sales calls
Manifestation: Not making the calls and end up feeling guilty; or making the call, not coming across well and feeling bad
Problem: Fear of rejection and of not being good enough
Solution: Determine why your services or products are good and how they can be of benefit or add value to your clients. Make a list of all the possible reasons why people might not buy your services. Write down all the objections they might have. Now write down the ways in which you can deflect these objections or handle them. Remember you are not trying to sell them anything on the telephone at this stage but you are trying to get an appointment which would allow you to identify their needs, and then determine whether they may have a use for your services

Clarify expectations

'The cause of almost all relationship difficulties is rooted in conflicting and ambiguous expectations around roles and goals,' suggests Stephen Covey, author of *The Seven Habits of Highly Effective People*. Try to clarify expectations in advance. When expectations are not clear and shared, personalities can clash and communications will break down.

Control your thinking

Our thinking creates much of our stress. Feelings are not caused by events themselves, but by beliefs we have regarding the event. Our self-talk and beliefs are based on our past experiences, some of which are self-defeating. Some negative beliefs are so deeply ingrained we don't realise we have them. One example of a negative belief most of us have at some stage or another is 'I'm not good enough'. Challenge the reality of these beliefs. Ask yourself how true your belief really is. If you believe it's so, then who says so and is this always the case? Think of examples that don't support this belief. You will often find that this belief isn't real and will be able to reduce its impact on you.

Breathe

You may think this is a joke, but it's actually measurable. Taking a few minutes to relax and breathe deeply will improve your 'heart coherence' and serve to increase the 'feel good' hormones being secreted into your system. For more information, see the fascinating research information at *www.hearthmath.org*.

Ask better questions

To change how you feel about anything, including stressors, you need to change what you are focusing on. Ask questions which give you useful answers. If you ask yourself negative questions you will get negative answers. Instead of asking why life is so unfair or why something always happens to you, seek out the positive aspects of your situation. Ask yourself what you can learn from this experience. Or what you can do differently to make you feel better or move towards your goal. This will get your brain thinking of solutions for you.

Be proactive

If the situation is controllable, take action to control the stressor. Any action you take will reduce the stress - when you shift into action, the body lowers its production of the stress hormone, epinephrine. Remember, you won't know if the decision is the right one until you have made it. Give yourself a pat on the back for taking action; proactivity will energise you.

If the stressor is uncontrollable, you will need to focus on controlling your emotions.

Reframe the situation to look for positive elements. Ask yourself what you might learn from the situation.

Be open to negative feedback; you may have to step back and adopt a new course of action. Robert Kohls, author of *Survival Kit for Overseas Living,* found the most important skill for living successfully abroad was the ability to fail. Keep looking for the positive in any situation and realise there is no failure, only feedback.

Get clear

Do not ignore the stressor, bring it into focus and get clarity about it. You won't be able to deal with it until you have understood it. It's usually much easier to see it in another person than to recognise it in ourselves. Ask for help from friends if you're stuck.

Pre-planning

Once you become aware of the stressor, prepare to handle it before it happens. Control your thinking, try to avoid exaggerating the situation and don't underestimate your ability for coping.

Pattern breaking

There are new forms of therapy which interrupt patterns in your brain to allow you to create new, healthier patterns. Thinking about the past and the future can be stressful. Try to bring your thoughts back to the present by centring your attention on your breathing, an object or another topic that interests and relaxes you. Doing something different such as laughing out loud or pinching yourself can also help as it breaks the pattern of our thoughts.

Well being

Take up aerobic exercise (it burns up stress hormones) and get enough rest as sleep is needed for physiological recuperation and is a close second to exercise for preventing stress. Eating healthily and not from a source of stress will boost your ability to deal with stress. Avoid the energy and emotional roller-coaster of a carb-loaded caffeine-fuelled existence.

'For me, probably reading works best. I am an avid reader. When I feel really fed up with the world I read a light historical novel, set in a world without the pressures of consumerism, commercialisation, globalisation, politics and global warming. Pure escapism. As well, I do Tai Chi, meditate, use Bach Flower Remedies and aromatherapy, and enjoy listening to music. If I have a block of time I like to paint. I also find stupid TV shows help on occasions when my brain just feels lazy! Oh, and I mustn't forget the pets. We have cats, fish and a rabbit who demand love and attention. That is remarkably relaxing, even cleaning out the litter tray can be done meditatively!'

Diane, Canadian in England, *www.expatwomen.com*

'For each person this can be so different. I find exercise, meditation, watching films, reading, writing and connecting with friends by phone or email are helpful ways to reduce stress.'

Megan, American in Italy, *www.careerbychoice.com*

'I sometimes write a thank you letter to a customer, ex-colleague, boss, etc. When I give I de-stress myself.'

Ursula, South African in America, *www.marketingmentorexpert.com* and *www.expatwomen.com*

'A beer always helps and having joined an expat group in Denver, it's a great release.'

Lizzy, British in America, *www.expatwomen.com*

Spirituality

Try to find time to be a human *being* rather than a human *doing*. It is easy to neglect being as we rush around busy doing and having. Try meditation as one way to become more grounded and balanced. There are CDs and books available to guide you in this process.

Time out

Every day make a point of relaxing, even if for only a few minutes. Try walking, stretching, yoga or taking up a hobby. We need to give our brain some quiet time when it is not nervously reacting to everything around it. The act of colouring in a Mandala is another way to use your right brain, re-charge your batteries and open up your creative abilities and thinking through the meditative activity of colouring these intricate repeating designs. Longchenpa describes a Mandala as 'an integrated structure organized around a unifying center' and these designs are now available in adult colouring books or to download from the Internet.

Devise your own anti-stress regime

Jutta König is a clinical psychologist and movement psychotherapist who offers workshops in a range of meditative arts. She suggests we should develop our own anti-stress regime. This should include learning a meditative art, such as Qi Gong, the Five Tibetans, Tai Chi, Yoga or Watsu and practise it daily to stay sane.

Jutta also believes it is vital to eat plenty of fruit and vegetables and to take exercise. She recommends consciously spoiling yourself with little attentions - flowers in your home, listening to music you love, drinking specialty tea, buying your favourite perfume.

Pick a theme song!

Is there a song that gives you a shot of optimism and energy? Choose a song to wake up to every day or to play when you need a pick-me-up. A song to play in the background of your mind as you go through your daily tasks. A soundtrack for this time of your life, this stage of your journey.

Some examples could be: *Life is a Highway, RESPECT, People Get Ready* and *Something's Got a Hold on Me.* I (Jo) picked Summertime as a theme song years ago and it never fails to revive my flagging spirits.

To expand your music repertoire, go to *www.allmusic.com* and search under the relevant themes for more ideas. Another idea is to go to *www.stereomood.com* and type in your mood. The website will create a playlist for your mood. On *www.npr.com* you can select the music to play during a work break.

My theme song(s):

_____

_____

Outside interests

In addition to the above methods, we have found that having an interest or hobby separate from work does wonders for taking the mind off your problems. There is a reason the word recreation stems from re-create! Making the time to pursue hobbies and interests will refresh and replenish. Start something new if what you used to do is no longer of interest or available in your current location. Use the same process to find a hobby as you did to find the work you love, as your hobbies are also based on your passion, values and skills.

I (Jo) realise writing poetry is my own kind of meditation, as is walking outside in nature. I (Colleen) also find getting outside in nature to be an effective way to deal with stress. I also use music. Sitting down at the piano to play and sing a song or two helps me to emote. A little dancing helps too and I have recently taken up Zumba so exercise and dancing can be combined.

Laughter

Spend a few minutes every day having a good laugh. Research has shown laughter relieves stress and makes us feel better — watch a movie or comedy show, listen to a tape, read some jokes or watch some funny stuff on YouTube. Look for the funny side of life and learn to laugh at yourself. Lighten up, stop taking yourself so seriously.

YOUR PERSONAL REWARD SYSTEM

Make a list of all the ways you can reward yourself for completing another small step on your journey. Is it a special cup of tea, a chocolate treat, a walk by the ocean, a new pair of shoes? Think about your *10 Things I Love to Do List* and *Eclectic Career List* from *Chapter 2 — Find Your Passion*. Are there any items on the list that could be a reward for you and help keep you going? The simpler they are, the more realistic it is you will do them. However, a nice big juicy reward is worth the effort as well! Make sure you aren't harder on yourself than the worst boss in the world. I (Colleen) add this last comment as I learned this first-hand when I become my own boss: be good to yourself and remember you're human.

1. _____
2. _____
3. _____
4. _____
5. _____
6. _____
7. _____
8. _____
9. _____
10. _____

Here are some additional examples: lunch out with a friend, a coffee break in the sun (yes, you deserve coffee breaks too), a spa treatment or massage, going to a concert, calling a friend in another time zone during your 'working hours'.

TEN TIPS TO A STRESS FREE BUSINESS LIFE

1. Take a five-minute break every hour and a half you work. Use the time to get up from your desk and stretch your legs, relax, breathe deeply, meditate or walk around.
2. Do not rush or leave things until the last minute. Try to arrive early for every appointment.
3. Recognise your boundaries. Learn to say no.
4. Organise yourself and your day according to your priorities. Exercise your right to adjust your schedule based on how the day is unfolding and your energy levels.
5. Notice the things you are grateful for. Say thank you.
6. Aim for a clutter-free desk and office.
7. Set aside a few minutes a day for worrying and refuse to focus on your worries randomly throughout the day.
8. Reward your achievements, it will encourage you to keep moving forward.
9. Admit you are responsible for your actions and move on.
10. Go easy on yourself. If you think a task will take one hour, allocate an hour and a quarter. If you think you will complete an assignment by Monday, say you will deliver it on Tuesday.

'For me motivation can only come from knowing that what I am doing is making a difference to other people's lives. Our business is after-school tuition in English and Maths, and we know for sure that many of our kids have gone on to have better lives than they would have done if we hadn't been able to help them. On a more mercenary level I am also motivated by the knowledge I am saving for my retirement, and helping my daughter have a better standard of living, and that helps to get me out of bed in the morning too!'

Diane, Canadian in England, *www.expatwomen.com*

'Setting goals and achieving them; trying projects that involve new research, techniques and information; sometimes having to give myself an occasional pep talk [keep me motivated].'

Carol, American in Saudi Arabia, *http://delhi4cats.wordpress.com*

'[To stay motivated I] read positive affirmations or poems when I feel lonely. Call peers and have a 5-minute marketing discussion with them. I have to pay my own medical insurance and bills - that motivates me. A big motivation is to have a goal and a vision board - write your goals and plans on this board, and when you get demotivated look at it. Make the vision board colorful, put pictures of things you would like to achieve, purchase on this board. In less good times, your vision board will be a good source of strength.'

Ursula, South African in America, *www.marketingmentorexpert.com*
and *www.expatwomen.com*

'I look at the Rocky Mountains on a daily basis and think how lucky I am. It's truly inspiring.'

Lizzy, British in America, *www.expatwomen.com*

'I stay motivated by sharing my ups and downs with my friends and with the women in a small Mum entrepreneurs group that we created a few months ago. Having a support group made of people in the same boat than you is in my opinion the best way of staying motivated. I guess the success of this group is also that all women onboard are dynamic, fun and positive.'

Jasmine, French in China, *www.inspiredbeijing.com* and
www.expatwomen.com

Need A Career Development Professional?

With all of the changes and developments occurring in the world, the skills needed and the process used to choose and find work have become more involved and complex. Just as you seek professional support for other complex life situations, you may choose to do the same for your career.

Career Development Professionals come in a variety of forms, and with a number of different titles: consultant, counsellor, advisor, coach and recruiter. The field, at this moment, is not professionally regulated and it does not always follow that one will do exactly the same work as another, even if they share the same title.

Much of what Career Development Professionals provide for their clients is intangible, consisting of information, coaching, counselling and advice. This is the major reason why it's not easy to be sure you've selected the right person and are getting the services you need.

In this section we want to give you a better idea of what Career Development Professionals do in order to help you decide if you can benefit from working with one. We also suggest guidelines to help you select a person who is qualified and well suited to help you.

What is career development?

First we need to define what we are talking about. Just as the professional roles within the field are not yet clearly defined and agreed upon, the use of the terms can also be confusing. For example 'career' and 'job' are often used interchangeably and this can lead to much confusion. Consult the glossary at the end of this book to see how the terms have been defined and used here.

Career development consists of the ongoing process of developing self-knowledge, gathering information about the world of work and combining the two in order to choose career direction and make informed career choices.

A holistic definition of career as stated by the Canadian Career Development Foundation is:

- Our life path
- The many roles we play along our life path
- The process by which we become the authors of our own futures and the creators of our own life stories

This broad definition allows the inclusion of the different roles we play in our life such as mother, student, volunteer, traveller and amateur musician to be seen as equal players in your career development. This definition is much more suitable to the way work is currently being packaged and opens up many different possibilities when one is generating career options. Instead of fitting your life around your work, you fit your work into your life.

A 2002 UNESCO *Handbook on Career Counselling*, available on the UNESCO website, defines career in this way:

> *'The interaction of work roles and other life roles over a person's lifespan including both paid and unpaid work in an individual's life. People create career patterns as they make decisions about education, work, family and other life roles.'*

The patterns created can also be called one's career development.

THE EVOLUTION OF CAREER DEVELOPMENT

As a distinct profession, career development is still so new its practitioners share no common background, preparation nor uniform standards. This is gradually changing with the availability of specific courses of study, increased emphasis on certification and membership in professional associations, and the development of standards of practice.

The diverse backgrounds of career professionals helps explain why it is difficult for the average person to evaluate and compare them on paper. This doesn't mean you need to resort to flipping coins or drawing straws. But it does put more responsibility on you as a consumer to do your research and make an informed, careful selection of the consultant you will use.

Here is a model I (Colleen) find very useful because it is in the form of the symbol for infinity - as long as you are living you will be engaging in this process in some way or form. It takes away the notion a career choice is a once in a lifetime thing and that there are 'right' and 'wrong' choices.

Career development process

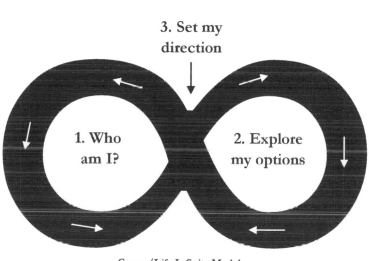

Career/Life Infinity Model
Pamela Lester

In this model there are three stages. The first stage focuses on everything that makes you who you are and is important to you. The second stage looks outside of you and explores what is available and developing in the world. The first two steps can take place simultaneously or sequentially. The third step is where you make a choice based on everything you have learned in the first two steps and take action. Action can involve setting goals and making plans and focuses on *doing*. Making a choice puts you into a new experience and context where you will continue learning about yourself and the world. Each choice provides you with new information that was not available until you took action. Do not second-guess choices. Accept the new learning and experience and use these to guide your next choice. You see now why it is called the infinity model — this process will continue over the course of your life. This is why it is important to understand your own career development and learn career development skills, with the help of a professional if you choose.

Why use a career development professional?

As mentioned, career development is a relatively new field and continues to evolve. As a result, you may not know what kinds of services a Career Development Professional can offer. Most often they will include:

- Self-discovery
- Occupational information
- Labour market information
- Planning
- Making choices
- Self marketing: CV, cover letter
- Networking
- Interviewing
- Staying organised and focused
- Troubleshooting and advice
- Support and affirmation

'I used a professional resume writer. He knew exactly how to take my experiences, achievements and strengths and put it into one document that presented who I am. I have a resume that is authentic and true to my career experiences and personality. They know what type of words to use to attract immediate attention.'

Ursula, South African in America, *www.marketingmentorexpert.com*

Who can help you with your career development?

The various types of Career Development Professional are:
- Coach
- Counsellor

- Therapist
- Consultant
- Advisor
- Recruiter
- Career Management firms

The terms are also used in different ways. For example, a Career Counsellor in one location would be considered a Career Advisor in another. Below you will find a description of the different types of Career Development Professionals as well as a number of criteria to help you make an informed choice.

THE DIFFERENCE BETWEEN COACHING, COUNSELLING AND THERAPY

Many people are confused about the differences between coaching, counselling and therapy. The table below from DoSo Coaching gives a brief overview of main differences between those three.

	Coaching	Counselling	Psychotherapy
Primary life focus	Coaching focuses on here and now in order to achieve future goals.	Counselling focuses on the present and past time in order to function better.	Psychotherapy focuses on the past (which often includes some form of trauma). It deals with the healing of emotional pain.
For whom	For people who want to achieve goals.	For people who want to overcome a temporary crisis, manage stress and create self-awareness.	For people who want to heal the past.
Goal	Learn new skills, achieve and set goals.	Understand and get insight.	Resolve old pain.
Subject focus	Action, goals.	Feelings, behaviour.	Feelings, traumas.
Questions asked	How? What?	What? Why?	Why?
Relationship	Partnership	Partnership	Patient-doctor
Timeframe	Short-term	Short / Medium-term	Long-term

Source: *http://www.dosocoaching.com/mission.php*

Coaches

There are many people offering coaching these days. They may call themselves a Life Coach, Business Coach, Executive Coach, Transformational Coach, Personal Coach, Expat Coach or a Career Coach. Some offer a combination of business and life coaching, others combine general life direction coaching with career advice. All coaches share one thing in common — *their goal is to facilitate positive change in their clients.* A coach does not tell you what to do, but helps you uncover your authentic desires and map out a plan for achieving them. They may also use formal or informal assessment tools as part of the coaching process.

Career counselling

While it is not universally the case, due to there being no regulation on the use of these terms, career counsellors are generally university educated and certified psychologists who specialise in career and vocation. Some of these also incorporate coaching techniques in their practice. Counsellors use more scientifically validated career development theories and approaches in their practices. Interpretation of psychological assessment results given by a counsellor can provide deeper insights and interpretations based on the depth of their experience, knowledge and training. Your counsellor needs to be registered with the regulatory body for psychologists in their region or country. Make sure your counsellor specialises in careers for the best results.

'I worked with a coach who successfully helped me to make the transition from working for corporate companies to starting my own business. His talents and expertise were just what I needed to transform my skills. His coaching and programs helped me to gain confidence to go out to start networking, presenting myself in a successful way and get more visibility. I am reaping the benefits of my hard work, perseverance and selecting the right coach!'

Ursula, South African in America, *www.marketingmentorexpert.com*

'I worked with Dori Weinstein *(lifematters@mac.com)*. She was amazing and it was something I had never encountered before, she made me think about things prior to reacting. Now I tend to think before jumping into a situation.'

Lizzy, British in America, *www.expatwomen.com*

Career consultants

Some career consultants teach people the skills they need to navigate their way through the career development process as described in the model at the beginning of this section. Others work specifically with people to guide them through one or more of the various elements of career development: learning more about yourself, conducting career assessments, understanding the labour market, making choices, setting career goals, writing CVs and cover letters, learning networking and interviewing skills, negotiating a salary and other aspects of career development and work search. Some consultants are also trained coaches or certified psychologists.

Career advisor

A career advisor is usually, but not always, someone who provides career services in a government or educational setting. They are more focused on providing information than supporting you through the career development process. The information they provide is related to programs of study or available occupations. They may also administer a form of assessment to allow them to match your skills and experience to an occupation or study. The amount of individual time and attention you will receive from a career advisor may be limited based on their funding source (e.g. a government service). This type of service can miss the deeper elements of your values and passion and miss some of the elements needed to discover the unique portable career paths open to you in your current situation.

Recruiters

This is a point of confusion for many people who expect career counsellors or consultants to find them jobs, and recruiters to help them with self-assessment. There is a distinct difference between them - career coaches, counsellors and consultants work for individual clients while recruiters work for client companies. Recruiters help companies to fill positions; they are in a position to recommend qualified candidates to companies, and sometimes conduct preliminary screening interviews. Recruiters are sometimes referred to as 'head-hunters' and are most interested in managerial and professional people who can command a salary of at least $50,000. In general, the higher your salary, the greater the chance of attracting recruiter interest. In addition, recruiters are often more interested in people who are already employed than in those looking for work.

Career or executive management firms

A career management firm offers services like those provided by career consultants. In fact, if you contract with a firm, you are likely to work with a particular consultant. Be aware that some of these firms promise more than they deliver and can cost a hefty sum, as much as 20 percent of a first year's salary. Some of these firms promise to connect you with important corporate 'decision makers', while just supplying you with a list of names obtainable from one of any number of databases. Some such firms have been accused of grossly misrepresenting themselves and found themselves dragged into court by irate clients. One large firm has found itself a frequent target of government investigation. Some firms contract to work with you for a year but internally plan to have you 'processed' within three months. You may end up being pressured into accepting a position that isn't what you were looking for. Remember work search for the average person is said to take from three to six months. For an internationally relocating, highly skilled professional this could take much longer. In times of economic upheaval, longer still.

This cautionary information does not mean you should never use this option - you need to research them thoroughly and ensure you have, in writing, details of the services they will provide and their cost.

HOW TO CHOOSE A CAREER DEVELOPMENT PROFESSIONAL

For the different Career Development Professionals described above, use these guidelines to compare and evaluate which one will best suit your needs best. Most will offer you a free session to meet (in person if possible), where you can ask your questions and determine if they are a fit for you.

a. **Experience**
While the profession is still relatively new, it is now old enough that a number of people have built up a significant amount of direct experience.

b. **Training**
Have they taken specific career development training and education? Are they committed to ongoing development of their skills?

c. **Certification**
Have they taken the time to certify themselves? Certification requires that professional skills are kept updated and ensures a person has met a

minimum standard for practice in the field. Always ask what the jumble of letters after their name stands for.

Certification can also apply to the use of assessment tools. What tools are they certified to use in their practice?

d. **Membership**

Are they a member of a national or international association in the field of career development?

e. **Specialization**

Which element(s) of the career development process do they provide or specialise in?

f. **Vision or mission of the professional**

What unique vision and mission do they bring to the field of practice? Do they practice what they preach?

g. **References**

Ask for testimonials and/or references from previous clients.

h. **Work Samples**

Ask to see examples of their work. These are often available on their website.

i. **Costs**

Get the costs from at least three different professionals so you can compare effectively. You wouldn't buy the first car you saw would you?

j. **Specific services offered**

Are services provided one-on-one or in a group or a combination of these approaches? Is it in- person or using Skype or telephone?

k. **Length of commitment or program**

How many sessions do they expect you will need?

How many sessions must you commit to in order to start?

l. **The fit**

Consider closely what your needs are and whether you believe this person can meet them.

Can you work closely with this person; do they inspire your confidence and trust?

Do they listen well and are they collaborative in their approach?

Career development professionals
for expatriates

As this book amply demonstrates with its numerous personal stories, pursuing career goals can be more complicated and more adventurous and fulfilling outside your passport country.

A growing number of Career Development Professionals are specialised and experienced in working with expat clients. They can assist with researching the prospects in the area you will be moving to. The professionals based in the country you move to should have a close acquaintance with the pertinent rules and regulations governing the work options of foreign nationals. Nevertheless, you may find it easier to work with somebody who is also part of the expatriate community, who understands the expat experience and is well connected with other expats.

Do not hesitate to access the services of a Career Development Professional. Just as you would call your doctor when you are sick, contact a Career Development Professional when you are not sure what direction to go in and feel like you are spinning your wheels. Don't miss out on all your global adventure has to offer and access the support that can make the difference you need to get, and keep, going.

For portable career case studies and the opportunity for you to add your own please go to *www.careerinyoursuitcase.com*

'In Malaysia work permits are impossible to get for spouses (because there is a protectionist policy) unless you are a teacher. However, I am able to continue environmental work on a short-term contract basis/freelance for organisations such as WWF, although it is only paid on a local volunteer 'pocket-money' basis.'

Yvonne McNulty, Author, Being Dumped In To Sink or Swim in *Human Resource Development International Journal*, 2012

Chapter 8: Resources for the Journey

Government of Alberta, Human Services, *Change and Transitions: The Path from A to B, www.alis.alberta.ca/publications*

Kennedy's *Directory of Executive Recruiters,* Recruiter Red Book

MS Peck, *The Road Less Travelled,* Touchstone

MJ Roy, *It's all about resiliency: Handle it!, www.iamexpat.nl*

M Pritchard, *Stressed? Turn to the Written Word,* Huffington Post online (accessed 13-11-2012)

R Bolles, *What Color is Your Parachute,* Ten Speed Press

R Sindemann *2010 Cultural Intelligence Study*

S Jeffers, *Feel the Fear and Do it Anyway,* Random House

W Bridges, *Managing Transitions,* Da Capo Press

Fluent

I would love to live
Like a river flows,
Carried by the surprise
Of its own unfolding.

John O'Donohue, theologian:
As found in *The Second Half of Life, Opening the Eight Gates of Wisdom*
by Angeles Arrien

Chapter NINE

My Career Passport

My Career Passport

This is a place to summarise your insights and key findings that will help you en route to your next career adventure. Throughout the book you have seen the

icon indicating this is something to include in this Career Passport. If you have not recorded your information here already, go back and revisit the previous chapters and summarise your insights in this section. Browse through here regularly as a touch point along your journey.

Chapter 2

FIND YOUR PASSION

Your passion provides the driving energy behind your career adventures. It is made up of various components all of which play a role in defining what your passion is.

Values

Values (p 47) provide a key to finding meaningful opportunities as they help you identify what is important to you. My top eight values are:

1. _____
2. _____
3. _____
4. _____
5. _____
6. _____
7. _____
8. _____

Patterns

The feedback (p 50) you receive from others is invaluable to opening up your eyes to new opportunities. *My 360° of Insight* summary:

1. _____
2. _____
3. _____
4. _____
5. _____

Seek to make choices that give you more *energy* (p 50—53) than they take and make time fly. I get energy from and the time flies when:

1. _____
2. _____
3. _____
4. _____
5. _____

Themes and commonalities between the activities you love will also help you uncover your passion. These are the themes and patterns I see in the *10 Things I love to do* (p 53—54) list:

_____

_____

_____

_____

Curiosity (p 54 — 55) can lead you to some interesting discoveries. Themes I am curious about:

1. _____
2. _____
3. _____
4. _____
5. _____

My hot tracks (p 55—57) seem to be pointing me in this direction at this point:

_____
_____
_____
_____
_____
_____
_____
_____

The memories that make up *my mental photo album* (p 57—59) focus around key events with these themes and lessons learned. Growing up, the main themes for a future career for me were:

_____
_____
_____
_____
_____
_____
_____
_____

People

My career ideas and aspirations are greatly influenced by the key players in my life. Summarise here what you have *inherited* (p 59—61) from your family and have made your own.

_____
_____
_____
_____
_____
_____
_____
_____

Summarise what you have accumulated from other role models and mentors.

_____
_____
_____
_____
_____
_____
_____
_____

Success

Set your focus on what you want to achieve with an awareness of what can hold you back and develop a proactive plan to deal with it (p 61—62).

My personal definition of success is:

_____
_____
_____
_____
_____
_____
_____
_____

I am successful when:

_____
_____
_____
_____
_____
_____
_____
_____
_____

The recurring themes in my *Shining Moments* (p 62—70) are:

_____
_____
_____
_____
_____
_____
_____
_____
_____
_____

The most important skills and competencies in these Shining Moments Stories, the red threads for happiness and achievement, for me are:

_____
_____
_____
_____
_____
_____
_____
_____
_____

These stories tell me that in order to shine I need:

_____
_____
_____
_____
_____
_____
_____
_____
_____
_____

An *eclectic career* (p 70—72) scenario based on my Shining Moments Stories is:

_____

_____

_____

_____

_____

_____

_____

_____

_____

Vision

Based on the visioning exercise (p 72—76), the key elements of my preferred future include:

1. _____

2. _____

3. _____

4. _____

5. _____

6. _____

7. _____

8. _____

My story (p 76—80) in a nutshell:

_____
_____
_____
_____
_____
_____
_____
_____
_____
_____
_____
_____
_____
_____
_____
_____
_____
_____
_____
_____
_____
_____
_____
_____
_____
_____
_____
_____
_____
_____
_____
_____
_____

Personality

My summarised personality profile based on the assessments I chose to do (80—85):

_____
_____
_____
_____
_____
_____
_____
_____
_____
_____
_____
_____

Take a week to reflect on all you have done.

On this date: _____I will read my *Career Passport* up to this point and summarise my key passions. They are:

1. _____
2. _____
3. _____
4. _____
5. _____

Chapter 3

WHAT CAN YOU DO?

My Career to Date

The top five things I have enjoyed most in my career experiences to date (p 90—91):

1. _____
2. _____
3. _____
4. _____
5. _____

Things to minimize in my next career move:

1. _____
2. _____
3. _____
4. _____
5. _____

Skills Summary

Skills are things you are capable of doing, things you have learned. Based on the Skills Inventory, complete the following sections (p 92—100):

Skills to reuse

1. _____
2. _____
3. _____
4. _____
5. _____

Skills to return

1. _____
2. _____
3. _____
4. _____
5. _____

Skills to recycle

1. _____
2. _____
3. _____
4. _____
5. _____

Skills to grow

1. _____
   How will I learn this:_____
2. _____
   How will I learn this:_____
3. _____
   How will I learn this:_____
4. _____
   How will I learn this:_____
5. _____
   How will I learn this:_____

My learning style:

I learn best when (p 101—102)_____

_____
_____
_____
_____
_____

My Possible Direction

Based on the different portable careers (p 103—111) profiled, I am considering these as possible directions:

_____

_____

_____

_____

_____

_____

_____

_____

_____

_____

_____

My mission statement (p113—116):

_____

_____

_____

_____

_____

_____

_____

_____

_____

_____

My six word memoir (p 116—117):

_____

_____

_____

Chapter 4

CREATE YOUR CAREER

Generate ideas on how to apply your passion and abilities. Put some additional details into your filters to help you sort through your options and find your perfect portable career.

Beliefs (p 122—124) guiding my career journey:

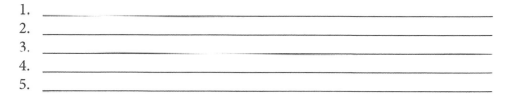

1. _____
2. _____
3. _____
4. _____
5. _____

Cultural values (p 127—128) that are essential to me are:

1. _____
2. _____
3. _____
4. _____
5. _____

Cultural values conflicts I can anticipate in my new location:

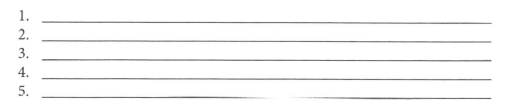

1. _____
2. _____
3. _____
4. _____
5. _____

Key *influencing factors* (p129—133) for my career:

How I want to live:

_____
_____
_____
_____

How I want to work:

_____

_____

_____

What I need from my career:

1. _____
2. _____
3. _____
4. _____
5. _____

My career serves these personal *purposes* (p 133—134):

1. _____
2. _____
3. _____
4. _____
5. _____

My ideal working environment contains these elements of *people contact and time alone,* and these *personal work preferences* (p 134—136):

1. _____
2. _____
3. _____
4. _____
5. _____

My thinking about careers and work has evolved (p 136—137) over the years and now mean the following for me:

_____

_____

_____

_____

_____

_____

Mindmapping (p 139—140) revealed these insights to me.

_____

_____

_____

Using the *25 ideas* (p 140—141) chart, the top 3 connections between my skills and passion are:

1. _____

2. _____

3. _____

Based on my analysis of what is reported in the *news* (p 142—145), and what I hear from the people around me, the ideas that hold the most potential for me are:

1. _____

2. _____

3. _____

4. _____

5. _____

Problems (p 145—146) I could possibly be the solution for:

_____

_____

_____

_____

My Blue Sky (p 148) insights are:

1. _____

2. _____

3. _____

4. _____

5. _____

My top rated way of *working* (p 149—155) looks like this:

_____

_____

_____

Companies or industry sectors of *interest* (p 156—158) to me for further follow-up and potential information interviews:

1. _____
2. _____
3. _____
4. _____
5. _____

SWOT (p 159—160)

The most important strengths and opportunities presenting themselves to me now are:

_____
_____
_____
_____
_____
_____

The most important weaknesses and threats I can identify at this moment are:

_____
_____
_____
_____
_____
_____

Living Your Mission (p 160—162)

Setting goals and making conscious efforts to bring your life activities in line with your mission will make it achievable.

My goals (p 164—165):

1. _____
2. _____
3. _____
4. _____
5. _____

My routemap (p 165—167) and action plan summary:

1. _____
2. _____
3. _____
4. _____
5. _____

I will *recognise* when I have arrived, because it will look and feel like this (p 168):

Preparing for other possibilities

These are some potential scenarios I want to be prepared for to open the doors for serendipity and to keep my momentum going (p 168—170):

Scenario B

_____
_____
_____
_____
_____

Scenario C

_____
_____
_____
_____
_____

Summing up your options (p 170)

Based on what you have done so far and what you have learned about yourself, using the chart on the following page, fill in the factors that are most important to you for your next career opportunity. Once you know which opportunities you are seriously considering, rate each factor out of 5 (5 being the highest) for each option. If you are unsure what to rate an option on a certain factor, put a temporary question mark and give yourself the time to get the missing information before you make you decision. Always take some after totalling the score for each option and check in with your gut feeling before making a definitive choice. Of course in this subjective scoring you may sway the results in favour of one option or another and that is something that also provides information as to which option you see as best.

Example:

Factors (values, goals, outcomes, lifestyle, location)	Current	Option A: Writing	Option B: Coaching	Option C: Facilitating
1. Meaningful	3	5	4	4
2. Nature	2	3	4	4
3. Work/life balance	2	4	4	4
4. Variety	3	2	3	4
5. Independence	4	3	3	4
6. People oriented	2	1	5	5
7. Commuting	1	5	5	3
TOTALS	17	22	29	29

Coaching and facilitating are tied as the most fitting options for me.

Factors (values, goals, outcomes, lifestyle, location)	Current	Option A: _____	Option B: _____	Option C: _____
1.				
2.				
3.				
4.				
5.				
6.				
7.				
8.				
9.				
10.				
TOTALS				

Note: Copies of this worksheet are available for download at *www.careerinyoursuitcase.com*.

Chapter 5

NETWORKING

I will meet and talk to people by joining these groups, taking part in these events and being open for conversation in these ways (p 176—193):

_____

_____

_____

I will further develop my networking skills (p 193—206) by:

_____

_____

_____

These are the people I would like to meet and talk to, potential mentors (p 206—207) for my journey:

_____

_____

_____

Information Interviews (p 207—212)
I am learning from my strategic information interviews:

_____

_____

_____

My Elevator Pitch (p 215—218):

_____

_____

_____

I will follow-up (p 218—219) with contacts and manage my contact database by:

_____

_____

_____

_____

Chapter 6

MARKETING YOURSELF

How I will learn about potential opportunities (p 224—239):

_____

_____

_____

_____

My brand (p 239—246):

_____

_____

_____

_____

These are the most fitting tools for marketing my portable career (p 247—263):

- ☐ My own website
- ☐ Proposal writing
- ☐ Portfolio
- ☐ CV
- ☐ Cover letters
- ☐ Reference list
- ☐ Follow-up plan consistent with my personal brand

Chapter 7

WORKING FOR YOURSELF

Potential collaborators and ways to collaborate are (p 268—272):

_____

_____

_____

_____

My business form is (p 273—274):

_____

_____

_____

_____

My main strengths as an entrepreneur are (p 275—277):

_____

_____

_____

_____

Chapter 8

FOR THE JOURNEY

Record here:

Skills I have learned in previous transitions, and lessons I want to take with me from previous experience with transitions (p 314—319):

_____

_____

_____

_____

_____

_____

_____

_____

Ways to manage stress and achieve my ideal work-life balance (p 320—336)

_____

_____

_____

_____

I will reward my efforts by (p 337):
1. _____
2. _____
3. _____
4. _____
5. _____
6. _____

Meet The Authors

Jo Parfitt
joparfitt.com

When professional writer Jo Parfitt joined her new husband in Dubai and received a stamp in her passport that read 'Not Permitted to Take up Employment' she was devastated. Since then she has let nothing prevent her from maintaining a professional identity regardless of regular intercontinental moves and the responsibilities of her family. Jo went on to create and sustain a shifting portfolio of portable careers, ranging from writing a cookbook called *Dates in Oman* through being a successful journalist in Dubai to running seminars and workshops worldwide from her current home in The Netherlands. In 1998 she realised it was time to write a book that would inspire and empower others to develop their own career in a suitcase too. 2013 sees the launch of the fourth edition of *Career in Your Suitcase*, this time in collaboration with Colleen. With a permanently evolving portable career to keep her busy, Jo has run Summertime Publishing since 1997 and now has 70 books in her stable, most of which are by or for other people living abroad. In 2012 she launched *ExpatBookshop.com* to enable her to promote them.

Find out more about Jo, her workshops, her consultancy and what makes her heart sing, through her blog at *JoParfitt.com* or via *SummertimePublishing.com*

Colleen Reichrath-Smith
cjscareers.com

Colleen believes in teaching people the skills they will need to make the most of their career journey, to make personally meaningful choices for their career. Colleen made an international transition in 2005 when she moved from Canada to the Netherlands for love after almost ten years working in the field of career development. Seeing it as the ultimate chance to apply the career development principles she teaches others, within two years she had learned the language and was again delivering career development training. This time in Dutch. After meeting Jo Parfitt at Connecting Women and the European Professional Women's Network, Colleen decided to follow her intuition and discuss the idea of a book further with Jo. This edition of Career in Your Suitcase is the result and incorporates lessons learned and the career development principles needed for today's mobile career adventurer.

To book Colleen as a speaker for your next conference or event, or to find out about Career in Your Suitcase workshops visit *CareerInYourSuitcase.com*

Glossary

Accompanying Partner — A person who moves internationally to support their partner's career. A new acronym coined by Apple Gidley is STARS: spouse travelling and relocating successfully. Also called an Enabling Spouse: Gives partner the means to do something, makes something possible by playing an active role in choices, rising to the challenges and approaching the new with a positive and optimistic attitude. Other names commonly used for this role: Trailing Spouse, Supporting Spouse. (adapted from *SustainableProspectsblog.com*)

Career — Career is a lifestyle concept that involves the sequence of work, learning and leisure activities in which one engages throughout a lifetime. Careers are unique to each person and are dynamic, unfolding throughout life. Careers include how persons balance their paid and unpaid work and personal life roles. (Canadian Standards and Guidelines for Career Development Glossary, 2012)

Career Development — Career Development is the lifelong process of managing your living, learning and earning in order to move to where you want to be. Decisions you make each day - how you spend your time and what you identify as priorities - affect your career development. Ultimately, your career development is much more than the jobs you pursue - it is about how you want to live your life. (Canadian Career Development Foundation, 2012)

Expat — From expatriate, meaning a person temporarily or permanently residing in a country and culture other than that of the person's upbringing. The word comes from the Latin terms ex ("out of") and patria ("country, fatherland"). (Wikipedia, accessed 21-05-2012)

Global Niche — Global niche is the intersection of all the worlds you belong to, where you can be most fully yourself. *(www.globalniche.net)*

Job — A job is a set of tasks that take place in a particular environment. Jobs may be paid or unpaid, part time or full time, and of short or long duration. (Canadian Standards and Guidelines for Career Development Glossary, 2012)

Occupation — A group of similar jobs found in different industries or organisations. (Canadian Standards and Guidelines for Career Development Glossary, 2012)

Passion — Intense enthusiasm. (Oxford Dictionary) Being wholehearted about an activity or a course of action. (adapted from David Whyte)

Personal Agency — Refers to people's beliefs about the extent to which they are active agents in their own life events, in contrast to being passive recipients in the events they experience. (Canadian Standards and Guidelines for Career Development Glossary, 2012)

Portable Career — A unique balance of paid and unpaid work and personal roles which one can take with them and are adaptable from one location to another. (Derived from Canadian Standards and Guidelines for Career Development Glossary, 2012)

Resilience — Holding the beliefs that enable flexibility in thought, behaviours and actions when facing adversity. (Carole Pemberton)

Self-efficacy — The belief that one is capable of performing in a certain manner to attain a certain set of goals. (Wikipedia, accessed 21-05-2012)

Third Culture Kid (TCK) — A person who has spent a significant part of his or her developmental years outside the parents' culture. The TCK frequently builds relationships to all of the cultures, while not having full ownership in any. Although elements from each culture may be assimilated into the TCK's life experience, the sense of belonging is in relationship to others of similar background. (Wikipedia, accessed 22-12-2012)

Transition — The psychological process one must go through to come to terms with a change. (William Bridges, Transition)

Work — Work is a set of activities with an intended set of outcomes, from which it is hoped a person will derive personal satisfaction and contribute to some greater goal. Work is not necessarily tied to paid employment, but to meaningful and satisfying activities, (e.g., volunteer work, hobbies). (Canadian Standards and Guidelines for Career Development Glossary, 2012)

books by people living abroad for people living abroad

ALSO AVAILABLE FROM
SUMMERTIME PUBLISHING

Where are you going? We'll meet you there.

Relocating or recently moved?
As you envision life in your new home, how are your dreams, goals and ambitions fitting into the picture?   REA has partnered with thousands of international men and women looking to redefine their careers in new locations. We can assist with-

- interest and skills assessments
- action plan development for long and short term goals
- identifying employment options for local markets
- networking strategies including social media use
- evaluation of work eligibility including licensing and visa requirements
- creating country specific self-marketing tools
- resume/cv and professional correspondence packages
- creative career options including remote businesses and entrepreneurial options

With over 2000 professionally certified coaches throughout the world, chances are we already have someone waiting to assist you.
See you there!

REA
Partners In Transition   www.r-e-a.com or +1.973.376.2020

Lightning Source UK Ltd.
Milton Keynes UK
UKOW06f2101130116

266375UK00012B/208/P